The Politics and Economics
of Park Management

The Political Economy Forum
Sponsored by the Political Economy Research Center (PERC)
Series Editor: Terry L. Anderson

The Politics and Economics of Park Management

Edited by
Terry L. Anderson and Alexander James

ROWMAN & LITTLEFIELD PUBLISHERS, INC.
Lanham • Boulder • New York • Oxford

ROWMAN & LITTLEFIELD PUBLISHERS, INC.

Published in the United States of America
by Rowman & Littlefield Publishers, Inc.
4720 Boston Way, Lanham, Maryland 20706
http://www.rowmanlittlefield.com

12 Hid's Copse Road
Cumnor Hill, Oxford OX2 9JJ, England

British Library Cataloguing in Publication Information Available

Library of Congress Cataloging-in-Publication Data

The politics and economics of park management / edited by Terry L. Anderson and Alexander
James.
     p.   cm. — (The political economy forum)
    Includes bibliographical references (p.).
    ISBN 0-7425-1155-3 (cloth : alk. paper) — ISBN 0-7425-1156-1 (pbk. : alk. paper)
     1. National parks and reserves—Management.   2. Natural areas—Management.
   3. Conservation of natural resources—Economic aspects.   I. Anderson, Terry Lee,
   1946-   II. James, Alexander, 1963-   III. Series.

SB486.M35 P66   2000
333.78'3—dc21   00-042559

Printed in the United States of America

∞™ The paper used in this publication meets the minimum requirements of
American National Standard for Information Sciences—Permanence of
Paper for Printed Library Materials, ANSI/NISO Z39.48-1992.

Contents

Part III: Opportunities for Institutional Change

Tables and Figures

Tables

Figures

Preface

ABOUT THE POLITICAL ECONOMY RESEARCH CENTER

The Political Economy Research Center (PERC) is the nation's oldest and largest institute dedicated to original research that brings market principles to resolving environmental problems. PERC, located in Bozeman, Montana, pioneered the approach known as *free market environmentalism*. It is based on the following tenets: (1) private property rights encourage stewardship of resources, (2) government subsidies often degrade the environment, (3) market incentives spur individuals to conserve resources and protect environmental quality, and (4) polluters should be liable for the harm they cause others. PERC associates have applied the free market environmentalism approach to a variety of issues, including national parks, resource development, water marketing, chemical risk, private provision of wildlife habitat, public land management, and endangered species protection.

PERC's activities encompass three areas: research and policy analysis, outreach, and environmental education. PERC associates conduct research, write books and articles, and lecture on the role of markets and property rights in environmental protection. PERC holds conferences and seminars for journalists, congressional staff members, business executives, and scholars. PERC also holds an annual free market environmentalism seminar for college students and sponsors a fellowship program that brings graduate students to PERC for three months of research and study on an environmental topic. PERC develops and disseminates environmental education materials for classroom use and provides training for kindergarten through twelfth-grade teachers.

ABOUT THE POLITICAL ECONOMY FORUM

In 1989, PERC organized the first of an ongoing series called the Political Economy Forum aimed at applying the principles of political economy to important policy issues. Each forum brings together scholars in economics, political science, law, history, and other disciplines to discuss and refine academic papers that explore new applications of political economy to policy analysis. From time to time, the series includes books not generated from PERC forums. These books are chosen based on their use of the free market environmentalism approach and their superior scholarship.

The chapters in this volume emanate from the Political Economy Forum, "The Politics and Economics of Park Management," held in October 1997. The forum was organized and directed by Terry L. Anderson. He was assisted in editing this volume by Alexander James. The purpose of the forum was to bring together a group of scholars, policy analysts, and policy practitioners to explore the economic and political interface that influences the way parks and protected areas are managed. It was hoped that we could learn from the broad range of management options that exist around the world and that this learning process could move the policy debate toward a more economically and environmentally sustainable approach to park management. It should be noted that because there has been a lag between the forum and this publication, some of the data may not be current.

PERC hopes that scholarship such as this will help advance the environmental policy debate and looks forward to further volumes in this series.

Acknowledgments

This volume resulted from a Political Economy Forum sponsored by the Political Economy Research Center (PERC) in October 1997. We are indebted to those foundations whose anonymous financial support made it possible to assemble such respected groups of scholars and policy analysts to focus on the important issue of park and protected area management.

Because this particular program involved authors from all corners of the world, hosting the forum and completing the volume required more effort and patience than usual. Thanks go to Colleen Lane and Monica Lane Guenther for making the forum run smoothly. As editors of the volume, we are especially appreciative of the effort and persistence that Dianna Rienhart maintained throughout the project. Without her we might have given up on the details that make this volume so useful.

Introduction: Parks, Politics, and Property Rights

Terry L. Anderson and Alexander James

THE LEGACY OF FORTRESS PARKS

Since the inception of the national park concept with the formation of Yellowstone in 1872, park management has been based on a military model. As in a war, commanders are appointed to protect the established boundaries from the enemy, usually the local people wanting to exploit valuable resources inside the boundaries. In fact, in the case of Yellowstone, the U.S. Army was the first agency in charge of protection. Under its guard, poaching of wildlife and defacing of natural features was effectively halted (Hampton 1971). Following on this model, other parks in the United States and in most of the rest of the world have used a hierarchical management organization patterned after the military. Especially in remote parts of Africa where wildlife has been under siege by poachers, insufficiently trained and equipped soldiers have tried to protect wildlife by shooting first and asking questions later.

The military or fortress model can be justified on the grounds that without limits on access and use, national parks would be subject to the tragedy of the commons. Whether from overexploitation of wildlife or overexploitation of natural wonders by overcrowding, complete open access and unlimited use of park resources would surely lead to tragedy. But the fortress model is encountering difficulties as demands on park resources have grown, particularly in developing countries. Fortress parks are not institutionally equipped to meet the challenge of protecting biological diversity while expanding access to resources. A fundamental problem for fortress-style management of national parks is deciding who should be protecting the parks from whom. Who should be denied access? In the case of war, the enemy is usually clear, but in the case of national parks, it is not. In the United States, clearly hunters, loggers, or miners inside parks are considered the enemy. But what about snowmobilers? What about foreigners who might carry in seeds of exotic plants?

What about the multitudes who crowd around wildlife or the wildlife itself that might be overgrazing vegetation? What about the fishers who trample the banks of streams or introduce exotic species? In developing countries the question becomes even more complex: Should traditional resource users be excluded from park resources? In chapter 9, Karl Hess Jr. puts forth the question "Management for whom?"

Generally the answer to this question has come from on high or, in other words, from a top-down hierarchy centered at the national level of government. Again, the U.S. National Park Service provides the quintessential model. Policy is set in Washington, D.C., far from the actual time and place where specific information is necessary for effective management. In developing countries, and Africa in particular, protected area policy is also set by national governments, reflecting traditions of central control established under colonial administration. In rich and poor countries alike, central government control and the fortress park tradition have similar shortcomings.

First, the fortress model generates "one size fits all" polices. In the United States, as well as in Argentina, state and provincial park agencies show greater creativity than federal agencies in raising revenues and working with the private sector, nongovernmental organizations, and local communities. In Argentina, for example, Javier Beltrán, Alexander James, and Mariano L. Merino show in chapter 5 that although their financial resources are much smaller, the provincial park agencies collaborate with a range of outside organizations to accomplish conservation objectives. In the United States, Donald Leal and Holly Lippke Fretwell (chapter 3) provide several examples of state parks that are better able to respond to local level conditions and financial opportunities than comparable national parks governed by rules originating at the national capital.

A second problem with fortress management is that it provides little or no scope for sustainable use of park resources. This is a particular problem in less developed countries, where strict preservation cuts off local people from resource use and denies the government development benefits from the natural resource base. In chapter 9, Karl Hess Jr. offers a wealth of examples where local communities have used biological resources sustainably as a matter of traditional practice. Hess argues that the imposition of "misanthropic parks" throughout the world has cut off these groups from the traditional use of resources, and a new park management ethic is needed where these use rights are recognized. Instead of strict preservation of resources by a centralized park agency, traditional patterns of sustainable use can provide the basis for park management regimes administered by the local people themselves.

Third, fortress management creates no incentive to increase park revenues. Typically, fortress agencies depend on government funds for their annual budgets and return any revenues raised in the parks to the national treasury. This has been a disaster for conservation in the developing countries where governments have rarely been able to supply adequate funds for park management. Protected areas contain valuable resources, which, if managed sustainably, could fund conservation activities, but the institutional structure of fortress park agencies has provided inadequate incentives to try to raise funds from visitors who enjoy the amenities. The list of possible funding sources includes trust funds endowed through debt for nature swaps or carbon offset deals, the participation of international nongovernmental agencies, donations from the voluntary and corporate sector, ecotourism, and joint ventures with the private sector. Fortress park agencies have little incentive to diversify into these activities when all revenues from the use of park resources are returned to the national treasury.

While many of these shortcomings are widely recognized, few examples of successful reform of park management agencies have received attention. Moreover, there is little theoretical guidance to draw upon in addressing the challenge of institutional change within park management agencies. The following chapters provide both theoretical insights and practical experience in successfully modernizing park management.

THE CHALLENGE OF INSTITUTIONAL CHANGE

Incentives guiding protected area management are created by the interaction of a country's conservation laws, social practices, and degree of enforcement of each, the subject of chapter 1 by Stephanie Presber James. She emphasizes that legislation is just a part of the institutional environment that guides protected area managers and other resource users. The informal institutions or social rules of conduct and traditional practice are often more important than national laws in determining the outcome of protected area management. These informal rules apply to the corporate culture within conservation agencies as well as to the expectations of park users. Especially in developing countries where the legal infrastructure may be as undeveloped as the economy and where local people have been accustomed to controlling access to the protected area commons, informal institutions must be considered as a critical part of institutional change. Therefore, institutional change requires more than simply changing the formal or legal rules that govern park management. Attention must also be paid to changing informal social expectations and practices. Though informal practices may be more important than conservation laws, the legal institutions are much easier to change. These changes require that legislative bodies recognize the incentive problems inherent in present management regimes and rewrite the laws to provide incentives more compatible with economic and environmental responsibility. In essence, property rights to the park revenues must be transferred to management agencies that are then required to cover most expenses out of revenues. Limits may be placed on revenue sources and expenditures. For example, a portion of revenues may be designated for parks that are not self-sustaining or for financing public goods for which it is impossible to collect fees. Generally, however, the goal should be decentralization of fiscal authority and responsibility.

These legal changes will not produce improved conservation performance, however, unless they are supported informally by protected area managers and other stakeholders in the park resources. Conservation agencies without the experience of financial independence will have informal institutions and practices unsuited to the new legal or administrative regime. Hence, managers steeped in the fortress paradigm may resist financial independence, and park users accustomed to a free ride may resist user fees. As Stephanie Presber James points out, the performance of protected area agencies will depend on how well the formal changes are supported by informal practice within the agency and among other park users.

SUCCESSFUL EXPERIENCES OF MODERNIZING PARK MANAGEMENT

Despite these challenges, many park agencies throughout the world have successfully reformed park management along the lines discussed in chapter 1. The experience of the Natal Parks Board in South Africa, as described in chapter 2 by its chief executive, George R. Hughes, is an outstanding example. The Natal Parks Board is a financially and administratively independent agency that has pursued a four-pronged strategy of park management that includes developing a sustainable wildlife industry, increasing ecotourism, forging links with private sector investors, and promoting the economic development of surrounding communities. The board raises considerable funding for conservation programs through the promotion of ecotourism and from the sale of live wildlife at regular auctions. It has also improved conservation on private lands through the Biosphere Reserve movement. Finally, the board has developed new means for community participation in the management of park resources to make biodiversity relevant to underprivileged and previously disadvantaged communities.

In chapter 3, Donald R. Leal and Holly Lippke Fretwell provide numerous examples of well-run state park systems, such as New Hampshire, California, and Texas, that internally generate all or nearly all of their funding requirements. The New Hampshire parks system, for example, is legally mandated to be financially self-sufficient. As a result, they have raised entrance fees, diversified the charges for campsites based on amenity values, and developed an extensive donor program and an ever-growing system of partnerships with companies. In 1992, volunteers contributed $2.8 million in labor and private funds. In contrasting the experience of financially self-sufficient Texas state parks with nearby government dependent national parks, the authors show that park managers can be highly responsive to incentives. At the financially self-sufficient Big Bend Ranch State Park in Texas, a wide range of innovative activities are offered to visitors including multiday rock art and desert survival courses, photographic expeditions, and an annual Longhorn cattle drive. Few, if any, of these activities are available at the federally funded and administered Big Bend National Park.

Financial independence of park agencies may be even more effective in raising funds in developing countries where government support for conservation is chronically weak. In chapter 4, Alexander James, Sam Kanyamibwa, and Michael J. B. Green compare the budgets of financially independent park agencies (in which the agency can raise and retain its own revenues) with government-funded agencies in comparable groups of developing countries. In Caribbean countries, the conservation budgets of financially independent agencies are twice as high per square kilometer as those of government-funded agencies. In Sub-Saharan Africa, financially independent agencies have fifteen times greater budgets than the comparable government-funded agencies. In both regions, the financially independent agencies actively take steps to expand tourism revenues, implement trust funds, solicit foreign and domestic donations, and invite the participation of the private sector.

OPPORTUNITIES TO MODERNIZE PARK MANAGEMENT

There is not one blueprint for modernizing protected area management applicable throughout the world. For example, in chapter 5 Javier Beltrán, Alexander James, and Mariano L. Marino argue that the flexible and dynamic provincial park system in Argentina ought to be maintained and strengthened, rather than consolidated under the management of the National Parks Agency (APN), as called for under a recent plan. APN is a centralized bureaucracy that imposes a regime of strict preservation of park resources, even to the extent of discouraging tourism. By comparison, the provincial protected area agencies show remarkable flexibility and innovation in attracting private investment, management assistance from universities and nongovernmental agencies, and the incorporation of local community representatives into park management boards. The authors suggest that an alternative plan might be to implement a provincial parks board as a focal point for donor assistance, the exchange of information and expertise, and joint implementation of a national biodiversity strategy.

Involving the private sector in park management is an attractive option and deserves closer examination. One strategy for involving the private sector is "contracting out" park operations, an option considered by Christopher Bruce in chapter 6. As Bruce discusses, Parks Canada's program of contracting out involves "employee takeovers" of the concessions at certain park operations. In the program, groups of employees form private firms that bid for the concession contract to supply defined park operations or services. After the employee firms have had a few years' experience, the contracting out of the service is then opened to all private sector bidders.

The management of Kruger National Park in South Africa provides a developing country example of a protected area in need of modernization. As Michael J. 't Sas-Rolfes and Peter W. Fearnhead discuss in chapter 7, during its century of operation, Kruger has typified the fortress park style. But as the authors argue, recent political changes in South Africa demand a broadening of the park's mandate to include providing new and different types of accommodation, offering a wider range of activities inside the park, and adopting more flexible pricing policies. Though the National Parks Board of South Africa, which manages Kruger, is a financially independent agency with broad flexibility to implement sustainable use and revenue raising activities, it remains to be seen whether and how the board will take advantage of its institutional flexibility.

In chapter 8, Terry L. Anderson and Holly Lippke Fretwell extend the concepts of modern park management to the Grand Staircase–Escalante National Monument (GSE) in the United States. They reason that a financially independent trust should be given the responsibility for management and administration of the area, instead of assigning it as another unit in the National Park Service. The GSE is a geographically large area with a wide range of potential sources of revenue, including tourism, coal, oil, gas, and minerals. As a unit in the National Park Service, no exploitation of natural resources will be allowed, and the area will be dependent on Washington for its annual budget. Anderson and Fretwell propose that a nonprofit, conservation-oriented trust be assigned to manage the GSE. As a financially self-sufficient entity, the trust would have the incentive to balance the revenues earned from natural resource exploitation with its conservation mandate.

In sum, parks have different values, different communities of stakeholders, and different pressures, as Karl Hess Jr. points out in chapter 9. These differences suggest that changes in protected area management must reflect each park's unique characteristics. Hess demonstrates this by presenting four case studies of the potential application of community-based conservation in established parks, two in Malawi and two in the United States. The author pays special attention to the question of institutional design for the new management regimes that must reflect both the underlying resource values and the social expectations of resource use.

CONCLUSION

Institutional change is a gradual and often contentious process. Kenya has taken vigorous steps to raise revenues, whereas Tanzania has not, despite incentives provided by the legal authority to retain park revenues within the system. This exemplifies the need for supportive informal institutions and organizational capacity, as discussed in chapter 4. Similarly, the South African National Parks Board has done little to raise and diversify its revenue base, a situation that the authors of chapter 7 attribute to informal practices associated with the fortress management mentality. Both of these chapters demonstrate that institutional change cannot be taken for granted just because the correct formal policies are in place. As George Hughes notes in chapter 2, "It has taken fifty years for the Natal Parks Board to evolve from a traditional nature conservation organization, with a commendable but narrow vision, to a modern body dedicated to making biodiversity relevant to all sectors of society." The purpose of this book is to plant the seeds for institutional change. It starts with a general theory of institutional change, shows how these principles have led to successful management in a range of protected area agencies throughout the world, and highlights the diversity of new institutions needed to improve conservation performance in several other countries. Before embarking on the course laid out by these essays, however, it is important to emphasize that the theme herein does not suggest that parks and protected areas are being managed by bad or insincere people. To the contrary, park managers usually care deeply about the resources under their control. It is the institutional constraints they face that dictate how and for whom parks are managed. Hopefully, the chapters that follow will help policy analysts and policymakers focus on how institutional change can better link management incentives with good resource stewardship.

REFERENCE

Hampton, H. Duane. 1971. *How the U.S. Cavalry Saved Our National Parks*. Bloomington: Indiana University Press.

Part I

Theoretical Approach

1

An Institutional Approach to Protected Area Management Performance

Stephanie Presber James

Studies concerning protected area management have identified a range of factors that influence conservation performance.[1] These factors include protected area legislation (Bell and McShane-Caluzi 1984; Spinage 1991; Heinen and Kattel 1992), protected area management plans (Bell and Clarke 1984; MacKinnon et al. 1986; Ndosi 1992), protected area budgets (Leader-Williams and Albon 1988; James et al. 1997), law enforcement (Martin 1990; International Union for the Conservation of Nature [IUCN] 1992; Spinage 1996), property rights to natural resources (IUCN 1993; International Institute for Environment and Development [IIED] 1994), and customary use of wildlife (Kiss 1990; Githinji and Perrings 1993).

Despite growing recognition that park management performance is affected by a number of interactive variables, and notwithstanding the impressive catalogue of anecdotal evidence of management challenges, the literature remains largely devoid of any theoretical underpinning. To date, the protected areas literature is essentially a collection of descriptive and prescriptive studies with little in the way of unifying structure, concepts, or terminology. Consequently, the analytical quality of the literature and the potential effectiveness of policy prescriptions are compromised.

The emerging paradigm of the new institutional economics, particularly the institutional framework outlined by Douglass North (1990), provides a suitable basis for developing an analytical approach to park management performance. Institutional theory provides the unifying structure, concepts, and terminology for protected area management studies that have been lacking. The framework is also capable of incorporating the wide range of legal, social, and economic variables that appear to affect protected area management performance.[2]

An analytical framework, based on North (1990), is outlined here. While some of the illustrative examples relate to protected areas, the discussion is predominantly abstract. This section is followed, however, by the development of an analytical approach to protected area management performance, the identification of desirable characteristics for good management results, and strategies for improving management outcomes.

THE INSTITUTIONAL FRAMEWORK

North's (1990) theory of institutions, institutional change, and economic performance is a response to the perceived failure of neoclassical economics to explain economic development adequately—specifically, the existence of radically different levels of wealth and income among the world's countries and the persistence of inefficient economies over time. Though the focus is on economic performance, the theory has the potential to be adapted to analyze other performance-related issues.

Herein, *institutions* are defined as the rules of the game and are not synonymous with organizations. Institutions are the constraints, restrictive or enabling, that direct human behavior in social, political, and economic exchange (North 1990). Organizations[3] and individuals are the players whose behavior is governed by these rules. Institutions comprise both the formal and informal rules that, with their respective enforcement characteristics, create a set of incentives that guide human behavior and, consequently, determine performance outcomes (North 1990).

The Institutional Environment

An institutional environment consists of three interactive aspects: formal institutions, informal institutions, and the type and level of their enforcement. These components are discussed in turn.

Formal Institutions

Formal institutions are the written instruments that provide a legally enforceable framework for the economic, political, and social activities of a society. They can include constitutions, laws, policies, regulations, and property rights. The legal system is the core of a country's formal institutional structure. Laws can either grow out of a society's social conventions (informal institutions) or be imported from another institutional environment—for example, where one country adopts another country's protected area legislation as the basis for its own. Policy measures such as taxes for "nonproductive" land use, agricultural subsidies, and regulations regarding park revenue are also formal institutions that function within the legal framework. In addition, the written specification of property rights (e.g., the property rights to wildlife resources and the statutes and contracts that render them legally enforceable) are another layer of a country's formal institutions.

Informal Institutions

While every country has a formal structure of laws, government policies, and property rights, an equally important parallel system of unwritten rules governs everyday human behavior in economic, political, and social exchange. These unwritten rules are the *informal institutions*.

Cultural norms, social conventions, mores, etiquette, traditions, and taboos are all examples of informal institutions. Informal institutions can and do vary widely among countries and social groups. This variation arises because informal institutions are expressions of culture-specific belief systems. A manifestation of variance in perceptions and social rules is seen when surveying different cultures on their beliefs and practices with regard to protected areas.

Like formal institutions, the purpose of informal institutions is to reduce uncertainty by making human behavior more predictable. Though informal institutions are unwritten, they form the basis for social expectations of individual behavior in everyday exchange and are therefore well known to all members of a society. For example, a society's informal institutions dictate what is appropriate and expected behavior when greeting others, making a purchase, or attending a social or business function. Such institutions can be more influential than a country's formal rules because they are deeply embedded in customs and represent an accumulation of social convention.

The relationship between informal institutions and formal institutions is interactive. In many instances, formal institutions are an outgrowth of a society's informal rules—a formalization of the cultural constraints (North 1990). Normally, however, there is influence in both directions, and changes in formal institutions can bring about changes in social behavior and expectations. Thus, while institutions can be informal or formal, they constitute more of a spectrum than two distinct domains (North 1990). Yet, when a country's formal institutions originate from a foreign institutional environment, its formal rules and informal rules can be unrelated. Foreign formal institutions may be adopted by or imposed on a country, depending on its history. The degree of difference between the characteristics of the indigenous informal institutions and the imported formal institutions often determines their relative levels of enforcement and therefore their relative influence on behavior.

Enforcement

The level of compliance with formal and informal institutions determines how effective they are in guiding human behavior. *Compliance* is the extent to which behavioral choices made by individuals and organizations reflect the purpose of the institution. Levels of compliance are normally a function of the type and scale of enforcement. If there is no enforcement, then compliance is likely to be limited, and an institution is ineffective in guiding behavior.

Different institutions have different enforcement mechanisms. Enforcement can be third-party (societal sanctions or enforcement by the state), second-party (retaliation), or first-party (self-imposed codes of conduct) (North 1994).

In theory, formal institutions, such as national parks legislation and written property rights to wildlife resources, are enforced by a third party (i.e., the state), normally through law enforcement agencies and the judiciary. In practice, third-party enforcement is rarely impartial because those responsible for enforcing have their own preferences that influence their perceptions and decisions (North 1990). Furthermore, if a society's informal institutions permit, the interests of the politically powerful can also interfere with a judiciary's independence.

Differences in informal institutions among countries mean that there is considerable variation in the level of impartiality among the judicial systems of the world. The extent to which the judiciary and law enforcement agencies approximate impartial third-party enforcement is largely determined by a country's informal institutions regarding the rule of law and social expectations for the honesty and integrity of judges (North 1990).

Enforcement of informal institutions can be the function of a social group or an individual. A social group could be civil society as a whole, a Mafia-type organization, a village council, or a family unit. Each group has its own enforcement methods and penalties, which may include humiliation, retaliation, or fines. Individuals can also regulate their own behavior, either in accordance with inner beliefs about acceptable standards of conduct or for reasons of self-preservation or personal reputation (such self-regulation, when consistent with the broader institutional incentives, can reduce the costs of enforcement at the group or state level). Most individuals and organizations comply with the prevailing informal institutions because it reduces their costs in everyday social, economic, and political exchange.

Institutional Incentives and Human Behavior

The incentives that guide human behavior derive from the interaction of the three components of an institutional environment (the formal institutions, the informal institutions, and their enforcement characteristics) and not from any one factor alone. For example, the extent to which protected area legislation is enforced often depends on the nature of the prevailing informal institutions. The interaction of the three components produces a set of institutional incentives that rewards certain types of behavior and penalizes others. By affecting the payoffs of different strategies of individual and organizational behavior, institutional incentives (along with other constraints such as budgets and technology) determine performance outcomes (North 1994).

Individuals and organizations normally comply with institutional incentives and thereby reinforce the characteristics and the legitimacy of the prevailing environment (North 1990). Successful organizations and individuals reinforce the existing environment because they are its greatest beneficiaries. These players have invested resources in learning the rules of the game and in acquiring the skills necessary to win. They are in powerful positions precisely because they understand, comply with, and reinforce the prevailing institutional incentives.

The institutional incentives facing various individuals and organizations can derive from many different layers of a country's overall institutional environment. This accounts for the variation in behavior among different groups within the same country. For example, at the local level, certain national institutions apply, such as national protected area legislation, but local cultural norms and property rights arrangements, ordinances, and by-laws interact with national institutions and their level of enforcement to create distinct subenvironments for local individuals and organizations. Frequently, these subenvironments are consistent with the broader formal and cultural constraints; however, marked variation can exist at different levels and among different groups.

Where variation in institutional incentive structures is often most obvious is among countries. Every country has a unique institutional environment and resulting set of incentives that guide the behavior of its citizens. Moreover, while two countries may have the same or very similar formal institutions, their informal institutions, enforcement characteristics, and the subjective mental models of their citizens may be totally different (North 1994). The result can be marked differences in human behavior and, consequently, in levels of wealth and economic development (North 1990).

Institutional Change

Institutional change occurs when a component of an institutional environment is modified or a new institution is introduced. Institutional change can alter incentives, behavior, and outcomes. Yet, in most instances, the "change" is largely consistent with the existing institutional environment, and the nature of the incentive structure is not substantially altered. It is perhaps more useful to think of institutional change as an evolutionary process rather than a revolutionary one. This said, however, the composition of an institutional environment can change considerably over time resulting in a different level and pattern of performance. (The complicated nature of institutional change is discussed later.)

As North (1994) notes, individuals and organizations continually invest in acquiring the skills and knowledge that will allow them to maximize their wealth (or other socially or privately defined objectives), given the institutional environment in which they exist. For example, if their institutional context rewards piracy, then they will work to become good pirates. If it rewards productive behavior and creativity, they will establish productive economic organizations and foster innovation. Occasionally, however, in an effort to advance, an individual or organization decides on noncompliance and deliberately attempts to initiate change to the institutional environment. These agents of institutional change are known as *institutional entrepreneurs*.

Institutional entrepreneurs are individuals (often the decision makers in organizations) who perceive that it has somehow become in their interest to initiate institutional change (North 1994). Potential entrepreneurs weigh the benefits and costs of devoting resources to changing the composition of the existing institutional environment. If they perceive that the benefits to be gained from altering the current rules outweigh the potential costs, then they may become agents for change. Their new perception of a potential benefit from institutional change usually stems from a change in prices or preferences or the acquisition of new knowledge (North 1990).

A change in relative prices can motivate an individual to initiate institutional change. Changes in prices can stem from (1) changes in the cost of information, (2) changes in technology, or (3) changes in the ratio of factor prices (land, labor, and capital) (North 1990). Shifts in these prices can alter the economic opportunity costs associated with particular activities. For example, an increase in the value of natural habitat, expressed through a rise in tourist visits to a country's parks, might cause the park management agency to perceive that it is in its interest to instigate a formal institutional change such as the transfer of the property rights to park revenue from the central treasury to the agency itself.

A change in preferences, due to a shift in relative prices or new information, can also motivate institutional entrepreneurs. For example, where a rise in international tourist visits to a country's parks brings an increase in foreign exchange, the government might perceive that it is in its interest to devise and implement policies that enable the nature-based tourism industry to grow. In this case, a change in prices (i.e., the value of foreign exchange) and new knowledge (nature-based tourism is a possible source of economic growth) causes entrepreneurs at the national level to initiate a formal institutional change (a new government policy). Yet while changes in prices can influence preferences, it is not a straightforward causal relationship because a change in relative prices is observed through a preexisting set of preferences (North 1990). Thus, in a given country, if a cultural tradition views strangers as threatening, then an increase in tourists and the foreign exchange they provide may receive less institutional support than in a country with a tradition of hospitality toward foreigners.

Potential entrepreneurs can also be encouraged to act by internal factors, such as the acquisition of new knowledge. Competition, due to scarcity, motivates individuals and organizations to acquire new knowledge to improve their position (North 1994). The rate of learning reflects the degree of competition, and where monopoly power exists, the incentive for learning is diminished (North 1993). The rate of learning determines the speed of institutional change, while the kind of learning that organizations decide to pursue is based on expected payoffs, which affects the type of institutional change that takes place.[4]

New knowledge might be acquired through exposure to new information—for example, as the result of a public awareness program. For instance, a campaign to reduce poaching in parks provides new information on the negative effect of poaching on tourist visits. This may cause certain individuals who benefit from tourism (e.g., because they run ancillary businesses) to perceive that the costs and benefits associated with poaching are different from what they had previously understood. This might spur a change in their beliefs about poachers (a modification at the informal level) and cause them to champion efforts to counter poaching at the informal and formal levels. Often, it is a combination of external change and internal learning that motivates entrepreneurs to modify the existing institutional structure (North 1994).

Institutional entrepreneurs benefit from an environment that displays the characteristic of adaptive efficiency. *Adaptive efficiency* exists where institutional incentives reward creativity, promote innovation, and encourage decentralized decision making (North 1990). This quality motivates people to act productively and discourage ineffectual rules and organizations (North 1990). Societies with a high level of adaptive efficiency are able to respond to new challenges in a more positive and proactive way than those with a low level of adaptive efficiency.

Even where adaptive efficiency exists or where changes in prices and preferences motivate individuals to act, institutional entrepreneurs still will have to work against substantial inertia (North 1990). Institutions exist to provide security and therefore most of society's individuals and organizations have a vested interest in maintaining the existing system. Any major institutional change represents new costs to those with vested interests, and they will oppose entrepreneurial activity. Consequently, the process of institutional change is relentlessly incremental and gradual, with change by entrepreneurs occurring largely at the margins of the institutional environment (North 1990).

North (1990) describes the process of institutional change as being "path dependent."[5] The large startup costs associated with creating institutions, formal and informal, and establishing monitoring and enforcement mechanisms creates momentum along one path of institutional development (North 1990). As a society's institutions evolve, social capital is invested in the institutional structure and the direction is reinforced, further reducing the margin for institutional change.

Even in cases in which dramatic institutional change seems to have taken place, such as in the case of a national revolution, an event does not happen in a historical or institutional vacuum. There is an institutional basis for a given occurrence, and even if the result is a substantial alteration to the formal rules, the old informal rules will continue to exert considerable influence over everyday activities at all levels (North 1990). Eventually, a new equilibrium is reached between the new formal institutions and the old informal ones, producing an institutional environment that is usually a much milder form than what the revolutionaries had articulated and predicted and that reflects its historical context (North 1993).

Summary

Performance is predominately a function of institutional incentives. The complex interaction of a myriad of formal and informal institutions and their enforcement characteristics create the incentives that guide the behavior of a country's individuals and organizations and thereby determine performance outcomes. The majority of individuals and organizations are stakeholders in the existing institutional environment and will oppose change; however, new prices, preferences, or learning can cause certain individuals' perceptions of costs and benefits to shift. These individuals can become institutional entrepreneurs for institutional change, but they usually encounter resistance due to the path-dependent nature of institutional change. As a result, most modifications to an institutional environment by entrepreneurs are minor, and institutional change is gradual and incremental. Yet, while individually small modifications barely affect the broad set of incentives, over time, a series of deliberate changes can alter the composition of the incentive structure, changing human behavior and performance outcomes.

AN INSTITUTIONAL APPROACH TO PROTECTED AREA MANAGEMENT

The institutional approach to protected area management uses the basic framework, concepts, and definitions of institutional theory to analyze protected area management performance. The premise of the approach is that a country's relevant formal institutions, informal institutions, and their enforcement characteristics interact to create a set of incentives that guide the behavior of its protected area stakeholders,[6] and it is this behavior that largely determines how closely protected area management outcomes reflect stated management objectives.

Formal Institutions

The central formal conservation institution is a country's protected area legislation, which normally gazettes a set of protected areas, defines their objectives, and specifies rules of access and penalties for noncompliance. Additional conservation legislation may exist at different levels, from national to local. Other relevant formal institutions include hunting, forestry, and fisheries legislation and laws covering the use of land, water, and minerals. The latter can be particularly relevant where the objectives of natural resource laws conflict with those of protected areas, and examples of resource exploitation within protected areas are not uncommon, particularly in the developing countries (Wilson 1995, 1996; Mittermeier, Werner, and Lees 1996). A review of each country's wildlife conservation and protected area legislation (and some of the relevant natural resource laws) reveals a wide variation around the world (IUCN 1992). For instance, legal specification ranges from the protection of biodiversity at the constitutional level in Namibia to the total absence of designated protected areas in Laos (as of 1992).

Government conservation policies are another layer of formal institutions. Policy measures may include a national biodiversity strategy (Glowka et al. 1994), a national conservation strategy (IUCN, United Nations Environment Program [UNEP], and World Wildlife Fund [WWF] 1980), protected area management policy (Bell and McShane-Caluzi 1984), a national environmental action plan, a national tourism plan, and an environmental impact assessment policy. Related economic policies might include subsidies for competing land uses such as agriculture and ranching (Anderson and Leal 1991; Williamson 1994; deMoor and Calamai 1997), tax incentives for protected areas (Loureiro 1996), and economic incentives for conservation in buffer zones (Lacher, Kennedy, and Ramirez 1996).

The written specification, or lack thereof, of property rights to the components of biodiversity are also relevant to protected area management. These formal property rights arrangements can pertain to biological resources inside parks, those in buffer zones (and beyond), and those that migrate in and out of parks. Degradation and overexploitation of these resources can be due to a lack of formally specified property rights, poorly defined rights, conflicting rights claims, or insecurity of tenure. An example of their impact is seen in countries where formal institutions specify a state property regime to protected areas, but there is little or no enforcement. In many instances, this leads to parks that have no management or budgets, known as "paper parks," which are essentially open access resources (IUCN 1994). The influence of property rights on conservation outcomes is discussed in numerous publications, including West and Brechin (1991); Lamprey (1992); Lusigi (1992); Matowanyika, Serafin, and Nelson (1992); WCMC (1992); Munasinghe, McNeely, and Schwab (1994); and UNEP (1995).

Informal Institutions

A wide range of informal institutions also can influence protected area management effectiveness. These include informal institutions that are general in scope and those that are specific to wildlife and protected areas. While potentially numerous, broad-based informal institutions that often influence conservation outcomes pertain to (1) the validity and role of formal institutions, (2) traditions of accountability, and (3) tolerance of personal initiative and decentralized decision making. These more general informal rules are reviewed first, followed by a discussion of informal institutions specific to wildlife and protected areas.

Social beliefs about the validity and role of formal institutions affect the extent to which a society's individuals and organizations comply with these written rules. For example, if protected area management personnel believe that conservation laws are valid, then their incentive to enforce is increased. In the case of park neighbors, beliefs that formal conservation institutions (particularly national-level institutions) are irrelevant or erroneous can lead to deliberate disregard for them. This is frequently the case where the property rights to the wildlife and land comprising a protected area were unilaterally appropriated by the state. Examples of how social beliefs and informal institutions regarding the validity and role of formal institutions influence behavior and outcomes are found in Poole (1989); West and Brechin (1991); Matowanyika, Serafin, and Nelson (1992); and IIED (1994).

Personal accountability refers to an individual's social or legal obligation to execute the formal responsibilities of a position, whether in public office, private enterprise, or as part of other organizations. Social expectations for personal accountability vary among cultures, and the resulting culture-specific informal institutions can influence protected area management performance. A lack of social expectation for personal accountability throughout a protected area management agency can contribute to a failure to achieve stated management objectives.

Tolerance of personal initiative and traditions of decentralized decision making can also affect conservation outcomes. Depending on social convention, individuals within a protected area management agency, for instance, may or may not be willing to act independently to achieve stated conservation goals. In countries with adaptive efficiency, social conventions reward personal initiative and decentralized decision making, enabling individuals to pursue creative solutions to conservation challenges. In countries without adaptive efficiency, the prevailing informal institutions impede innovation,[7] obstructing behavior that could contribute to good performance.

In addition to the more general informal institutions described earlier, specific cultural beliefs and conventions regarding the value and role of wildlife and protected areas also influence stakeholder behavior. These informal institutions can be shaped by a range of factors, from religion to physical environment (Kiss 1990; Barzetti 1993; Ostrom and Schlager 1996; Noss 1997). Over time, belief systems in different countries and among different groups have translated into a range of conservation practices and traditions (Gadgil and Guha 1992; Maybury-Lewis 1992; Suzuki and Knudtson 1992; Gadgil, Berkes, and Folke 1993; Western and Wright 1994). For example, some countries hold the widespread belief that wildlife is there to be consumed. In others, the idea of the consumptive use of wildlife is contrary to dominant social preferences. Each belief system gives rise to a different set of informal rules and practices that are perceived as legitimate within their own context.

In the developing countries, conflicts frequently arise between the nationally designated formal property rights regimes governing wildlife and protected areas and local informal institutions pertaining to the same resources. For example, at the national level, the state creates a protected area on the behalf of the entire country, a public good. Yet at the local level, there may be long-standing informal property rights regimes governing access to the same area and the natural resources it comprises.

Competing claims to wildlife and other protected area resources can create substantial management challenges. Indeed, disputes between local informal institutions and broader formal institutions are often at the heart of many protected area management conflicts. Where the informal rules have a long history, more recent state control over protected area resources may be seen as invalid and ignored by non–rights holders. And, if formal enforcement is also low, then prospects for good conservation outcomes are reduced.

An additional protected area management challenge occurs when the property rights to land and wildlife bordering parks are poorly defined, monitored, and enforced, resulting in open access. These conditions often stem from the imposition of formal institutions from a different institutional context (national or foreign), leading to confusion and conflicting rights claims. Arbitrary appropriation of rights to land and wildlife without compensation can be made worse by subsequent non-enforcement. The damage to the surrounding local environment resulting from open access conditions can place pressure on nearby protected areas.

Enforcement

A country's protected area management agency normally enforces the protected area laws (within the broader national framework for legal enforcement). Other enforcement agencies with related duties can include the army, the police, customs, and other government departments like those responsible for forestry and fisheries.

The extent of conservation law enforcement is strongly influenced by the relevant informal institutions and social expectations of personal accountability (budgets and technology can also be factors). If social constraints do not require that the responsible agencies actually enforce the law, or perhaps even penalize enforcement, then the agencies will be ineffective in their role as enforcer. This will increase the incentive to violate conservation laws.

The behavior of protected area management agency field personnel is particularly important to conservation outcomes. The social beliefs of field staff regarding the law enforcement component of their job, as opposed to the conservation/management function, depends on the informal institutions within the management agency, as well as broader social expectations for formal enforcement. Protected area managers may neglect certain aspects of the enforcement function, particularly where social support is lacking. For example, if field staff are responsible for collecting fees in parks where visits were previously free of charge, then the cultural expectation that visiting parks should be free will clash with the new formal institution, and park personnel may be reluctant to collect fees (Egan 1997). This situation can be exacerbated by low social expectations for personal accountability (though some individuals may have internally held beliefs that are consistent with their duties to monitor and ensure compliance).

The judicial system also plays an important role in enforcing a country's formal conservation institutions. The effectiveness of the judicial system in its role as an impartial enforcer depends on the extent to which the judges' own utility function, and that of others, influences their decisions. Both the integrity and honesty of judges and the extent of political interference in the judiciary are a function of the relevant informal institutions and social expectations for personal accountability.

Social beliefs regarding wildlife and protected areas can be translated through court rulings by the members of the judicial branch. For example, court rulings on poaching, and the penalties assessed, might be moderated by sympathetic informal institutions. Where the judicial system is vulnerable to political pressure, the interests of the politically powerful are frequently reflected in judicial decisions. Low levels of formal enforcement due to political interference indicate a lack of social support for the rule of law.

Institutional Incentives, Stakeholder Behavior, and Management Outcomes

The interaction of formal institutions, informal institutions, and enforcement variables creates the overall incentives for human behavior. Furthermore, these incentives can derive from many different layers of a country's institutional environment. Thus, the behavior of protected area stakeholders is not the consequence of one law or social custom but of the interaction of a complex and multilayered institutional environment. Yet different stakeholder groups within a country may behave differently because they are subject to distinct institutional subenvironments, often reflecting discrepancies in interests and informal institutions.

While the number and type of protected area stakeholders varies among countries, some common examples include (1) protected area management agency personnel; (2) personnel in other government agencies with compatible or conflicting responsibilities; (3) politicians; (4) local people; (5) protected area visitors; (6) tour operators; (7) foreign nongovernmental organizations, donor agencies, and consultants; and (8) domestic conservation nongovernmental organizations.

Institutional incentives guide stakeholder behavior, and it is the combined behavior of the full range of a country's protected area stakeholders (along with other constraints such as budgets and technology) that decides long-term performance outcomes. If, overall, the institutional incentives governing stakeholders reward behavior that enables (or at least does not impede) a management agency to meet its formally stated conservation objectives, then outcomes are more likely to be consistent with stated goals. If, by contrast, the overall mix of institutional incentives rewards behavior that prevents a management agency from meeting stated goals, then poor performance is likely.

While all three components of an institutional environment contribute to the incentives guiding stakeholder behavior, the influence of the informal rules cannot be underestimated (North 1990). Informal institutions are particularly important in determining the level of enforcement of, and voluntary compliance with, a country's formal conservation institutions. Where formal enforcement is inadequate, it is often because the informal institutions of those responsible for enforcing conflict with the formal rules. Where voluntary compliance with formal conservation institutions by other protected area stakeholders is low, it is normally due to hostile informal institutions.

Dissonance can also occur when a country's formal conservation institutions originated from a foreign institutional context, because they were imposed by another country, adopted from another country, or crafted largely by individuals from another country. In such cases, the formal institutions are not an outgrowth of the informal rules and may not reflect domestic social beliefs and preferences. Consequently, the influence of these formal institutions on stakeholder behavior is normally low, and behavior is instead largely determined by the prevailing informal institutions. By contrast, where the formal institutions are an outgrowth, or formalization, of a society's informal rules, levels of voluntary compliance and formal enforcement are naturally higher. In such cases, good conservation performance is more likely because the institutional incentives reward behavior that supports stated objectives.

Understanding the composition of a country's institutional incentives, and their relationship to stakeholder behavior and to conservation performance, offers some insight into why two countries can have very similar formal conservation institutions but have totally different levels of protected area management performance. The distinct cultural beliefs and social rules of each country produce different levels of formal enforcement and voluntary compliance.

The institutional framework also helps explain the persistence of poor performance in countries that have received considerable foreign inputs of expertise and financial resources. The influence of informal institutions means that unless social expectations and conventions are consistent with donor objectives, outcomes will remain largely unchanged regardless of external assistance. In addition, while increasing levels of formal enforcement can improve outcomes in the short term, sustained progress requires increasing social support for conservation objectives.

IMPROVING PROTECTED AREA MANAGEMENT PERFORMANCE

The first step in improving a country's protected area management performance is to diagnose the root causes of current shortcomings using the institutional framework and language. The second step is to specify the components of a more desirable institutional environment. The third step is to determine how to progress from the first step to the second. While the preceding section focused on the first step, the following discussion considers the second and third steps.

Institutional Characteristics for Successful Management Performance

Those looking for simple prescriptions and specific measures to improve conservation outcomes will be disappointed with the institutional approach. Just as there is no one tax law, banking code, or attitude toward risk that guarantees sustained economic growth, the institutional approach does not provide a single set of protected area management guidelines designed to produce good results wherever applied. The substantial variation in national institutional environments, and particularly countries' informal institutions pertaining to the role of wildlife and protected areas, means that one model or set of prescriptions cannot be suitable for all countries. Thus, no one institutional mix creates the "right" incentives for every country. This said, certain institutional characteristics, as opposed to specific laws or policies, appear to lead to good performance outcomes (North 1990). Such institutional characteristics can facilitate the creation of incentives that are suitable for the unique circumstances of individual countries. Yet within these broad confines, considerable flexibility is possible to reflect the wide variation in social beliefs, preferences, and traditions that exist among the world's nations.[8]

Almost all countries have a mix of institutions pertaining to protected areas, some that facilitate and others that impede effective management. What is desirable is to encourage an institutional mix that, on balance, creates incentives that enable, or at least do not hinder, the ability of the responsible organization(s) to meet stated objectives.

Formal Institutions

Institutional theory suggests that a country's formal protected area institutions should be well defined, appropriate, and enforceable (North 1990). Well-defined formal institutions include comprehensive conservation legislation, transparent government policies, and highly specified property rights arrangements and contracts. Appropriate formal institutions are compatible with a country's objectives, capabilities, and social values.[9] When formal institutions are well defined and appropriate, then they are more likely to be enforced.

Well-defined protected area legislation is up-to-date, comprehensive, and specific. It reflects current management capabilities, knowledge of ecological and human systems, and social preferences regarding the use of resources. Comprehensive conservation legislation is highly specific regarding the status and objectives of protected areas, the property rights to the country's biological and base resources, and the penalties for noncompliance. Yet, the legislation should also be "user-friendly" so that those charged with interpretation and enforcement are comfortable and familiar with the content.

Protected area legislation should reflect a country's unique history, capabilities, conservation philosophy, and traditions. Making legislation appropriate should not be confused, however, with eliminating all current protected area laws or lessening protected areas' conservation objectives.[10] Instead, appropriate legislation provides for protected area management through achieving compatibility with the relevant informal institutions, thereby increasing social support and compliance.

Property rights regimes to wildlife and protected areas should also be well defined and appropriate. Most countries' conservation legislation creates a well-defined state property regime, but it is not always enforced, often because of institutional factors, as discussed.[11] While state property regimes are the prevalent form of ownership and management of protected areas, some countries may find alternative structures to be more appropriate and therefore more enforceable. Alternative arrangements may include creating a parastatal management agency or other private sector solutions or possibly implementing common property regimes to manage protected areas if the institutional capacity exists and is socially appropriate.

Well-defined and appropriate policy instruments also contribute to effective protected area management. Policies that support conservation objectives may be based on a national action plan, such as a national biodiversity strategy. The main concern is that the policy is suitable for the country; otherwise, its content is likely to be diluted down in the political market and then ignored. Thus, international guidelines may offer a skeletal framework for policy, but the actual instruments need to reflect the social preferences of the country.

All other things being equal, legislation, property rights, and policies that are well defined and appropriate are more easily enforced. Such laws will have social support and the advantage of being written instruments. If the written instruments governing protected areas are comprehensive and harmonious with the prevailing social conventions regarding wildlife and protected areas, enforcement costs are reduced because the voluntary compliance of stakeholders is more forthcoming.

Informal Institutions

The great variation among the world's cultures prevents the identification of a specific set of cultural attributes (and their related informal rules) that create incentives for good conservation performance. Certain beliefs and corresponding informal institutions, however, can improve the likelihood of a positive institutional mix for protected area management.

Clearly, broad-based informal institutions that validate the rule of law and create social expectations for honesty and integrity are desirable for a positive institutional mix. This applies equally to society at large, to enforcement agencies, and to the judiciary. In some rare instances, a country's informal institutions alone may provide an adequate basis for good conservation outcomes, but normally a written structure of rules is necessary that, if complied with, indicates inter alia a respect for the rule of law and an adequate level of enforcement.

Informal institutions that reward personal accountability, personal initiative, and decentralized decision making can also foster good management performance. These social characteristics can indicate the presence of adaptive efficiency, which rewards innovative responses to new challenges and individual pursuit of improved performance outcomes.

No specific informal institutions pertaining to wildlife and protected areas are requisite for good management performance. Thus, countries can have disparate beliefs and rules about who owns and manages the benefits related to wildlife and protected areas. If the model is consistent with a country's history, traditions, and social expectations of resource use, then it is more likely to engender social support and ensure the continuation of a country's protected area system.

Enforcement

The most important characteristic of enforcement is that it is impartial (North 1990). While total impartiality is impossible, the approximation of impartial third-party enforcement is integral to enhancing the likelihood of good performance outcomes. Impartial enforcement usually leads to a better public opinion of enforcement agencies, increased respect for the formal rules, and greater voluntary compliance. Again, the degree of impartiality on the part of enforcement agencies and the judiciary when invoking the formal institutions governing protected areas is predominantly a function of the prevailing social rules.

Improving Performance through Institutional Change

Modifying a country's institutional environment, or mix, so that it contains more desirable characteristics requires directed institutional change. As discussed previously, institutional change involves altering one or more of the components of the institutional environment, resulting in modified institutional incentives, human behavior, and outcomes. Yet most modifications to the institutional environment actually reinforce the prevailing institutional composition; therefore, institutional change is more evolutionary than revolutionary. By contrast, directed institutional change occurs when purposeful efforts are made to change the nature of the incentive structure to modify behavior and outcomes (i.e., to achieve new outcomes).

Institutional theory suggests that institutional entrepreneurs are required to initiate the process of directed institutional change (North 1990). Institutional entrepreneurs are motivated by shifts in prices, preferences, the acquisition of new knowledge, a combination thereof, or some internally held beliefs (North 1990). In the case of improving protected area management performance, "conservation entrepreneurs" are needed to undertake directed institutional change.

Conservation entrepreneurs are individuals whose personal and/or professional objectives are compatible with, or promote, stated conservation objectives. They can be primary or secondary. Primary conservation entrepreneurs initiate directed institutional change and can be domestic or foreign, internal to protected area management or external; they may act independently or on behalf of an organization, and they may operate at the national, regional, or local level.

Regardless of origin and role, the success of primary conservation entrepreneurs in executing institutional change is determined by how accurately they gauge the institutional environment. A successful conservation entrepreneur will have an intimate understanding of the institutional context of protected area management. With this knowledge, the entrepreneur will attempt to achieve as much change as is perceived to be possible given the institutional environment in place. For example, if a country's political marketplace is particularly hostile to institutional change at the formal level, an entrepreneur may decide that working at the grassroots level for gradual changes to some of the relevant informal institutions is the best strategy.

Ignorance of a country's institutional environment, particularly its informal institutions, can stymie efforts by conservation entrepreneurs to direct institutional change. Such unfamiliarity may explain why the efforts of foreign conservation entrepreneurs working in developing countries are often ineffective. Foreign conservation entrepreneurs may possess inaccurate mental models of the institutional environment of the host country, due to preconceived assumptions about local institutions, simple naïveté, or both. Consequently, they may design inappropriate programs and have unrealistic expectations about what a project can accomplish and the time necessary to effect change.

Once individuals are motivated to become primary conservation entrepreneurs, their efforts to direct institutional change often involve altering various components of the environment so that secondary entrepreneurs emerge. Secondary conservation entrepreneurs are those stakeholders who respond positively to the changes made to the institutional mix and reinforce the new institutional incentives. This can result in a path of institutional evolution that increasingly favors protected areas. An example from Nepal illustrates this dynamic.[12]

In 1985, concerned about the rapid environmental degradation in the scenic and biologically rich Annapurna area, His Majesty's Government of Nepal (HMG) wished to establish a national park. Yet poor management performance and conflict with local people in other Nepalese protected areas caused HMG to perceive that a new approach and set of institutions were needed. For example, in an effort to secure social support from local communities in the area, HMG surveyed them on their feelings about the proposed park. The communities were against the idea because they associated parks with the armed enforcement and resettlement practices that had occurred in other protected areas under the direction of the government management agency, the Department of National Parks and Wildlife Conservation (DNPWC). This information motivated government officials to undertake directed institutional change so as to increase the likelihood of a good conservation outcome.

In 1986, national legislation established the Annapurna Conservation Area (ACA), not as a national park but as a multiple-use area. As such, the ACA's principal management objective is the long-term conservation of biodiversity, though the area is zoned for different land uses including wilderness, limited use, and intensive use. To generate local support, hunting and the collection of forest products are allowed in certain areas, visitor use fees are earmarked for local development, and some management authority is devolved to the village level. The introduction of appropriate formal institutions changed the opportunity costs for resident communities of supporting the establishment of the ACA and its management objectives. New perceptions of formal protected area institutions and objectives were created that subsequently led to greater social support, as described later.

HMG vested the management authority for the ACA in a parastatal organization rather than in the DNPWC, seemingly based on the new information acquired regarding public perception of the DNPWC. The parastatal, the King Mahendra Trust for Nature Conservation (KMTNC), already had some smaller conservation successes to its credit. Whereas the Department of National Parks and Wildlife Conservation had a history of poor relations with local people, the KMTNC was known to regard the conservation of biodiversity and the welfare of local people as equally important and interdependent.

The KMTNC enjoys autonomy in its management decisions regarding the ACA, and it controls its own revenue and budget (though HMG maintains regulatory authority). The KMTNC has the power to raise funds from the international community for management of the ACA, including local development projects. Due to its autonomy, the KMTNC has been able to avoid many of the problems associated with DNPWC management and to execute projects efficiently and effectively.

The positive institutional incentives created by HMG encouraged KMTNC personnel to try to create additional secondary conservation entrepreneurs from among the ACA's resident communities. For example, the KMTNC decided to reduce the costs of sound environmental practices for the proprietors of local businesses. Local people had started businesses catering to the thirty thousand tourists who "trekked" through the area each year, but sewage and rubbish disposal were inadequate, and forests were cleared to supply fuel, causing numerous environmental problems. A KMTNC training program changed the costs of information and technology for local people. The program provided new knowledge that resulted in improved service, standardized menus and prices, and better sewage and rubbish disposal practices. Information on alternative technology, such as solar panels, was distributed, and financial support was provided to allow hotels and restaurants to switch from wood to kerosene. By changing the cost of information and technology, the KMTNC encouraged local businesspeople to become secondary conservation entrepreneurs and behave in a manner that supports stated ACA management objectives. The modified social preferences were evidenced, for example, when local businesses reinvested a portion of their profits (furnishing up to 50 percent of the costs) into trail upgrading and maintenance in the ACA.

The example of Nepal demonstrates how primary conservation entrepreneurs (in this case national-level politicians) can direct institutional change so that the institutional mix comprises more desirable characteristics for protected area management. Yet in many developing countries, where domestic political and legal support for protected areas is limited and a supportive national framework is lacking, incentives for domestic primary conservation entrepreneurs are weak or nonexistent. These situations represent an area of opportunity for foreign individuals and organizations to act as primary conservation entrepreneurs. Foreigners, such as those working for an international conservation NGO or aid agency, are less constrained by a host country's institutional environment than its citizens and normally have informal institutions that are supportive of conservation objectives (as evidenced in their chosen occupation).

Foreign conservation entrepreneurs can deliberately work to change prices, preferences, or introduce new knowledge, encouraging the emergence of domestic conservation entrepreneurs. A sound understanding of a country's institutional environment and of the dynamics of institutional change can make foreign conservation entrepreneurs more effective. Otherwise, as has been the case in the past, their objectives will likely be overly ambitious and their time frame too short. In addition to being ineffective, their prescriptions and projects may have unintended and perhaps even undesirable consequences. For example, when a project changes the value of natural resources (e.g., wildlife), the underlying property rights may require alterations, or the outcome may be accelerated exploitation or a new distribution of wealth and associated social effects. In some instances, these institutional changes may actually disadvantage groups that the project was designed to help and lead to reduced social support for conservation objectives. A thorough understanding of a country's institutional incentives prior to implementation provides a way to anticipate potential side effects and to better direct efforts to improve outcomes.

The characteristics of institutional change suggest that in most cases sustained progress in protected area management performance can be expected to be gradual and incremental. Clearly, where there is little or no evidence of domestic conservation entrepreneurship, and therefore no individuals or organizations with a stake in good performance outcomes, progress will be much slower than in countries where the institutional incentives already reward activity by conservation entrepreneurs. This is where the state of a country's current institutional mix and its level of adaptive efficiency figure prominently into determining the possible degree of change and the time necessary to effect it.

Despite cautions against overly optimistic expectations for rapid improvements to conservation outcomes through directed institutional change, it is possible to effect favorable changes to a country's institutional mix (North 1990). The strategy of creating domestic conservation entrepreneurs suggested by the institutional approach has the advantage of eventually shaping endogenous preferences for conservation, creating a sense of ownership over the new institutional environment among stakeholders. Consequently, while directed institutional change and the creation of domestic conservation entrepreneurs requires a long-term perspective, improvements in performance are likely to be self-sustaining.

CONCLUSION

Protected areas represent a potential source of biodiversity, ecosystem services, watershed protection, and opportunities for recreation, education, and research. Yet, throughout the world, poor management performance significantly compromises these values. Furthermore, poor management persists in many developing countries despite substantial financial assistance and expert advice designed to improve conservation outcomes. While this is an enduring concern, the related literature lacks a theoretical basis for understanding the persistence of poor protected area management performance and the variations in performance among countries. Consequently, analysis and policy prescriptions appear to be compromised.

The institutional approach to protected area management offers a framework and language for analyzing the numerous variables influencing stakeholder behavior and for understanding the relationship of these variables to one another and to management outcomes. As such, the institutional approach has value for scholars interested in better understanding protected area management issues and for policymakers and practitioners wishing to generate more appropriate and effective prescriptions

While many of the conclusions of the approach are not new—for example, that cultural characteristics influence management outcomes or that a change in prices can increase preferences for conservation—it does offer a theoretical context for these aspects that has been absent from the literature. As North (1990) points out, the main strength of an institutional framework is that it can transform a collection of ad hoc descriptions into a meaningful story. That the protected areas literature is characterized by anecdotal evidence of management challenges suggests that the institutional approach has considerable potential for making the lessons from case studies more meaningful.

In addition to improving the analytical quality of the protected area management literature, the approach can increase the possible effectiveness of policy prescriptions. For instance, understanding the pivotal role that informal institutions play in reducing the costs associated with monitoring and enforcing protected area laws can lead to targeted efforts to change any hostile informal institutions. Depending on a country's circumstances, primary efforts may be directed at those responsible for law enforcement, while secondary efforts focus on other key stakeholders such as park neighbors. Strategies for increasing social support for enforcement duties might include making enforcement methods more acceptable or improving morale through innovative compensation schemes or education programs. Other options include making formal institutions more appropriate so that they reflect the history, philosophy, and preferences of the country in question, which then creates greater social support for protected area laws and management objectives. Another possibility is to strengthen both formal and informal institutions simultaneously.

An institutional analysis of a country can suggest a preferred course of action to improve its protected area management performance. Yet any policies or projects that change prices or preferences, be they foreign or domestic in origin, are likely to have additional institutional side effects, which may be unanticipated by the implementing agencies. Thus, prescriptions should reflect, as best they can, the multidimensional and interactive nature of a country's institutional environment.

The implications of the institutional approach for improving management performance are not without complication. For example, if a country chooses to make its formal provisions for protected areas more appropriate (e.g., through modifying laws imported or imposed from a foreign institutional context), it creates an obligation to meet the newly stated objectives, which cannot be as easily dismissed as when formal institutions were not indigenous. Furthermore, there are no simple prescriptions for improving protected area management performance; there is no one model of good protected area management. In addition, the path-dependent nature of institutional change suggests that any improvement in performance outcomes will most likely be gradual and incremental. Moreover, while foreign conservation entrepreneurs can be important catalysts for institutional change, sustained improvements in management performance require domestic conservation entrepreneurs with a stake in perpetuating these conditions. The time required to motivate domestic conservation entrepreneurs, for them to change the incentive structure, and to improve management outcomes, depends on the institutional conditions of the country in question. In most instances, a long-term perspective is best.

On a more positive note, while the strategies suggested by the institutional approach involve considerable time, effort, and patience, the resulting protected area management practices and objectives are more likely to be appropriate and realistic and therefore have greater potential for stakeholder support and for sustained improvements in outcomes. Furthermore, many of the desirable characteristics for good protected area management outcomes, such as well-defined property rights, respect for the rule of law, and an impartial judiciary can also contribute to improving a country's economic performance, a win-win situation.

Finally, the institutional approach to protected area management should not be seen as an excuse for a country to dismantle all its conservation laws or to eliminate protected areas in the name of appropriateness. Protected areas are needed for the long-term conservation of biological diversity. As long as this remains their primary management objective, then a country can decide on how best to achieve this goal in accordance with its own unique values and preferences. Yet the institutional approach is not just a call for greater cultural sensitivity. It is a balanced perspective that also stresses the importance of formal institutions, such as protected area legislation, and the need for impartial law enforcement.

NOTES

1. In this chapter, *conservation* is defined as any activity that maintains the long-term health of biodiversity (at the ecosystem, species, and genetic levels) and therefore includes preservation and sustainable use. Performance is assumed to be measured against the stated objectives of a given protected area, as specified in legislation, policy, or management plans. Good performance is equated with outcomes that closely reflect stated objectives, while poor performance is equated with outcomes which are far from the stated objectives.

2. The institutional approach to protected area management developed herein is designed to apply equally to all countries, regardless of levels of wealth or income. Much of the analysis and many of the examples, however, will pertain specifically to the world's poorer countries because that is normally where protected area management challenges are the greatest.

3. Organizations are defined as groups of individuals bound by some common purpose to achieve objectives (North 1990).

4. Personal interview with Douglass North, Henry Luce Professor of Law and Liberty, Department of Economics, Washington University, 23 May 1995, at the Judge Institute of Management, University of Cambridge, United Kingdom.

5. The theory of path dependence, as developed by Arthur (1988), illustrates how minor historical occurrences can result in one technology being favored over another. Arthur uses the example of typewriter keys to illustrate how technologies develop due to a series of small choices over time, resulting in the current level and type of technology employed. The example is interesting because of the nonalphabetical placement of letters on the keyboard, yet the arrangement endures. North (1990) develops the theory of institutional change within the context of path dependency.

6. Protected area stakeholders are individuals and organizations with a political, economic, or social interest in management outcomes. A country's stakeholders might include protected area management personnel, national and local politicians, park neighbors, park visitors, academics, foreign donors and consultants, domestic NGOs (nongovernmental organizations), foreign NGOs, tour operators, and other private sector concerns.

7. It is recognized that individuals within an organization may be very creative or innovative in pursuing objectives that are contrary to those that are formally stated. In this instance, however, creativity and innovation are assumed to facilitate stated management objectives.

8. It is assumed that countries have stated conservation objectives, as embodied in national-level institutions such as protected area legislation. This assumption makes possible the discussion of desirable characteristics for achieving the stated objectives. If a country has no interest in conservation and no stated objectives, then this discussion does not apply.

9. This assumes that a country's formally stated management objectives are consistent with the long-term conservation of biodiversity. Clearly, if there is no social preference for wildlife conservation and protected areas, it is undesirable to have formal institutions reflect such preferences, and other measures, such as changing beliefs to be supportive of basic conservation goals, are the best strategy.

10. Also, making legislation appropriate does not negate the need to have some protected areas managed for nonconsumptive uses (Categories I–III). However, in countries where consumption of wildlife has a long history, then sustainable use protected areas (Category VI) may dominate. Yet, like all protected areas, to meet the formally stated conservation objectives of Category VI (see IUCN 1994) requires effective management.

11. It could be argued that the failure to enforce on behalf of the state is largely due to budget constraints, but budgets are determined by national governments, and the meager parks budgets in many counties merely reflect the low social and economic values assigned to protected areas. National governments usually can find funds to secure state property if it is perceived as valuable (e.g., mines).

12. The example summarizes a case study from Wells and Brandon (1992), with additional information from Heinen and Kattel (1992), but recasts the information in an institutional context.

REFERENCES

Anderson, Terry L., and Donald R. Leal. 1991. *Free Market Environmentalism*. Boulder, Colo.: Westview.

Arthur, W. Brian. 1988. "Self-Reinforcing Mechanisms in Economics." In *The Economy as a Complex Evolving System*, ed. P. Anderson, K. Arrow, and D. Pines. Reading, Mass.: Addison-Wesley, 9–31.

Barzetti, Valerie, ed. 1993. *Parks and Progress: Protected Areas and Economic Development in Latin America and the Caribbean*. Cambridge: IUCN and WCMC.

Bell, Richard, and C. Clarke. 1984. "Why Have Master Plans?" In *Conservation and Wildlife Management in Africa*, ed. Richard Bell and E. McShane-Caluzi. Proceedings of a workshop organized by the U.S. Peace Corps at Kasungu National Park, Malawi, October. Produced through the Office of Training and Program Support, Forestry and Natural Resources Sector, U.S. Peace Corps, 503–26.

Bell, Richard, and E. McShane-Caluzi, eds. 1984. *Conservation and Wildlife Management in Africa*. Proceedings of a workshop organized by the U.S. Peace Corps at Kasungu National Park, Malawi, October. Produced through the Office of Training and Program Support, Forestry and Natural Resources Sector, U.S. Peace Corps.

deMoor, Andre, and Peter Calamai. 1997. *Subsidizing Unsustainable Development: Undermining the Earth with Public Funds*. San José, Costa Rica: Earth Council.

Egan, T. 1997. "Adapting to Fees for Enjoying Public Lands." *New York Times*, 21 August.

Gadgil, Madhav, F. Berkes, and Carl Folke. 1993. "Indigenous Knowledge for Biodiversity Conservation." *Ambio* 22: 151–56.

Gadgil, Madhav, and Ramachandra Guha. 1992. *This Fissured Land: An Ecological History of India*. Berkeley: University of California Press.

Githinji, Madhav, and Charles Perrings. 1993. "Social and Ecological Sustainability in the Use of Biotic Resources in Sub-Saharan Africa." *Ambio* 22, nos. 2–3: 110–16.

Glowka, Lyle, Françoise Burhenne-Guilmin, Hugh Synge, Jeffrey A. McNeely, and Lothar G'ndling. 1994. *A Guide to the Convention on Biological Diversity*. Environmental Policy and Law Paper No. 30. Gland, Switzerland: IUCN.

Heinen, Joel, and Bijaya Kattel. 1992. "A Review of Conservation Legislation in Nepal: Past Progress and Future Needs." *Environmental Management* 16: 723–33.

International Institute for Environment and Development. 1994. *Whose Eden? An Overview of Community Approaches to Wildlife Management*. Nottingham, U.K.: Russell.

International Union for the Conservation of Nature. 1992. *Protected Areas of the World: A Review of National Systems*. Vols. 1–4. Gland, Switzerland: Author.

———. 1993. *Parks for Life: Report of the IVth World Congress on National Parks and Protected Areas*. Gland, Switzerland.

———. 1994. *Protecting Nature: Regional Reviews of Protected Areas*. Gland, Switzerland.

International Union for the Conservation of Nature, United Nations Environment Program, and World Wildlife Fund. 1980. *World Conservation Strategy: Living Conservation for Sustainable Development*. Gland, Switzerland: World Conservation Union.

———. 1991. *Caring for the Earth: A Strategy for Sustainable Living*. Gland, Switzerland: Author.

James, Alexander, Jeremy Harrison, Michael Green, and James Paine. 1999. "A Global Review of Protected Area Budgets and Staffing." *WCMC Biodiversity Series*. Cambridge: World Conservation Monitoring Center.

Kimmage, Kevin. 1990. "Nigeria's Home-Grown Dust Bowl." *New Scientist* (July): 42–44.
Kiss, Agnes, ed. 1990. *Living with Wildlife: Wildlife Resource Management with Local Participation in Africa*. Washington, D.C.: World Bank.
Lacher, Thomas, James Nations, Elizabeth Kennedy, and Manuel Ramirez. 1996. "Conservation Strategies and Incentive Mechanisms Implemented within the La Amistad Conservation and Development Initiative for Costa Rica and Panama." Paper presented at the Global Biodiversity Forum, Montreal, Canada, 31 August–1 September.
Lamprey, Hugh. 1992. "Challenges Facing Protected Area Management in Sub-Saharan Africa." In *Managing Protected Areas in Africa*, ed. Walter Lusigi. Paris: UNESCO–World Heritage Fund.
Leader-Williams, Nigel, and Steve Albon. 1988. "Allocation of Resources for Conservation." *Nature* 336: 533–35.
Loureiro, Wilson. 1996. Ecological ICMS. Economic Incentive toward Biodiversity Conservation: A Successful Experience in Brazil. Paper presented at the fourth session of the Global Biodiversity Forum, Montreal, Canada, 31 August–1 September.
Lusigi, Walter, ed. 1992. *Managing Protected Areas in Africa*. Paris: UNESCO–World Heritage Fund.
MacKinnon, John, Kathy MacKinnon, Graham Child, and Jim Thorsell. 1986. *Managing Protected Areas in the Tropics*. Gland, Switzerland: IUCN.
Martin, Rowan. 1990. "Appendix 1: Analysis of Conservation Success." In *African Elephants and Rhinos: Status Survey and Conservation Action Plan*. Gland, Switzerland: IUCN/SSC African Elephant and Rhino Specialist Group.
Matowanyika, J., R. Serafin, and J. Nelson. 1992. *Conservation and Development in Africa: A Management Guide to Protected Areas and Local Populations in the Afrotropical Realm*. Gland, Switzerland: WWF International.
Maybury-Lewis, David. 1992. *Millennium: Tribal Wisdom and the Modern World*. New York: Viking.
Mittermeier, Russell A., T. Werner, and A. Lees. 1996. "New Caledonia: A Conservation Imperative for an Ancient Land." *Oryx* 30, no. 2: 104–12.
Munasinghe, Mohan, Jeffrey A. McNeely, and Aldelaida Schwab, eds. 1994. *Protected Area Economics and Policy: Linking Conservation and Sustainable Development*. Washington, D.C.: World Bank.
Ndosi, O. 1992. "Preparing Management Plans for Protected Areas." In *Managing Protected Areas in Africa*, Walter Lusigi, ed. Paris: UNESCO–World Heritage Fund, 117–24.
North, Douglass. 1990. *Institutions, Institutional Change, and Economic Performance*. Cambridge: Cambridge University Press.
———. 1993. "Economic Performance through Time." Presentation as the Prize Lecture in Economic Science in memory of Alfred Nobel, 9 December, Nobel Foundation, Stockholm.
———. 1994. "Constraints on Institutional Innovation: Transaction Costs, Incentive Compatibility, and Historical Considerations." In *Agriculture, Environment and Health: Sustainable Development in the 21st Century*, ed. Vernon W. Ruttan. Minneapolis: University of Minnesota Press, 48–70.
Noss, A. 1997. "Challenges to Nature Conservation with Community Development in Central African Forests." *Oryx* 31, no. 3: 180–88.
Ostrom, Elinor, and Edella Schlager. 1996. "The Formation of Property Rights." In *Rights*

to Nature: Ecological, Economic, Cultural, and Political Principles of Institutions for the Environment, ed. Susan Hanna, Carl Folke, and Karl-Goran Maler. Washington, D.C.: Island, 127–56.

Poole, P. 1989. *Developing a Partnership of Indigenous Peoples, Conservationists, and Land Use Planners in Latin America.* Washington, D.C.: World Bank.

Spinage, Clive. 1991. *History and Evolution of the Fauna Conservation Laws of Botswana.* Gaborone: Botswana Society.

———. 1996. "The Rule of Law and African Game: A Review of Some Recent Trends and Concerns." *Oryx* 30, no. 3: 178–86.

Suzuki, David, and Peter Knudtson. 1992. *Wisdom of the Elders.* New York: Bantam.

United Nations Environment Program. 1992. *The Convention on Biological Diversity.* Chatalaine, Switzerland: Interim Secretariat for the Convention on Biological Diversity.

———. 1995. *Biodiversity Assessment Global.* Cambridge: Cambridge University Press.

Wells, Michael, and Katrina Brandon. 1992. *People and Parks: Linking Protected Area Management with Local Communities.* Washington, D.C.: World Bank, World Wildlife Fund, and USAID.

West, Patrick C., and Steven R. Brechin, eds. 1991. *Resident Peoples and National Parks: Social Dilemmas and Strategies in International Conservation.* Tucson: University of Arizona Press.

Western, David, and R. Wright, eds. 1994. *Natural Connections: Perspectives in Community Based Conservation.* Washington, D.C.: Island.

Williamson, Doug. 1994. *Botswana: Environmental Policies and Practices under Scrutiny.* Cape Town: Lindlife.

Wilson, Jane. 1995. *Lemurs of the Lost World: Exploring the Forests and Crocodile Caves of Madagascar.* 2d ed. London: Impact.

———. 1996. "Conservation and Ecology of a New Blind Fish, *Glossogobius ankaranensis* from the Ankarana Caves, Madagascar." *Oryx* 30, no. 3: 218–21.

World Conservation Monitoring Center. 1992. *Global Biodiversity: Status of the Earth's Living Resources.* London: Chapman & Hall.

Part II

Applications: Successful Park Institutions

2

The Natal Parks Board Experience in Southern Africa

George R. Hughes

The slaughter of wildlife in South Africa during the colonial expansion period, especially in the nineteenth century, resulted in declines in many large mammal species. At least twenty-one species of large animals neared extinction or actually became extinct in South Africa during this period, including the elephant, lion, white rhino, buffalo, hippopotamus, giraffe, and numerous ungulate species. Twelve of these species became locally extinct in KwaZulu-Natal.

The cause of these declines was trade and commerce in wildlife (Pringle, Bond, and Clark 1982). As a result, early conservationists developed a clear conviction that commercial exploitation of wildlife and conservation were incompatible. The creation of laws protecting wildlife and especially the proclamation of wildlife reserves was not universally applauded as progressive steps, however (Ellis 1975). Such laws were resisted strongly by an uncaring electorate and resented intensely by indigenous peoples when traditional lands became unavailable to them (Kemf 1993).

The first formal protected areas in Africa, specifically for large mammal conservation, were established in KwaZulu-Natal in 1895 (Ellis 1975). Since then, the protected area system in KwaZulu-Natal has grown to cover 6,752 square kilometers, or 8.4 percent of the provincial land area. In addition, 28 percent of the KwaZulu-Natal coastline has been officially protected. The KwaZulu-Natal conservation areas are a part of a larger South African system of protected areas that covers 69,283 square kilometers and includes the Kruger National Park, established in 1898.

The Natal Parks Board was formed in 1947 as a parastatal agency to manage the protected area system in what is now the KwaZulu-Natal province. The Natal Parks Board (the board) is South Africa's first parastatal conservation body at the provincial level. At the federal level in South Africa, the National Parks Board is also a parastatal agency. A parastatal conservation agency is a legally separate entity from the government, though not a private company. The agency is overseen by a politically appointed board of trustees, has the legal authority to raise and retain its own revenues, and receives a yearly subvention from the national or provincial government.

The parastatal structure has provided the Natal Parks Board with the flexibility and incentives to achieve a number of outstanding conservation successes. Since its creation in 1947, the board has overseen the return of many large mammal species to the parks and elsewhere and the incorporation of local communities and landowners in a model of modern conservation management. Over the past fifty years, the Natal Parks Board has evolved from traditional protectionism to a balanced, people- and economics-oriented biodiversity conservation authority that has achieved some of the "benchmark" conservation successes in Africa.

EARLY CHALLENGES TO CONSERVATION, 1947–1960

In the 1950s, the board's conservation strategy was dominated by a law enforcement philosophy aimed at controlling the use of wildlife outside of protected areas, consolidating and increasing the size of the early game reserves, and adding new nature reserves. This was a difficult period, as little headway was made in changing the prevailing public attitudes, and considerable hostility was experienced from private landowners (mainly whites) and rural indigenous communities. In the coastal areas, where the province was responsible for all shore-based exploitation of marine resources, the gradual introduction of legislative control was poorly received.

The board gradually achieved control over this period and began to earn a grudging respect from resource users. There is little doubt that the positive change in attitudes was as a result of the board's early belief that people should enjoy the parks. People who visited the parks were made welcome, particularly those with influence. The board made some far-sighted decisions at this time to expand the modest overnight accommodation that had been available since 1928, when the first tourist facility, a guest house, was built in Hluhluwe Game Reserve. The capacity of the new facilities reached fifty beds. Though the accommodation remained simple, these new facilities contributed in no small part to the popularity of the parks in Natal.

Of even greater importance were the clear indications that wildlife populations, even white rhinoceros, were beginning to show noticeable and, in some cases, surprising growth within the protected areas (Player 1967; Vincent 1970).

THE EMERGENCE OF A CONSERVATION INDUSTRY, 1960–1980

An enormous change in attitudes toward conservation occurred in South Africa after 1960. The board received benevolent financial support from the provincial legislature, which, coupled with the flexibility of the parastatal structure, permitted considerable freedom to experiment. In addition, the board's reputation as an authority that was clearly different soon attracted resource managers, biologists, and other scientists, all of whom have played a pivotal role in developing the board's management skills and policies.

As a result, the board recorded a number of conservation successes in the 1960–1980 period. The board gradually brought back animals that had become extinct in the province, with the ultimate reintroduction being that of elephant in 1982. The populations of many of these species in the province expanded exponentially, and the board began efforts to spread these populations into private land areas.

During this period, large mammal populations grew at rates that presented new management challenges, and the board took the first steps to develop census techniques and control methods. Large-scale culling of surplus impala and nyala became a management tool but was not universally popular and considered wasteful. The board, therefore, encouraged experimentation to improve the capture and translocation of surplus animals, and after some disappointing failures, even rhinoceros were translocated safely to other parks in Natal. New techniques were developed, better equipment was designed, and soon a steady stream of animals were being moved from Natal parks to the rest of South Africa and even overseas.

The white rhinoceros story is illustrative of this program. By 1895, fewer than fifty white rhino were left in South Africa, all existing in the Natal province. One hundred years later, the number of white rhino in KwaZulu-Natal had grown to several thousand and had spread throughout the province in a number of separate populations. In addition, 2,635 white rhino had been relocated to other provinces in South Africa, 566 to other countries in Sub-Saharan Africa, and 673 to other countries. Since 1962 the board has captured and translocated over a hundred thousand animals, including four thousand rhinoceros. No less than 20 percent of all white rhinoceros in South Africa are privately owned (Buijs and Papenfus 1996), demonstrating that the board has achieved its goal of making wildlife a valued economic asset for the private sector. From a program started in 1962, the Natal Parks Board now earns over $1 million per year from sales of white rhino and other large game animals. These funds make a valuable contribution to the costs of conservation management, as they do have to be returned to the provincial government.

In 1963, the board, realizing that successful biodiversity conservation must involve private landowners, started the first Extension Service designed to encourage the proper management and care of wildlife on private land. The availability of surplus mammals from the Natal Parks Board became a critical tool in building constructive relationships with farmers and other landowners. Hunting was encouraged on private lands (Mentis 1972–73), and the board made many species available at heavily subsidized prices for restocking game farms and other conservation areas. The aim of the board's policy was to spread wildlife populations throughout the province, making species less vulnerable and giving them an economic value. Even the hunting of white rhinoceros was encouraged, and trophy animals were made available for this purpose.

Other notable conservation successes during this period were Operation Rhino (Vincent 1970), the loggerhead and leatherback sea turtle protection program (Hughes 1974 and 1989), and the establishment of the conservancy movement (Kotze 1993). These achievements were the result of sound teamwork between resource managers and scientists that also produced the first management plans for protected areas. These early opportunities for experimentation created the springboard that, in the 1980s, launched the board into its present goal-oriented management strategy, supporting biodiversity conservation through social awareness and economics.

INTEGRATING CONSERVATION AND DEVELOPMENT, 1981–1997

In the 1980s, the stage was set for a paradigm shift in management style of the Natal Parks Board. The board's policies began to achieve focus, management became goal oriented, and strategies for species survival were developed. At the same time, there was a growing awareness that, in the rest of Africa, wildlife was faring badly as were the departments responsible for biodiversity conservation. In contrast, the Natal Parks Board began to exploit the opportunities made available by its abundant wildlife resources and ever-increasing expertise and confidence.

By the 1980s, the board had developed a viable wildlife conservation industry with the full participation of local communities and landowners. The board's strategy was to develop four components of the wildlife industry in Natal: the sale of wildlife, ecotourism in the parks, the emergence of private nature conservancies, and the growth of local economic benefits from the park system. The successful development of these four components represents the culmination of fifty years of effort by the Natal Parks Board to create a viable and integrated wildlife conservation industry in the province. In the 1990s, the board began to receive significant financial benefits from these earlier efforts.

The Natal Parks Board's annual revenues have increased nearly fivefold since 1989, as shown in figure 2.1. These revenues represent funds raised and retained by the agency, primarily from ecotourism and wildlife sales, but do not include the annual allocation from the government. While much of the board's revenues must be set against costs, particularly with respect to the operation of visitor facilities, a yearly surplus from operations is generated. In the fiscal year ending in 1997, the surplus from ecotourism operations amounted to $1.8 million (Natal Parks Board 1997). This surplus represents additional funds that directly support biodiversity conservation activities and community outreach efforts. In recent years, the annual subvention from government has decreased, and the surplus revenue has allowed the board to continue to fund its activities adequately.

Another source of revenue for the board is the Natal Parks Board Conservation Trust. The trust, established in 1989, is a capital fund that accepts donations from

Figure 2.1
Natal Parks Board Revenue

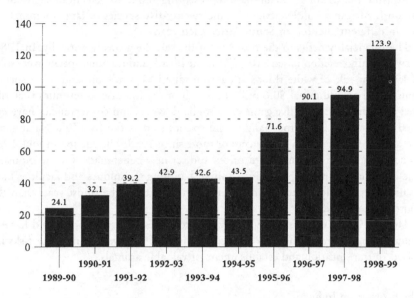

Source: Natal Parks Board, Pietermaritzburg, KwaZulu-Natal.

public and private sources creating a permanent endowment for the parks in KwaZulu-Natal. The trust provides an annual flow of funds to the board in an amount equal to the interest earned on the capital endowment. The trust's contributions to the board have grown fairly rapidly, now having contributed nearly $400,000 to operations. With its steadily growing endowment, the trust has unlimited potential to contribute to biodiversity conservation in the future. The Conservation Trust fund is an excellent indicator of the public's acceptance of the board's mission as the growth in donations is a demonstration of the willingness to pay for biodiversity conservation.

The following sections will review the more recent results of the board's strategy of developing a viable wildlife conservation industry and integrating it with society in KwaZulu-Natal. The four components of the strategy include wildlife sales, ecotourism, support for private conservancies, and community involvement in resource management.

Wildlife Sales

In 1988, board policy changed from making wildlife available at subsidized prices to selling through auction to let market forces drive the prices of wildlife. The first Natal Game Auction took place in 1989, and it has since become the premier game auction in South Africa. Sales of wildlife at this auction now set the benchmark indicator of wildlife values. The game auction in 1996 raised $1.9 million for the board from the sale of 1,546 animals, representing about 40 percent of the value of all South African wildlife auctions. Some twenty-five species of large mammal are sold in different auctions in South Africa each year.

The financial benefits to the board from the sale are growing annually. In 1986, the white rhino auction raised $10,327 for the board, and no other species were sold. In 1996, the sale of white rhinos at auction raised $1.2 million, and other species contributed an additional $0.6 million. Much of the increase in revenues is attributed to higher prices for live game as more landowners and conservancies have entered the market. Prices for many of the species sold at the KwaZulu-Natal game auction have increased by 100 percent or more since 1988. The auction in June 1998 broke many South African record prices and set new benchmarks for the industry. The care and commitment put into animal handling techniques and facilities have resulted in prices for board animals being significantly higher most years than the South African average.

The board also delivers game to buyers' properties at market prices and has encouraged the insurance industry to become involved to cover the inherent risks involved in translocation and establishment of valuable animals.

The Ecotourism Industry

In 1958, the Natal Parks Board was the first conservation authority in South Africa to establish wilderness trails for visitors (Player 1967). Although the board had, for many years, encouraged tourists to visit the protected areas and had continued to develop overnight facilities, the basic goal had been one of providing a social service rather than running a profit-earning activity. In fact, when the running costs and income were thoroughly examined in the late 1980s, it was found that overnight visitors were being subsidized. This analysis resulted in a change in policy to develop tourist facilities that would cater for all levels and operate at a profit.

Over time, the board has become the single largest ecotourism provider in KwaZulu-Natal, as a result of a major effort to improve visitor facilities. This effort has included tapping into the private financial markets to fund capital investment in tourist facilities in the parks. Over the past eight years, the board has invested over $8.9 million in tourist developments, of which $7.1 million was borrowed from finance houses, $1.6 million was raised from joint venture/donor schemes, and the balance came from internal resources. The results of these efforts have been dramatic. Tourist numbers have risen substantially through the 1990s as the world ecotourism industry has recognized the outstanding offerings of the Natal Parks system. In 1997, surplus revenues from tourism contributed $1.8 million to the board's biodiversity conservation activities.

The board expects to benefit from the continuing strong growth in tourism to South Africa, particularly international ecotourism. Accordingly, the board is planning to expand its facilities by creating a number of new camps. A borrowing facility of $26.0 million has been arranged to fund these developments.

Private Conservancies and Biosphere Reserves

In 1977, fifteen years of extension effort saw the establishment of the first conservancy in KwaZulu-Natal, a grouping of private properties into a cooperative unit for the conservation of wildlife (Kotze 1993). In contrast to surrounding private land areas, wildlife inside the conservancies is recognized as a legitimate and valued asset as landowners seek ways to benefit financially and ecologically from conservation. The growth of the conservancy movement has been exponential and continues to this day. By 1997, there were 218 established conservancies in KwaZulu-Natal alone.

The demonstrated success of the conservancy movement in KwaZulu-Natal has led to its spread throughout South Africa. The concept is also being developed in other African countries, particularly in the southern region. At present, there are at least 355 established conservancies, mostly in South Africa but also in Zimbabwe, Botswana, Namibia and Kenya.

In addition to the extension services, the board supports the conservancies in a number of other ways. The board offers a 25 percent discount on wildlife species for first time introductions of any appropriate species (NPB Policy Document 3.I). In addition, the freedom for landowners to use wildlife and benefit directly from its sustainable use has been made extremely simple. For example, through registration as a commercial game reserve, landowners acquire total and absolute ownership of their wildlife (Natal Parks Board Ordinance 15 of 1974).

Over time, the conservancy movement has broadened its vision. An active Conservancy Association is now playing an increasingly prominent role in environmental matters, and this vision has seen the creation of urban conservancies and even industrial and commercial park conservancies. Many conservancies have committed themselves solely to wildlife management and ecotourism, both consumptive and nonconsumptive.

Encouraged by the success of the conservancy movement, the board launched the Biosphere Reserve concept, including some of its formally protected areas as required under the Man and Biosphere Charter (International Union for the Conservation of Nature [IUCN], United Nations Environment Program [UNEP], and World Wildlife Fund [WWF] 1991). The biosphere reserves are operated similarly to the conservancies, where a range of commercial activities are allowed in harmony with wildlife conservation.

The conservation activities promoted by the conservancy and biosphere movement have resulted in a dramatic increase in large mammal populations outside the park system. Sampling of wildlife populations within conservancies over time shows impressive growth in many large mammal species. For example, common reedbuck numbers in a sample of ten conservancies increased from 500 in 1984 to about 2,750 in 1996.

The commitment of the conservancies and biosphere reserves to the sustainable use of wildlife is exemplified by the Thukela Biosphere Reserve. Thukela is a private and community-owned biosphere reserve (including the Weenen Nature Reserve of the board), established in 1994, whose members have invested over $1.7 million in developing a major ecotourism destination. Eleven private landowners and local communities comprise the ownership of the biosphere reserve. They have invested in game reintroductions, infrastructure, training and human capacity development, and tourist facilities, including lodges, tented camps, rustic cottages, and a conference center. Sixty permanent and 105 temporary jobs have been created in the reserve. Thukela is an example of the many conservancies and biosphere reserves within KwaZulu-Natal and in southern Africa in general that are successfully integrating conservation and development.

Community Development

In KwaZulu-Natal, as well as the rest of Africa, biodiversity conservation has been perceived as a cost for society and not an investment that produces a stream of benefits. The Natal Parks Board has made strenuous efforts to rectify this view by not only developing a viable wildlife conservation industry but also by making sure that the benefits are spread throughout society. Accordingly, the board's most recent strategy has been to make biodiversity conservation relevant to poor, underprivileged, and previously disadvantaged communities. This is a strategy deemed necessary by conservation theorists for some time and has been tackled with vigor by only a few conservation authorities worldwide.

In 1991, the board launched its Community Outreach Program in partnership with a large community development nongovernmental organization, the Rural Foundation. This partnership and its objectives were formalized in a Natal Parks Board policy document (no. 5, xiv). At the time, the board committed a small number of staff to the program who were enthusiastic about the challenge of turning hostile communities into supportive communities. The program established discussions with local communities, called Neighbors' Forums, aimed at creating trust through improved communication. These fora established agreements for responsible access to surplus natural resources, the creation of small and medium business enterprises, and investments in community infrastructure through fund raising efforts by the board. Capacity building and empowerment through training were central to the success of this endeavor.

Under the program, local communities receive tangible benefits from three principal sources: the value of harvested natural resources, employment and earnings from entrepreneurial activities, and contributions made by the board to community infrastructure and other activities. Resources harvested by neighboring communities include thatch, reeds, wood, poles, hay, bamboo, gum, meat, mussels, and other commodities. The values are difficult to calculate, but the benefits to communities have been widespread throughout the province. Employment in the Natal Parks produces income of over $1 million per year for at least five communities, and it makes a contribution in the hundreds of thousands annually for another fourteen communities. Entrepreneurial activities by communities created over $250,000 in extra income in the fiscal year ended 1997. The board has contributed $4.4 million to community projects since the program inception in 1991. In 1997, these projects included cattle breeding training, indigenous nurseries, medicinal plant propagation training, organic vegetable gardening, sewing workshops, craft training, block making, community committee training, civic education training, adult education, literacy training, and many other projects (Natal Parks Board, various years).

The Community Outreach Program has recently been developed further, and it is now known as the Eco-Partners Program. New legislation will establish local conservation boards, designed to ensure broad participation in the board's biodiversity conservation and community development activities. A new innovation to assist in community development work has been the establishment of a Community Trust, which will be overseen by a board of trustees representing local community interests and the provincial government. It will be funded by a levy on visitors to the Natal parks, including a one-rand entrance fee, a ten-rand bed fee, and a five-rand camping fee.[1] The trust will make annual disbursements to the local conservation boards, based on their annual requests for support. The local conservation board will collect and prioritize project funding requests from adjacent communities on an annual basis. The local board will also be responsible for monitoring the implementation of the community projects throughout the year. The local conservation boards will give communities a direct stake in the management of a share of the resources from the wildlife conservation industry in KwaZulu-Natal.

The latest of the board's efforts to create new institutional structures for the involvement of local communities is the proposal for a Greater St. Lucia Wetland Park Company. The Wetland Park Company would be formed by aggregating the land areas of the current park, private landowners, and local communities into a single conservation unit. The company would issue shares to the owners based on their contribution of land to the new park. The Natal Parks Board will manage the entire area and seek additional investment in tourism infrastructure from private sector sources and international development banks. The adjacent local communities will have a substantial share of the equity ownership of the company based on their land contribution, giving them a strong incentive to participate fully in the management of the resources. A full feasibility study has been carried out (Leo-Smith 1997), and the board has placed a high priority on completing the model for implementation.

CONCLUSION

It has taken more than fifty years for the Natal Parks Board to evolve from a traditional nature conservation organization, with a commendable but narrow vision, to a modern body dedicated to making biodiversity relevant to all sectors of society. In accomplishing this transformation, the board has been guided by four principal strategies. The first has been to develop a viable wildlife conservation industry to demonstrate the economic value of biodiversity to KwaZulu-Natal and to contribute additional financial support for the board's conservation activities. The second has been to promote ecotourism, for several reasons. Ecotourism is the primary way to realize the financial values of biodiversity, it creates employment opportunities at all levels of society, and it promotes popular acceptance and enjoyment of the parks. Third, the board has sought to increase the involvement of private citizens and landowners in biodiversity conservation, through the conservancy and biosphere movement. Finally, the board actively develops new institutions for community participation in the management of resources from the parks to make biodiversity relevant to underprivileged and previously disadvantaged communities.

The success of this strategy shows that biodiversity conservation does not have to be a loss making activity for governments and taxpayers. The modest cost of the annual government subsidy, plus the revenues raised within the system, has created the basis of enormous economic benefits for the province (see also Creemers and Wood 1997). The parastatal structure has ensured, to some degree, that budget cuts in provincial subsidies will not cripple the achievements of the past. The board has no intention of becoming self-sufficient, however. Law enforcement, research, and environmental education are all important functions of a conservation agency, and these activities are seldom income generators.

By developing a viable wildlife conservation industry in KwaZulu-Natal, the board continues to strengthen its financial position and gain widespread acceptance at all levels of society, thereby ensuring the long-term survival of biodiversity in the province. This is balanced conservation built on a stable economic and social foundation that promises a future for biodiversity conservation in Africa.

ACKNOWLEDGMENTS

Thanks are due to the Center for Wildlife Economy, Potchefstroom University; Stockowners Cooperative, Pietermaritzburg; and Vleissentraal Pty Ltd of Louis Trichardt, all of which willingly provided their wildlife auction results. Janet Channing of the Thukela Biosphere Reserve cheerfully provided data. Other contributors are Eugene Geel, Mike Thayer, Pat Wilson, and Dr. Hans Grobler, all of the Natal Parks Board. My thanks to the board for permission to deliver the paper on which this chapter is based. Finally, I would like to acknowledge the vision, commitment and leadership of the board's first two directors, Colonel Jack Vincent and

John Geddes Page, without whose talents the Natal Parks Board would never have succeeded.

NOTE

1. Conversion rate: $1U.S. equals six South African rands.

REFERENCES

Buijs, Daan, and Tom Papenfus. 1996. *Survey: Rhinos on Private Land.* Pretoria: African Rhino Owners Association.

Creemers, Geert, and Libby Wood. 1997. *The Economic Contribution of Tourism to the Province of KwaZulu-Natal.* Report to the Interim Provincial Tourism Steering Committee, Durban.

Ellis, Beverley. 1975. "Game Conservation in Zululand, 1824–1947." Honors thesis, History Department, University of Natal, Pietermaritzburg.

Hughes, George R. 1974. *The Sea Turtles of South East Africa*, vol. 1. Investigational Report No. 35. Durban: Oceanographic Research Institute.

———. 1989. "Sea Turtles." In *Oceans of Life off Southern Africa*, ed. Rob Crawford and Andy Payne. Cape Town: Vlaeberg, 230–43.

International Union for the Conservation of Nature, United Nations Environment Program, and World Wildlife Fund. 1991. *Caring for the Earth: A Strategy for Sustainable Living.* Gland, Switzerland: IUCN.

Kemf, Elizabeth, ed. 1993. *The Law of the Mother.* San Francisco: Sierra Club Books.

Kotze, Stephen, 1993. "Conservancies in Natal, 1978–1993." Bachelor's (honors) thesis, University of Natal, Pietermaritzburg.

Leo-Smith, Kevin. 1997. *Proposed Greater St. Lucia Wetland Park Company.* Natal Parks Board and Conservation Corporation Africa Report to the Natal Parks Board.

Mentis, Michael. T. 1972–73. "Game on the Farm." *Farmers Weekly*, Series 1-29.

Natal Parks Board. Various years. *Yearbook.* Natal Parks Board, Pietermaritzburg, KwaZulu-Natal.

Player, Ian. 1967. "Translocation of White Rhino in South Africa." *Oryx* 9, no. 2: 137–50.

Pringle, John, Creena Bond, and James Clark. 1982. *The Conservationists and the Killers.* Cape Town: Books of Africa and T. V. Bulpin.

Vincent, John. 1970. "The History of Umfolozi Game Reserve, Zululand, as It Relates to Management." *Lammergeyer* 11: 7–49.

3

Back to the Future to Save Our Parks

Donald R. Leal and Holly Lippke Fretwell

Our national parks are in trouble. Their roads, historic buildings, visitor facilities, and water and sewer systems are falling apart. The Park Service says it has a $4.5 billion backlog of construction improvements and an $800 million backlog of major maintenance.[1] Even Yellowstone Park, the crown jewel of the national park system, is crumbling. To repair infrastructure and cover needed resource projects, it will cost $700 million.[2]

What has gone wrong? "Decades of forced neglect" is the answer given in a 1995 article in *U.S. News & World Report*, implying that the parks have not received enough money from Congress (Satchell and Tharp 1995, 25–36).

But Congress has not been all that stingy. Indeed, since 1980, the total budget for the National Park Service has nearly doubled, increasing from almost $700 million to about $1.3 billion.[3] From 1980 to 1995, spending on park operations grew at a healthy annual rate of 3.1 percent after adjusting for inflation, and full-time staff increased from 15,836 to 17,216 employees.[4] While spending on the agency itself increased, spending for major park repairs and renovations fell at an inflation-adjusted annual rate of 1.5 percent.[5] It appears that long-term investment in our national parks has played second fiddle to bureaucratic growth.

Could a business survive for long if most of its budget went to organizational growth rather than to ensuring the quality of its product? Certainly not. Park management continues "as is" in spite of the parks' deterioration only because the money to operate the parks comes from taxes, not from customers. If we are to improve the condition of our parks, the incentives governing our parks must change. The

This chapter was previously published as *PERC Policy Series*, PS-10 (June 1997). Copyright © the Political Economy Research Center.

goal should be to make them financially self-sufficient, supported by those who use them.

Fortunately, we are seeing signs that this is happening. Pushed by budget-conscious legislatures, fifteen state park systems now obtain at least half of their operating support from visitors, rather than taxpayers. Even national parks are testing the waters of greater user support. Congress recently authorized a three-year demonstration program that, on average, doubles entrance fees at up to a hundred parks. Those parks will get to keep 80 percent of the revenue from fees. Previously, they could keep only 15 percent of the revenue.

When they were established, our national parks were supposed to be self-supporting. This chapter examines the prospects for actually achieving this goal with our state and national parks. Going "back to the future" will enable our parks to solve fiscal problems while protecting the resources such as wildlife habitat that make parks such cherished treasures.

SELF-SUFFICIENCY BEGINS WITH REALISTIC FEES

Very simply, self-sufficiency means relying on park visitors, not Congress, for operating support. (True self-sufficiency would mean covering the costs of capital improvements, too, but self-sufficiency in operations would be an important start.) Attaining self-sufficiency will require, among other things, charging higher fees and practicing greater diligence in fee collection.

In the past, park fees have been a subject of controversy in the halls of Congress and state legislatures. But public sentiment has been changing. A 1995 nationwide survey by Colorado State University revealed that 80 percent of those surveyed did not oppose higher fees as long as all the fees went to the parks where they were collected (National Parks and Conservation Association 1995).

When it comes to realistic fees that can support our national parks, we have a long way to go. In 1995, proceeds from park recreation fees totaled $80.5 million, or about 7.5 percent of the total cost of park operations.[6] At approximately 270 million park visitors, 1995 proceeds from all 369 parks represented an anemic $0.30 per visitor.[7]

A primary reason for the low per-visitor return is the fact that over two hundred park units did not charge entrance fees, and those that did charge fees at the gate charged by the carload per week. At $10 per vehicle, a family of four could visit in Yellowstone Park for a week for $0.36 per person per day in 1996. Furthermore, entrance fees have failed to keep pace with inflation. Beginning 1 January 1997, Yellowstone's annual vehicle pass, which provides the user unlimited visits for the year, was raised from $15 to $40. But this hefty hike did not bring the price anywhere near the $133 (in 1995 dollars) that visitors paid in 1916 (Mackintosh 1983, 2). At $75, an annual pass to visit California's state parks is more realistic.

If national parks are to be self-sufficient, park managers must not only be allowed to charge more realistic fees, but they must be allowed to retain most of the proceeds to enhance their parks. Most of the receipts from fees go to the federal treasury instead of the parks themselves. Most national parks give up 85 percent of their proceeds to the treasury. Not being able to keep the lion's share of the proceeds weakens the incentive for park managers to maximize revenue.

Indeed, a 1993 audit by the U.S. Department of the Interior's (USDI) Office of Inspector General found that the Park Service collected $59 million from user fees in fiscal year 1991, but it could have collected $105 million more from entrance fees alone without raising existing fees (USDI 1993, 22). One of the chief reasons was weak fee collection. Of the 136 units authorized to collect entrance fees and retain only 15 percent of the proceeds, 131 had made inadequate collection efforts. For example, fees were collected from only half the 409,352 vehicles that entered Olympic National Park and from only 5 percent of the 356,238 vehicles that entered Cedar Breaks National Monument and Capitol Reef National Park.

Furthermore, hardly any national parks charge fees for popular activities such as hiking, nature tours, or fishing. Yet trails need upkeep, fisheries need monitoring, and interpreters have to be paid. An additional $123 million could have been collected if fees for these activities were charged, according to the audit (USDI 1993, 22).

SELF-SUFFICIENT AT THE START

At first, the national parks were supposed to be self-supporting. Congressional appropriations were to be limited to initial investments in roads and visitor facilities. Ferdinand Hayden, one of the early explorers of Yellowstone, the country's first national park, assured Congress that the park would require no appropriated funds. Yellowstone's first superintendent, Nathaniel Langford, even suggested that toll roads be leased through the park to pay for road maintenance (McDaniel 1996, 3).

This attitude was still strong in 1916 when Congress authorized the creation of the National Park Service. Interior Secretary Franklin Lane appointed Stephen Mather to run the fourteen existing parks on a self-supporting basis. In Mather's first report on parks to the secretary, he stated:

> It has been your desire that ultimately the revenues of several parks might be sufficient to cover the costs of their administration and protection and that Congress should only be requested to appropriate funds for their improvement. It appears that at least five parks now have a proven earning capacity sufficiently large to make their operation on this basis feasible and practicable. (Government Accounting Office [GAO] 1982, 2)

The five parks were Yellowstone, Yosemite, Mount Rainier, Sequoia and General Grant (now part of Kings Canyon/Sequoia).

By 1916, at least seven parks had seasonal auto fees, from $2 in Glacier and Mesa Verde to $10 in Yellowstone ($26 and $133 in 1995 dollars, respectively). Auto fees increased revenues, which reached over $65,000 in 1916 ($858,000 in 1995 dollars). Mather noted that "no policy of national park management has yielded more thoroughly gratifying results than that which guided the admission of motor-driven vehicles to the use of the roads of all parks" (Mather 1916, 6).

The receipts from these fees were held in a special account, accessible to the Park Service without congressional appropriation, that could be used for road maintenance, park development, and administration. Mather considered agency control of the funds important for responsible management. But the legislation that created some parks—Rocky Mountain, Mesa Verde, Crater Lake, Hawaii Volcano, and Lassen—required these parks to turn their receipts over to the federal treasury. Mather tried to persuade Congress that revenues collected at these parks should be returned to the parks, but he was unsuccessful (McDaniel 1996, 18).

Succumbing to Politics

It did not take long for Congress to take full control of the purse strings. In 1918, two years after the creation of the National Park Service, Congress began to require that all park fees revert to the federal treasury (Mackintosh 1983, 3). This broke the link between park revenues and park spending, and expenditures have become political footballs ever since.

In 1965, the Land and Water Conservation Fund Act was passed to help finance the establishment of more parks. The act also redirected all national park user fees from the treasury to the Land and Water Conservation Fund. Through this act and subsequent amendments, Congress dictated what fees could be charged, how much could be charged, and which parks could charge them. Throughout the 1970s and 1980s, entrance fees were minimal, and sometimes not collected at all, and camping fees were permitted only in "developed" campgrounds.

A Reversal of Sorts

A reversal of sorts began in the early 1990s. Some parks discovered the benefits of charging fees for special use permits. Unlike other revenues, these receipts could stay in the park.[8] Yellowstone, for example, began charging $5 for an annual fishing permit in 1994. The program brought in $425,000 to the park in 1995. The fee was doubled in 1996 (*Billings Gazette* 1996), and revenues rose to $660,000.[9] In addition, beginning in 1993, parks were allowed to keep 15 percent of fee revenues to pay for the cost of fee collection.[10]

An even more important policy change came in 1996 when Congress authorized the Recreational Fee Demonstration Program, which went into effect 1 January 1997. This gives the Park Service the authority to select up to one hundred park units to participate in a three-year fee demonstration program. Entrance fees at these parks have more than doubled, on average, and the price of annual park passes has nearly doubled.[11] Some parks initiated entrance fees for the first time, and some began charging fees for the first time for interpretive nature programs, backcountry use, boating, and snowmobiling (USDI 1996).

Initially, each unit was allowed to keep up to 80 percent of fee revenues in excess of a base amount equal to 104 percent of the amount collected in fiscal year 1995, with this amount adjusted upward by 4 percent annually. In 1998, the program was adjusted to allow 80 percent of *all* fee revenues to stay in the unit of collection. The remaining 20 percent goes to those parks most in need. The new revenues are to be used for maintenance, enhancement of facilities, resource preservation, and annual operations. The initial base amount was still returned to the federal treasury. Though earmarked for the National Park Service, Congress had to reappropriate these revenues.

While the fee demonstration program is a step in the right direction, it does not address all the obstacles that prevent popular national parks from becoming self-supporting (see Fretwell 1999). For one thing, it applies to only 100 out of 369 park units. Second, the lion's share of park operational funding still comes from tax dollars, and thus financial control of the parks remains with Congress. Finally, the demonstration program creates no pressure to minimize operating costs.

WHY SELF-SUFFICIENCY?

Our park systems should move toward self-sufficiency for several reasons. First, self-sufficiency would give park managers an incentive to provide more services and maintain parks in good condition. Park managers who depend on visitors for funds want them to have a memorable experience that brings them back. Unhappy customers will be less likely to return.

Self-sufficiency would also encourage more realistic pricing—that is, prices that cover the cost of services—and careful attention to collecting lawful fees. In contrast, a tax-financed park offers limited service, fails to collect fees, and encourages park overuse by subsidizing goods and services.

Self-sufficiency would also give park management an incentive to balance costs and benefits. Since costs must be covered out of revenues, managers would add services that covered costs and eliminate those that did not. In contrast, when park operations are mostly funded by taxes, management can ignore such economic realities. In the summer of 1996, Yellowstone Park managers closed a campground to "save" money. The campground earned more than it cost to operate, but since the revenues went to the treasury, not to the park, the managers had little incentive to keep it open.

Self-sufficiency would also free park managers from a major obstacle to protecting park resources—politics. Because most national park funding is controlled by Congress, park managers must cater to politicians and special interests. Politics is making it difficult to control runaway elk populations in Yellowstone and Rocky Mountain national parks, keep "exotic" mountain goats from eating rare plants in Olympic National Park, and protect wildlife from snowmobile use in Yellowstone Park. Self-sufficiency would give park management the incentives and the freedom to avoid congressional meddling.

Politics, in fact, tends to keep public funding low. Parks that rely on tax revenues for operating support are at the mercy of legislatures or Congress and the mood of the taxpayer. Public spending on state park systems averaged only 0.023 percent of total state spending in 1997 (National Association of State Park Directors [NASPD] 1998). As taxpayers rebel against higher taxes, the outlook for growth is poor for both state and federal funding. Also, when public funds are appropriated, they tend to flow to bureaucratic support and not to the parks themselves.

Self-sufficiency alone, however, will not necessarily lead to the lowest possible costs. Unlike private business, government managers are not motivated to maximize "profits." To deal with this problem, some state park systems have created incentives for government managers to find cost savings or have "contracted out" park support functions to private sector organizations that can provide services at lower cost. These actions are in addition to the move toward self-sufficiency.

The great benefit of self-sufficiency is that it is a spur to provide more services. While it is difficult to say whether a park with many services is "better" than a park with fewer services, revenues tend to grow. This indicates that the parks with more services are pleasing their customers. At the same time, we have found no evidence that greater services damage the environment of the parks; indeed, the greater flexibility and availability of funds suggest the opposite.

Lessons from State Parks

Since 1980, many state park systems have felt the pinch of fiscally tight legislatures. General tax support for state parks has risen from $619.7 million in 1980 to $638.49 million in 1997 (NASPD 1981, 1998). This is a small increase, given that prices rose by 77 percent over this period.

As general support lagged, state park managers began to rely more on fees. In 1980, user fees collected at all state parks totaled $181.7 million, or about 17 percent of total park spending. Seventeen years later, in 1997, user fees totaled $588.5 million, or about 34 percent of total park spending (NASPD 1981, 1998).

Fifteen park systems regularly obtain more than half their operating costs from user fees. These include New Hampshire, Alabama, Arkansas, Colorado, Kentucky, Michigan, Nebraska, Oklahoma, South Carolina, South Dakota, Tennessee, Indiana, West Virginia, Wisconsin, and Vermont. In fact, both New Hampshire and Vermont fund their entire operating budgets out of user fees.

In spite of this trend, many states still receive only a small return per visitor. As we see in table 3.1, Alabama, New Hampshire, and Vermont collected $4 or more

Table 3.1
Annual Revenue per Park Visitor, FY 1997

0 – $0.50	$0.51 – $1.00	$1.01 – $1.50	$1.51 – $2.00	$2.01 – $6.50
Hawaii .02	California .55	New Mexico 1.04	South Carolina 1.54	Delaware 2.05
Illinois .13	Texas .59	Minnesota 1.23	Arkansas 1.67	Alabama 4.00
Washington .22	North Dakota .66	Georgia 1.24	Florida 1.71	Kentucky 4.86
Iowa .23	Virginia .79	Mississippi 1.26	Louisiana 1.85	Vermont 5.52
North Carolina .24	Wisconsin .79	Oklahoma 1.29	Arizona 1.91	New Hampshire 6.13
Massachusetts .27	New York .81	Nebraska 1.29	West Virginia 1.95	
Wyoming .31	Montana .82	Indiana 1.33		
Oregon .32	Tennessee .83	Michigan 1.39		
Missouri .35	Maine .84	Idaho 1.46		
Pennsylvania .35	Colorado .87			
Ohio .40	Utah .90			
Connecticut .44	Maryland .91			
Natl Park Service .44	South Dakota .97			
Alaska .48	Rhode Island 1.00			
Kansas .48				
Nevada .49				
New Jersey .49				

Note: For each park system, total park-generated annual revenue was divided by annual visitation.
Source: Calculated from NASPD (1998).

Table 3.2

Changes in Annual Revenues per Visitor

State	1980	1997
Texas	$ .40	$ .59
New Hampshire	.61	6.13
California	.26	.55
Washington	.06	.22

Source: NASPD (1981, 1998). See the chapter appendix for data from which these figures were derived.

per visitor in fiscal year 1997. States such as Alaska, Pennsylvania, and Wyoming, however, collected less than 50 cents per visitor, and the National Park Service collected 44 cents per visitor. One reason for these low average returns is the failure to collect an entrance fee from many day visitors. The percentage of day visitors not paying entrance fees at parks in Alaska, Pennsylvania, and Wyoming was 88, 99, and 72 percent respectively (NASPD 1998).

A more detailed look at several representative state park systems sheds additional light on how states finance their state parks. The four states listed in table 3.2—Texas, New Hampshire, California, and Washington—have all increased revenues from park users since 1980. Texas has accomplished this by expanding visitor services, and, to gain additional income, it recently replaced per-vehicle entrance fees with per-person entrance fees. New Hampshire has diversified its camping fee structure to reflect different demands for campsites and has raised entrance fees. California has raised entrance and camping fees. Washington has increased fees, too, but the voters have restricted increases to camping fees. We will look more carefully at these representative park systems (see also a comparative summary of these four states' park systems in the appendix to this chapter).

New Hampshire State Parks: A Self-Supporting Park System

We begin with New Hampshire State Parks, an agency that is legislatively mandated to be self-supporting. The system's eighty-nine recreational, historical, and natural sites cover nearly seventy-five thousand acres of land, with more than six thousand miles of trails. The park system attracts about 1.2 million visitors a year. It has nationally recognized natural areas, with several sites on the National Register of Natural Landmarks.

New Hampshire finances all of its nearly $5 million operating budget from fees and has some left over for construction improvements. It was the first to implement different prices for campsites, reflecting the different levels of amenities offered and the different levels of demand for various parks. It was one of the first park systems to charge entrance fees per person instead of per vehicle. In 1996, prices for campsites ranged from $12 to $30, and entrance fees were $2.50 per adult. The annual pass to all state parks costs $35. (Children twelve years and under and resident adults over sixty-five are admitted free.)

Although New Hampshire has a long history of heavy user support, mandated self-sufficiency did not come until 1991. In the midst of a growing general fund crisis, the legislature required the park system to rely solely on park-generated revenue. Park revenue had actually exceeded operating expenditures for three consecutive years prior to passage of the act, but park receipts had been handed over to the state treasury (LaPage 1995, 29). The 1991 act let receipts flow into a park fund that carries over unspent park monies from year to year. This approach encourages self-sufficiency because park officials know they have a reliable source of money dedicated to parks over the long term.

In addition to operations, some major maintenance and capital improvements are now being financed through park income. Allison McLain, director of Recreation Services, calls the current backlog of park maintenance and capital projects "manageable," averaging $333,000 per park but growing.[12]

The system has taken other initiatives to make ends meet. It has an extensive donor program and an ever-growing system of partnerships with companies (LaPage 1995, 29). In 1992, volunteers contributed $2.8 million in labor and private funds.

An example of company partnerships is the agreement with PepsiCo, Inc., which has an exclusive five-year right to beverage sales in all state parks. PepsiCo won this agreement through a competitive bid process. As part of its proposal, the company promised to fund an education and awareness program for state parks. This has produced an album of songs about New Hampshire and its parks, concerts highlighting these songs, and four park activity books featuring animated Chumley Chipmunk, who also helps promote safety and environmental education in the parks. None of these would have been affordable without the partnership with PepsiCo. Coca-Cola, Inc., has since outbid PepsiCo for this agreement.

Texas State Parks: Heading toward Self Support?

With over half a million acres and over twenty-four million visitors a year, the Texas state park system is the fourth largest in the United States, after the national park system and the state park systems of Alaska and California. The system encompasses forty-one state parks, forty-four recreation areas, forty historic sites, and seven natural areas.

In 1991, the state legislature changed the rules: Beginning in 1994, there would be no general funds for operations, except for a small tax on recreational equipment sales designated for parks.

At first, prospects looked bleak. Prior to 1991, general tax funds had made up 60 percent of the operating budget of the park system (Holliday 1995, 24), and only a handful of units were operationally self-sufficient. Park officials contemplated closing a number of highly subsidized parks. However, a "partners-in-parks" program, which brought in volunteer workers and community donations totaling $1 million, staved off immediate closure.

Then the department launched a dramatically different long-term approach to running the parks. That approach has come to be known as the *entrepreneurial budgeting system* (EBS). It is a financing system that provides managers at individual parks incentives to save money and raise revenue.

At the heart of the EBS is the performance agreement, essentially a contract between the park manager and the department hierarchy to meet certain performance standards, including a spending limit goal for the upcoming year. Department officials pledge to reward the manager if he or she spends less than the spending goal. The reward is the return of all the cost savings to the park's budget the following year in the form of an enhancement—not an offset—to the park's budget.

The park manager also pledges to raise revenue equal to the previous year's revenue plus 0.5 to 3 percent. If the park manager surpasses the revenue target, department officials pledge to return as much as 35 percent of the surplus to the park budget the following year. The park manager will be free to spend the extra money as he or she sees fit for park improvements. Twenty-five percent of the remaining surplus goes to a seed fund to help other parks initiate EBS programs, and the remaining 40 percent goes to park units of ecological value that may never attract enough visitors to be self-supporting. In this way, the program creates a safety net for less visited parks.

The system has spawned attractive services that earn revenue. For example, visitors at Brazos Bend State Park can enjoy a two-hour nocturnal "owl prowl" for $3 per prowler. They can watch alligators from a pontoon boat for $8 per person. At South Llano River State Park, a refurbished 1951 Chevy bus (donated by the local fire department) takes visitors on wildlife safaris through the park for $3 per passenger. Huntsville State Park holds an annual canoe rendezvous, Rocky Raccoon Trail Runs, and fifty- and hundred-mile "fun" runs that generate between $5,500 and $7,000 annually in additional funds. Activities such as these raise revenues without detracting from natural amenities. As an added safeguard to protect the parks' environment, regional managers must approve all customer services proposed by field personnel. Says Huntsville State Park Superintendent Wilburn Cox, "Protection of our natural resources remains our first priority."[13]

Initially, EBS was a financial success. During the planning stage, department officials anticipated that the program would yield $1 million in additional revenue. By fiscal year 1995, additional revenue had reached $1.1 million and cost savings totaled nearly $685,000 (King 1995, 56). Tyler State Park Superintendent Steve Powell says that the program "makes you more thrifty because you have an incentive to save."[14] The year before EBS began, nine parks took in more revenue than they spent. After three years of operating under the program, twenty-two parks took in more money than they spent.[15]

EBS gave park managers discretionary funds to enhance park amenities and improve park facilities. Hakeem Elahi, assistant park manager at Brazos Bend, says that with additional money generated under EBS, his park purchased a plant shredder that is now used to create small openings for wildlife in areas of dense vegetation. EBS money has also financed the upgrading of maintenance vehicles and equipment at Garner State Park.

In addition to using the entrepreneurial budgeting system, parks have opened up their own souvenir shops, and park officials recently began operating a centralized reservation system for state parks. Both of these innovations make money. The centralized reservation system helps tourists find alternative parks or dates for camping when their first choice is filled up. It also increases park revenue by steering people toward underutilized parks. During the system's first six months of operation, 30 percent of the reservations were made by campers whose first choice was filled, but who agreed to an alternative park or date.

The Texas parks made steady progress toward the goal of operational self-sufficiency. Revenue hovered around $12 million annually from 1989 to 1991 but rose steadily in the next four years, reaching nearly $20 million in 1995, or two-thirds of the operating budget. Texas officials said parks could make further gains if, among other things, they were given complete control over pricing park services and facilities and over the park system's funds, including interest earned from those funds. The legislature retains authority over both.

As with any new system of operation, there have been growing pains. A drought year in 1996 reduced visitation far below normal levels, wiping out funds that were supposed to reward the parks that had gained revenue in 1995. Similarly, floods in 1997 discouraged park visitors, again reducing funds available for reward payments. The glitch occurred because payments to parks came out of anticipated revenue from the next year, not actual earnings. To avoid such a problem, rewards should be paid out of actual earnings. Unfortunately, this onus accounting system brought the demise of EBS and its incentives for Texas state parks.

In addition, officials are trying to cope with a substantial capital backlog, estimated to be as high as $185 million. The most pressing need is to modernize outdated sewage and drinking water systems, which pose potential health risks to park visitors and whose improvement will cost $50 million (Dawson 1996b). The huge backlog stems from the late 1970s and 1980s when general tax dollars and oil and gas revenues flowed into the park system. Political pressures directed the money to land acquisition rather than to needed repairs and renovations. Says one park official, "People don't like to cut ribbons on new roofs and sewer systems" (quoted in Dawson 1996a).

To raise capital, Texas officials have turned to the park user. In May 1996, per-vehicle entrance charges (which averaged $3) were replaced with per-person entrance fees ranging from $0.50 to $5 at all parks. In addition, the annual pass to state parks was raised from $25 to $50. Officials had hoped that the new entrance fees would raise an additional $5 million to $7 million to fund park renovations (Taylor 1996, 63), but the 1996 drought reduced revenues. While the parks' gross revenues were 7 percent greater in May 1996 than in the same month in 1995, they fell 11 percent in July when the drought was at its peak (Dawson 1996b). Even under the duress of the drought in 1996 and floods in 1997, park revenues were up nearly $2 million from 1995 levels.

California State Parks: Standing on the Threshold

Composed of 275 units, the California state park system is the largest state park system in the nation after Alaska's. It is the most visited state park system, with more than 115 million visitors in fiscal year 1997 (NASPD 1998). Amenities at California state parks include coastal beaches ranging from serene to rugged, expansive deserts, majestic redwoods and sequoias, and landmarks illustrating the state's rich history.

Like many others, the California state park system is in transition. Shrinking general funds and a maintenance backlog estimated at $75 million have prompted park officials to search for ways to reduce operating costs and increase visitor revenue.

In 1996, the system's operating budget was $180 million, but this amount was $45 million less than the system's operating budget four years earlier, largely due to lower general fund appropriations. Park receipts increased by $15 million over this period, but the increase covered only half the loss from general funds. The 1996–97 budget for parks included a $16.4 million emergency augmentation from state general funds, with the provision that it be phased out over five years as new efforts are implemented to save money and raise revenue.

The Department of Parks and Recreation has already taken several steps to save money and raise revenue. Some fees have increased; the annual park pass went from $50 in 1990 to $75 in 1994. New partnerships with corporate sponsors and volunteer work projects have provided services for parks. A revamped state park store in Sacramento is earning money. Private contracting has reduced operating costs, and some lightly visited units have been transferred to local or nonprofit entities.

California's parks generate substantial revenue from entrance fees, camping fees, cabin rentals, and concessions, at least in comparison with other state systems. In 1995, revenue from entrance charges, including a per-vehicle fee of $5 and the annual parks pass of $75, totaled over $26 million. Camping fees ranging from $7 to $20 for primitive sites and $12 to $25 for developed sites were the next largest source of revenue, totaling $19 million. Concession fees, averaging 7 to 8 percent of lodging and restaurant sales and 4 to 10 percent of merchandise sales, totaled nearly $8 million. All park receipts are kept in the State Parks and Recreation Fund, from which allocations are made annually by the state legislature.

Perhaps the most promising change in the California system occurred in July 1996. The department began allocating park budgets through a process that rewards local managers for generating more revenues or saving money. California's park system has twenty-three districts. The new budget allocation program allows each park district to retain all the revenues earned from its parks above a historical base (but not to exceed $63 million for all parks). Budgeted funds not spent can be used the following year at the discretion of the district. Any shortfall in revenues will be taken from the following year's budget. This system gives district managers incentives to save money and to earn revenue.

Still, there appear to be untapped opportunities to increase revenues. In 1994, only 30 percent of the more than sixty-five million visitors went to areas that charged fees. The remaining forty-six million visitors are an important potential source of revenue.

Washington State Parks: Mired in Red Ink

The Washington State Parks and Recreation Commission administers 105 developed state parks, some satellite properties, and about twenty sites held either for preservation or future park development. Together these areas constitute 232,000 acres. Recreational and educational facilities abound, with nearly 8,000 campsites and 6,000 picnic sites, 122 boat launches, 699 miles of trail, 10 environmental learning centers, 13 interpretive centers, and 17 historic sites. With so much to offer it is easy to see why the system is so popular. In fiscal year 1997, over forty-eight million people visited Washington's state parks (NASPD 1998). This was the fourth highest visitation among all state park systems in the nation.

Despite its popularity, Washington park system is experiencing serious financial problems. A 1994 report by the State Parks and Recreation Commission, the administering agency for Washington's parks, said that the parks are "crumbling under the weight of recurring budget cuts, staff losses, and increasing public demands" (Washington State Parks 1994, 1). In addition to a substantial decline in onsite staff, thirty parks that were once open year-round have been closed seasonally; deferred maintenance projects now top $40 million; and during peak usage times, there is a shortage of campsites.

The reasons for this distress are not hard to find. The system is funded entirely from the state general fund and is one of only ten state park systems that do not charge a day use fee at any park. Camping and concession fees are collected, but they go into a state park fund, and the legislature must reappropriate them for park use. Camping fees are significant. In fiscal year 1997, they totaled over $7 million, accounting for 23 percent of the parks' operating budget.

Dissatisfaction with the current funding process and recommendations for change are surfacing, albeit slowly. In its report, the commission considered a day use fee but did not propose it, fearing a public outcry. General sentiment in the state clings to the notion that park access must remain free. This perception is unfortunate because down the coast, California, with nearly twenty million "fee area" visitors, generated nearly $28 million from entrance fees alone in 1994.

The commission also assumed that camping fees had reached adequate levels. In fact, however, Washington's campsite fees are typically under half the price charged in California and several other western states.

The commission did propose that the parks be allowed to keep all user fees in an unappropriated fund, avoiding the legislative process. In July 1995, a special park fund for park-generated revenues was created, but legislative approval is still required to use these revenues. The commission also proposed increases in fees to concessionaires, river guides, and other commercial operations and the establishment of more "friends of parks" groups to raise funds and donate volunteer work.

Recently, volunteer programs, friends' groups, and other donors have become more active. The commission has also implemented a centralized reservation system (in coordination with Oregon) for campsites. This should increase attendance and revenue. To help with capital improvements, the 1996 legislature authorized the use of certificates of participation (essentially, bonds) for park improvements. The state treasurer, acting as broker, sold ten-year bonds at 4.5 to 5.5 percent variable interest to private investors, raising $310,000 for improved lodging and campgrounds in Fort Warden State Park. Repayment of the bonds is made with revenues earned by the new facilities.[16] However, a 1994 initiative approved by voters limits fee increases and removes entrance fees as a viable option for raising revenues. Hence, Washington's parks still have a long way to go in addressing their funding problems.

COMPARING STATE AND NATIONAL PARKS

The best way to illustrate the differences that stem from self-sufficiency is to compare adjacent parks that differ in their reliance on user fees. State and national parks in Texas and South Dakota provide such a one-on-one comparison.

Big Bend Ranch State Park versus Big Bend National Park

Big Bend Ranch State Park and Big Bend National Park are located next to each other in southwest Texas.[17] Both parks feature mountain, river, and desert habitats in a setting as rugged as any in the western United States. Both parks border the Rio Grande River and include huge sections of Chihuahuan Desert wilderness. Both parks are home to a rich variety of wild animal and plant species. Beaver, summer tanagers, painted buntings, vermilion flycatchers, sandpipers, and killdeer bobs reside along the Rio Grande and its flood plain. White-tailed deer, mountain lions, and peregrine falcons inhabit the mountainous regions of both parks. Roadrunners, Lloyd's mariposa cactus, and lechuguilla, to name just a few species, occupy the desert.

At 801,163 acres, Big Bend National Park is over two and a half times the size of Big Bend Ranch State Park. Established in 1935, it has been around longer and has more facilities for park visitors, providing lodging, dining, gas, groceries, showers, and laundry. It also has 194 developed camping sites complete with water, outdoor toilets, and electrical hookups, as well as an area with utility hookups for recreational vehicles.

Big Bend Ranch State Park, a former private ranch generally called "Big Bend Ranch," became a state natural area in 1989 and a state park in October 1995. It first catered to tourists in 1991. The park has two lodging facilities, one bed-and-breakfast-style and one dormitory-style, located on the edge of the park. Together they can accommodate thirty-eight visitors. Gas and groceries are available just outside the park. As of 1995, there were only sixteen campsites, all considered primitive. Five of the sixteen have pit toilets; the rest have none. Young and relatively undeveloped, Big Bend Ranch receives far fewer visitors than Big Bend National Park—56,697 visits compared with 314,209 in 1995.

With the nearest city over two hundred miles away, Big Bend Ranch and Big Bend are both considered "destination parks." Such parks attract people who can afford to travel a considerable distance and spend a few days in or near the parks. Visitors can enjoy the same basic activities at both parks, such as hiking and wilderness backpacking, nature tours, horseback riding, camping, fishing, river rafting, and bird watching. However, most of these will cost extra at Big Bend Ranch, and there are more offerings at Big Bend Ranch than at Big Bend. There are other differences, too, in the way that the parks are maintained and in their ability to protect their natural resources.

Big Bend National Park

Hiking, birding, horseback riding, river rafting and canoeing, fishing, and swimming are free at the national park, and a few naturalist workshops are offered at no charge. Valerie Naylor, chief of interpretation and visitor services at Big Bend, says they are always trying to improve on the interpretive offerings at Big Bend but are "limited by staff and budget."

Maintenance in Big Bend National Park has suffered in recent years as a result of budget cuts. Periodic repair and rehabilitation of facilities are lagging and, "in some cases, have the potential to threaten public and employee health and safety" (Big Bend National Park 1996, 7). Deterioration of facilities and trails has become a major concern.

Visitors are free to roam the national park as they please. Big Bend does not have a visitor management policy to protect its natural features from human impact.

Big Bend Ranch

The state offers a wide variety of fee-based activities. Bird watching, river rafting, canoeing, hiking, fishing, horseback riding, and swimming cost an additional $3 beyond the $3 per-person entrance fee. (The entrance fee is waived if the visitor has purchased the annual Texas Conservation Passport.) Overnight fees are $6 per night per person, of which $3 is the entrance fee and $3 is the activity fee.

But these basic activities are just the beginning. Three-day rock art and desert survival courses are available for $300. A three-day desert photography course is available for $450. Interpretive bus tours into the interior of the park cost $60. In addition, visitors can see the botanical desert garden and museum exhibits at the Barton Warnock Environmental Education Center near the southeast entrance or the historical site, Fort Leaton, on the west side of the park. These options cost an adult an additional $2.50 and $2.00 respectively ($1.00 per child).

One program that has generated a lot of interest is the Longhorn Cattle Drive and Campfire. For $350 and your own horse and tack, or $450 if the park provides the horse, visitors can assist park rangers as they move the small resident herd of Texas longhorns from winter to summer pasture and vice versa. The drive lasts three days and includes meals, lodging (trailside tents or cabins), and evening campfire entertainment. Visitors participate in the roundup and branding and vaccination of cattle. Offered twice a year for up to twenty participants, the cattle drive has the longest waiting list of all the activities offered in the park.

Big Bend Ranch's housing and facilities were in pretty good shape when the state purchased the ranch, says Exhibit Technician David Alloway, but improvements are being made. To facilitate university research on geology, wildlife, botany, and archaeology, the park has renovated and expanded a laboratory for graduate students, complete with lodging facilities. Additional lodging, showers, hiking trails, campgrounds, and equestrian and mountain bike trails are planned.

The park is divided into zones where the number of visitors at any given time is strictly controlled. Sensitive areas within the park are monitored to assess the effects of public use, and visitors can be rerouted if necessary to minimize harmful human impacts (Texas Parks and Wildlife Department [TPWD] 1994, 21).

The differences noted earlier stem in large part from the different ways that Big Bend and Big Bend Ranch are financed. The lion's share of Big Bend's funding comes from the federal treasury, while Big Bend Ranch depends much more heavily on revenue from fees.

As table 3.3 shows, Big Bend Ranch's cost-saving incentives and dependence on user fees result in lower expenses and higher returns per acre than Big Bend. Big Bend Ranch earned more per acre although it had far fewer visitors. Also, the state park had much lower operating expenses per acre and a much smaller staff but managed to provide more services (see table 3.4).

Since general fund support for the operation of Texas's state parks ended in 1994, the staff at Big Bend Ranch have had a strong incentive to generate more revenues from user fees. They have done this by creating a proliferation of fee-based activities. Since Big Bend Ranch operated under the EBS program, Superintendent Luis Armendariz has been rewarded as much as 35 percent of any revenue above his tar-

Table 3.3
Summary of Comparisons, FY 1995

	Big Bend Ranch Complex[1]	Big Bend National Park
Acreage	300,000	810,763
Staff size	14	94
Visits[2]	56,697	314,209
Operating budget	$ 463,165[3]	$ 3,951,000
Revenue	$ 176,042[4]	$ 337,103
Revenue per acre	$ 0.59	$ 0.42
Expenses per acre	$ 1.54	$ 4.87

[1] Includes ranch area, Fort Leaton, and Warnock Center.
[2] Visits include waived per-person entrance fees for children under 12 and adults who have the Texas Conservation Passport.
[3] About 67 percent of the operating budget comes from fees collected at all state parks and redistributed throughout the system and 33 percent is derived from a dedicated tax on recreational equipment sales.
[4] Revenue originating from complex only.

Sources: Data for Big Bend Ranch Complex provided by Luis Armendariz, Superintendent, Big Bend Ranch State Park, telephone interview, October 1996. Data for Big Bend National Park provided by Valerie Naylor, Chief of Interpretation and Visitor Services, Big Bend National Park, telephone interview, March 1996, and Andrew Teter, Budget Analyst, U.S. Department of the Interior, National Park Service, Budget Division, by fax, 11 April 1996.

get level that he generated from new services, plus all cost savings he achieved. He spent these revenues as he chose on the park. In 1996, his "profit" paid for a new pickup truck, radios for rangers in the field, dishes and a freezer for the visitors' lodge, and repairs to a road grader.

Custer State Park versus Wind Cave National Park

The prairie lands in the southwest corner of South Dakota contain two parks with a common border: Wind Cave National Park and Custer State Park. The parks share similar features. With rugged mountains surrounded by prairie, the land is populated with bison, pronghorn antelope, deer, coyote, turkey, and prairie dogs. Both parks offer numerous activities including hiking, horseback riding, scenic drives, picnicking, camping, and wildlife viewing. The national park also offers caving. Both are destination parks, attracting visitors from distant regions. Other nearby attractions include the Black Hills and Mount Rushmore. Many of the features of the parks are similar, but their administration is not.[18]

Table 3.4
Services Available, 1995

Big Bend Ranch Complex	Big Bend National Park
Museum/historical site tours ($2/$2.50)	Bird watching (free)
Bird watching ($3)	River running (free)
Rafting, canoeing ($3)	Camping ($5)
Camping ($3 per night)	Hiking (free)
Wilderness backpacking ($3)	Fishing (free)
Hiking ($3)	Nature workshops (free)
Fishing ($3)	
Swimming ($3)	
Horseback riding ($3)	
(horses leased for $50)	
Longhorn cattle drive ($350 each)	
Interpretive bus tours ($60)	
Weekend nature seminars ($300/3 days)	

Sources: Data for Big Bend Ranch Complex provided by Luis Armendariz, Superintendent, Big Bend Ranch State Park, in a telephone interview, October 1996. Data for Big Bend National Park provided by Valerie Naylor, Chief of Interpretation and Visitor Services, Big Bend National Park, in a telephone interview, March 1996, and Andrew Teter, Budget Analyst, U.S. Department of the Interior, National Park Service, Budget Division, by fax, 11 April 1996.

Wind Cave National Park

Established in 1903, Wind Cave National Park is not considered a major national park, but it has distinguishing features that attract tourists. The cave has more than seventy-six miles of passages, reaching as far as five hundred feet below the surface. Its walls are covered with distinctive crystal formations unlike the stalactitic and stalagmitic growths found in most other caves. Ranger-guided cave tours are scheduled daily year-round at a cost of $3 to $15, depending on the extent of the tour. (Children under six are free but are not allowed on all cave tours; persons aged six to fifteen or persons holding a Golden Age Passport receive a 50 percent discount on tours.) Ranger-led hikes across the park's surface lands depart daily in the summer, free of charge.

Although the cave is an important asset, only one-sixth of the park visitors actually tour the cave. The park offers much more. Its more than twenty-eight thousand acres include the cave and grasslands, pine forests, hills, and ravines. In 1912, a game preserve was created to reintroduce many species previously eliminated by uncontrolled hunting. Originally, the preserve contained fourteen bison, along with elk, deer, antelope, and prairie dogs. The bison herd has since grown to several hundred animals. Much of the wildlife can be observed from the road, but thirty miles of trails weave through the park's rolling prairie grasslands, ponderosa pine forests, and riparian habitat. Fencing encloses the preserve, preventing most of the animals from migrating out of the park.

Wind Cave Park has a bison-carrying capacity of about three hundred animals. To keep the bison at this level, the park removes about sixty-five bison each year. They are sold to Native American tribes at an average price of $275 per head, just enough to cover the costs of roundup and sale. Elk are managed in a similar manner every three to five years. Hunting is not allowed.

The park offers no lodging, gas, or groceries. Only one developed campground is available, for a fee of $10 per night during peak season, $5 during the shoulder season. There is no entrance fee into the national park and no other user fees.

Custer State Park

Located directly north of Wind Cave, Custer State Park was established in 1919 to preserve wildlife, open prairie, granite spires, and pristine lakes. The park, which extends seventy-three thousand acres, is about two and a half times the size of Wind Cave. It also has abundant wildlife, including one of the world's largest bison herds, plus bighorn sheep, mountain goats, elk, and burros. Like Wind Cave, the southern end of the park has rolling hills, grasslands, and pine forests. The northern end, higher in elevation, has granite spires and spruce forests. Mountain streams run across the park, flowing into pristine lakes.

Activities abound at Custer; some are free of charge (except for the entrance fee). These include fishing, climbing, swimming, boating, mountain biking, and wildlife viewing. (Custer has more water than Wind Cave, so there are more water-based activities.) Fees are charged for horseback riding, hayrides, pack trips, "Buffalo Safari Jeep Rides" to the park interior, chuck wagon dinners, and theater performances (Custer State Park 1996). The park offers a full range of accommodations, from rustic to deluxe, in its four developed resorts, which have dining, lounges and general stores. The park hosts 321 campsites, from primitive to full-service, at a cost ranging from $2 per person per night to $12 per site per night. An entrance fee of $3 per person ($2 during the winter months) or $8 per vehicle ($5 in the off-season) is charged. An annual license can be purchased for $20 per vehicle.

Custer State Park generates substantial revenues through its animal management program. The park range has a winter carrying capacity of 950 bison. Spring calving increases the herd to nearly 1,500 head, so each fall Custer has a roundup and buffalo auction. The roundup has become a festive affair, attracting several thousand bystanders to watch Bob Landis and other local volunteers on horseback herd together the more than one thousand bison. In fiscal year 1996, the auction generated more than $800,000, at a cost of $135,000. Prices of the bison varied. One bull was sold for $8,000; a more typical price per animal was $2,200.

The park also has a limited hunting season for game animals, including elk, bison, bighorn sheep, and wild turkey. Hunting licenses earn money for the park and keep the number of animals within the park's carrying capacity. Game licenses brought in over $100,000 in 1996, at a cost of $35,000 for one full-time employee.

Because of its large acreage, Custer State Park has been allotted its own division under the South Dakota Department of Game, Fish, and Parks. All park revenues go into a revolving fund held specifically for Custer. Annually, the park creates a budget plan under which it must operate. Funds are returned to the park via legislative appropriation, but generally the park receives the amount requested, and any funds not used are maintained in the fund, with interest, for Custer. The park is self-supporting in its day-to-day operations but receives some tax dollars for maintenance.

In 1989, the park needed $7.8 million for rehabilitation and development. To foot that bill, the park renegotiated with concessionaires, increasing the franchise fee to 18 percent of gross proceeds. The first $100,000 of the fee goes to the Custer State Park fund for operating expenses; 3 percent of the fee is used for maintenance, to be appropriated by the Game, Fish, and Parks Commission; and the remainder repays the state revenue bonds that were issued to complete the project. A 3 percent tax on all goods and services sold in the park helps finance marketing and promotion.

Table 3.5
Summary of Comparisons, FY 1995

	Custer State Park	Wind Cave National Park
Acreage	73,000	28,292
Staff size	51	37
Visits	1,600,000	1,094,933
Operating budget	$ 3,019,922	$ 1,212,000
Fees	2,500,000	389,735
Total revenue	$ 3,607,500	$ 389,735
Revenue per acre	$ 49.42	$ 13.78
Expenses per acre	$ 41.37	$ 42.84

Sources: State park data provided by Craig Pugsley, Supervisor of Visitor Services, Custer State Park, telephone interviews, July and November 1996; Roger Bamsey, Business Manager, Custer State Park, fax dated 12 April 1996; and a Custer State Park Resort Company publication, *1996 Lodging Rates and Information.* Data for Wind Cave National Park provided in a letter from Paul Menard, Chief of Administration, Wind Cave National Park, dated 12 August 1996; and from the park's annual publication, *Passages 1995: A Visitor's Guide to Wind Cave National Park.*

These promotional efforts have increased visitation, filling campgrounds during peak periods, compared to only 40 to 50 percent of capacity previously.

In sum, Custer State Park is much more entrepreneurial than Wind Cave National Park when it comes to generating revenue. As table 3.5 indicates, in fiscal year 1995 Custer collected $566,125 more than its operating budget of $3.02 million. Part of this surplus was invested in wastewater treatment. Custer also appears to be run more efficiently. It spent slightly less per acre operating the park than did Wind Cave but provided more customer services and more park management activities.

While Custer earns a surplus, Wind Cave loses money—nearly $0.75 for every visitor. Its budget is much smaller than Custer's, only $1.2 million, and revenues are less than $400,000. Like other national parks, Wind Cave has little incentive to generate revenues.

BACK TO THE FUTURE FOR OUR PARKS

Only by making those who run our parks financially accountable to users can we spur effective management and stable funding for our parks. Toward that end, we recommend several policy changes. If enacted, they would unleash entrepreneurial abilities, increase revenues, save money, and enable park managers to refurbish visitor facilities and protect natural resources.

- Congress and state legislatures should establish a fixed schedule that gradually reduces annual appropriations for park operations over a ten-year period until they reach zero.
- Congress and state legislatures should allow park managers to institute their own fee programs.
- Most of the fees collected in these parks, about 95 percent, should remain in the park in which they were collected, to be used to fund operations there. A small amount, perhaps 5 percent, could be used to fund systemwide administration. Any revenues in excess of costs should be retained by the parks.
- Park managers should have the authority to raise fees or establish new fee-based services as demand dictates, without having to obtain approval from Congress or state legislatures.
- Each park should have a special "park endowment fund" for capital improvements and repairs. The fund would be allowed to invest in financial assets such as high-quality stock-and-bond funds and treasury bills. A percentage of concessionaire sales as well as park road tolls should also contribute to the fund (Anderson and Liffmann 1996). Interest from the fund should be used for annual repair and renovation to buildings and roads.
- Initial investments in the fund could be raised through a variety of private contractual arrangements such as corporate sponsorship of individual parks. Sponsors could pay for exclusive rights to sell or advertise their products in the park for a limited time as long as doing so did not detract from park amenities.

- As an interim step, park managers should be allowed to keep all cost savings and apply them to the budgets for subsequent years. These funds would be treated as budget enhancements, not offsets to subsequent funding.
- To curb incentives for bureaucratic growth in the long term, private competitive bids should be sought for park support functions such as security, fee collection, trash and campground cleanup, and interpretation tours. If these bids indicate that the private sector can provide these services at a much lower cost, then these functions should be provided by contract by the private sector. Government support staff would, in turn, be reduced.

Some parks will not attract enough visitors or have enough other commercially valued assets to be self-supporting. If these parks are to remain public, they should be funded separately out of general funds. Another option is to turn them over to private, nonprofit groups, with a onetime endowment fund for maintenance.

Other parks that may not attract many visitors or that require some seclusion from the public to protect environmental assets may have commercially valued assets such as oil and gas deposits. In these cases, management by a quasi-independent "park endowment board" would be appropriate (Stroup 1990).

Requiring popular parks to be self-sustaining is the surest way of spurring responsible management and financial stability. This is, after all, what Stephen Mather and other early park supporters had in mind near the turn of the century when we were a much poorer nation than we are today. Surely, with our higher incomes today, we as users can afford to pay for these amenities and help make our parks the treasures they should be.

NOTES

1. Data provided by fax from Andrew Teter, budget analyst, U.S. Department of the Interior, National Park Service (USDI, NPS), Budget Division–Operations Formulation Branch, Washington, D.C., dated 11 April 1996.

2. Financial data provided by Don Striker, comptroller, Yellowstone National Park, during presentation at PERC's 1999 National Conference for Journalists, "Market Approaches to Environmental Problems," Mountain Sky Guest Ranch, Emigrant, Montana, 1 October 1999.

3. Data per Teter fax, 11 April 1996.

4. Data per Teter fax, 11 April 1996.

5. Data per Teter fax, 11 April 1996.

6. Kathy Poole, budget analyst, USDI, NPS, Budget Division–Operations Formulation Branch, telephone interview, 23 January 1997.

7. Data provided by fax from Carol Wellington, Socio-Economic Studies, USDI, NPS, Denver, Colorado, dated 8 July 1996.

8. The Appropriations Act of 1991 allowed fees from special use permits to be retained within individual parks to cover the costs of allowing such uses. Permit revenues could be

used to support park operations and carry over to the following fiscal year. In 1994, special permit revenues totaled $3.8 million. See USDI (1995, 1).

9. Don Striker, comptroller, Yellowstone National Park, telephone interview, 22 April 1997.

10. In prior years, park management chose whether to use personnel for fee collection or in other areas. Fee collection did not receive a budgetary stipend, and with all fees going to the treasury, park personnel had a disincentive to collect fees since it took support away from other activities.

11. Yellowstone now charges entry fees of $10 per person, $20 per vehicle and $40 for an annual pass. Previously the fees were $4, $10, and $15.

12. Allison McLain, director of recreation services, New Hampshire Division of Parks and Recreation, telephone interview, November 1996.

13. Wilburn Cox, superintendent, Huntsville State Park, telephone interview, January 1996.

14. Steve Powell, superintendent, Tyler State Park, telephone interview, January 1996.

15. Mike Crevier, director of revenue management, Public Lands Division, Texas Parks and Wildlife Department, telephone interview, October 1996.

16. Mike Clarey, senior accountant, Management Accounting, Washington State Office of the Treasury, telephone interview, 21 October 1996.

17. Unless otherwise cited, information in this section was gathered in telephone interviews with Valerie Naylor, chief of interpretation and visitor services, Big Bend National Park, and Luis Armendariz, park superintendent, Big Bend Ranch State Park, October 1996.

18. Unless otherwise cited, information in this section was gathered in telephone interviews with Paul Menard, chief of administration, Wind Cave National Park, April and November 1996; Ross Rice, chief ranger, Wind Cave National Park, November 1996; Craig Pugsley, supervisor of visitor services, Custer State Park; and Roger Bamsey, business manager, Custer State Park, July and November 1996.

REFERENCES

Anderson, Terry L., and Mark Liffmann. 1996. "Making 'Crown Jewels' Pay: Congress Gives Parks a Golden Opportunity." *Rocky Mountain News*, 1 September.

Big Bend National Park. 1996. *State of the Park Report: Big Bend National Park Rio Grande Wild and Scenic River*. Big Bend National Park, Tex.: Author.

Billings Gazette. 1996. "Yellowstone's Fishing Fees to Double." 5 March.

Custer State Park. 1996. *Come to Custer State Park*. Custer, S.D.: Custer State Park Resort Company.

Dawson, Bill. 1996a. "Falling Down, Falling Apart: Repair Urgency Is Mounting." *Houston Chronicle*, 19 July.

———. 1996b. "Parks and Wildlife Face Fewer Visitors, Less Funds." *Houston Chronicle*, 29 August.

Fretwell, Holly Lippke. 1999. "Paying to Play: The Fee Demonstration Program." PERC Policy Series, PS-17. Bozeman, Mont.: Political Economy Research Center.

General Accounting Office. 1982. *Increasing Entrance Fees—National Park Service*. GAO/CED-82-84. Washington, D.C.: U.S. Government Printing Office.

66   *Donald R. Leal and Holly Lippke Fretwell*

Holliday, Ron. 1995. Texas' Entrepreneurial Budget System. *Different Drummer* (Summer): 24–28.

King, Merrill S. 1995. "The Entrepreneurial Budgeting System of the Texas Parks and Wildlife Department." Master's thesis, University of Texas, Austin.

LaPage, Wilbur. 1995. "New Hampshire's Self-Funding Parks." *Different Drummer* (Summer): 29–32.

Mackintosh, Barry. 1983. *Visitor Fees in the National Park System: A Legislative and Administrative History.* Washington, D.C.: U.S. Department of the Interior, National Parks Service, History Division.

Mather, Stephen. 1916. *Progress in the Development of the National Parks.* Washington, D.C.: U.S. Department of the Interior.

McDaniel, R. Andrew. 1996. "The National Parks on a Business Basis: Steve Mather and the National Park Service." Working Paper 96-8. Bozeman, Mont.: Political Economy Research Center.

National Association of State Park Directors. 1981. *1981 Annual Information Exchange: State Park Statistical Data for the Year Ending June 30, 1980.* Tallahassee, Fla.: Author.

———. 1995. *1995 Annual Information Exchange: State Park Statistical Data for the Year Ending June 30, 1994.* Tallahassee, Fla.: Author.

———. 1996. *1996 Annual Information Exchange: State Park Statistical Data for the Year Ending June 30, 1995.* Tallahassee, Fla.: Author.

———. 1998. *1998 Annual Information Exchange: State Park Statistical Data for the Year Ending June 30, 1997.* Tallahassee, Fla.: Author.

National Parks and Conservation Association. 1995. *National Public Opinion Survey on the National Park System.* Washington, D.C.: Author.

Satchell, Michael, with Mike Tharp. 1995. "Trouble in Paradise." *U.S. News & World Report,* 19 June.

Stroup, Richard L. 1990. "Rescuing Yellowstone from Politics: Expanding Parks While Reducing Conflict." In *The Yellowstone Primer,* ed. John A. Baden and Donald R. Leal. San Francisco: Pacific Research Institute, 169–84.

Taylor, Gene. 1996. "Per-Person Pricing Now in Effect." *Field & Stream* (July).

Texas Parks and Wildlife Department. 1994. *Big Bend Ranch State Natural Area Management Plan.* Austin: Author.

U.S. Department of the Interior. 1993. *Recreation Fee Charges and Collections.* Audit Report 93-I-793. Washington, D.C.: National Park Service.

———. 1995. *Special Use Fees, National Park Service.* Audit Report No. 96-I-49. Washington, D.C.: National Parks Service.

———. 1996. *Interior Department Announces Test Project to Fund Needed Improvements on Public Lands.* Office of the Secretary, news release, 26 November. Washington, D.C.: Author.

Washington State Parks. 1994. *Restructuring Washington State Parks and Recreation.* Olympia: Author.

Appendix
Statistics on Four State Park Systems

State Parks	Acres (thousands)	Visits (thousands)	Receipts (thousands of $)	Budget (thousands of $)		
				Operating	Capital	Total
New Hampshire						
FY 1980	70	3,662	$ 2,245	$ 3,721	$ 5,555	$ 9,276
FY 1997	153	910	5,574	5,345	248	5,593
Texas						
FY 1980	134	14,022	5,581	12,272	12,742	27,014
FY 1997	629	21,818	20,393*	32,585	7,008	39,593
California						
FY 1980	1,005	58,024	15,338	69,755	245,813	315,568
FY 1997	1,355	115,740	63,183	183,531	17,585	201,116
Washington						
FY 1980	86	37,154	2,219	15,359	3,219	19,271
FY 1997	263	48,539	10,905	30,514	22,980	53,494

* Receipts data provided by e-mail from John Emerson, finance department, TPWD, 2 June 1998.
Sources: NASPD (1981,1998).

4

Sustainable Financing for Protected Areas in Sub-Saharan Africa and the Caribbean

Alexander James, Sam Kanyamibwa, and Michael J. B. Green

Evidence suggests that most of the protected areas of the world are managed on very small budgets. Figure 4.1 shows that protected areas in Africa and Latin America are managed on less than $150 per square kilometer on average, well below the benchmark level of $250 per square kilometer required for adequate conservation (James, Green, and Paine 1999; Leader-Williams and Albon 1988). Government funding of protected area agencies in the developing countries amounts to only one-third of the funding required to achieve their stated conservation objectives (James et al. 1999). Furthermore, examples of "paper parks," or government gazetted protected areas that have no administration or budget, are common in many parts of the world (International Union for the Conservation of Nature [IUCN] 1992; McNeely, Harrison, and Dingwall 1994). As one study notes, "Budget constraints make it unlikely that a system will receive enough funding from the central government to effectively manage all protected areas" (Dixon and Sherman 1990, 78).

An alternative to the dependence on governments for conservation funding is offered by parastatal protected area agencies. A *parastatal protected area agency* is a semiautonomous organization that receives a yearly grant from government but also has the right to raise and retain its own revenues. Parastatals often take advantage of their greater financial independence by diversifying their sources of revenue beyond the collection of park fees and the provision of visitor services. Other sources of funds tapped by parastatals include investment and trust fund income, subscriptions and donations, and foreign assistance. Parastatal agencies typically pay no dividends or taxes, so surplus revenues from operations can be reallocated to conservation activities within the protected areas. Governmental control over parastatals is exercised through protected area legislation and by representation on a board of directors, which often includes a broad range of stakeholders.

Figure 4.1

Average Protected Area Budget, by Geographic Region

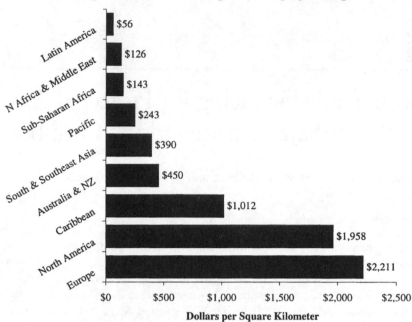

Note: Budget data is presented in 1996 U.S. dollars. The data pertain to one year within the 1990–1998 period, as was reported.
Source: James, Green, and Paine (1999).

As a framework for analyzing the performance of protected area agencies, institutional theory states that the incentives governing environmental performance, at any level, stem from three national characteristics: the formal or written laws (and property rights), the social conventions and constraints, and the level of enforcement of each. The interaction of the formal structures with the social codes of behavior create an institutional environment that provides the set of incentives. When the formal laws, policies, and programs are supported by the social expectations and conventions, and both receive adequate enforcement, an institutional incentive is created (United Nations Environment Program [UNEP] 1996; James 1996; North 1990). A parastatal agency is an example of the institutionalization of a new incentive structure for the management of national parks and protected areas that depends upon both a formal change in the agency's legal designation and an informal change in the attitudes and strategies of the agency managers.

The difference in formal institutions between government and parastatal protected area agencies is embodied in the structure of property rights over the park revenues. A *property right* is the claim on the benefit stream arising from an asset. This claim must be enforceable over other individuals and organizations through a set of property rules (Bromley 1991). In the case of a parastatal, the control over the stream of revenue arising from the operations of a protected area is a property right that has been transferred from the government to the conservation agency. The property right over protected area revenue creates the incentive to optimize the value of the benefit stream from the protected area assets. Optimization of the benefit stream requires that the managers of the parastatal agency maximize the revenues flowing from the protected areas subject to the constraint of maintaining adequate conservation of the biodiversity resources. This constraint is enforced formally through government regulation and oversight of the protected areas and informally through the stewardship ethic of the park managers.

Thus, the creation of a parastatal protected area agency can be expected to result in a range of outcomes, depending on the response of protected area managers to the institutional incentives. An improvement in financial performance cannot be taken as a given once the property rights to the protected area revenues have been transferred to the agency. This modification of property rights is strictly a formal measure; its success in improving the financial performance depends on the support of the informal rules and modes of operation within the conservation agency. Thus, this study will attempt to determine whether, in practice, the creation of parastatal protected area agencies has resulted in better financial performance than comparable government funded conservation agencies. Whether financial performance translates into improved conservation results is not easily measured and remains outside of the scope of this analysis.

METHODS

Data

A number of parastatal protected area agencies were identified in an ongoing project on national budgets for protected areas, conducted by the World Conservation Monitoring Center (WCMC) (James et al. 1999). These parastatal agencies and a control group of government-funded agencies were sent a survey questionnaire requesting information on protected area funding. The questionnaire asked respondents for data on their annual budgets, including the total amount of funds allocated to protected areas, the sources of funds, and a self-assessment of the adequacy of funds relative to the agency's stated conservation objectives.[1]

Response to the survey was incomplete, but not out of line with previous WCMC experience in collecting data on protected area budgets. Completed questionnaires were received from eight out of the thirty countries contacted. Six parastatals provided detailed budgets along with comments on their financial activities. Four of the responding parastatals were located in the Caribbean region and two in Africa. Due to the low survey response, the data were supplemented with information on protected area budgets from other sources, primarily from previous WCMC protected area surveys (James et al. 1999). As a result of the limitations on data, the study compares the financial performance of protected area agencies in the Caribbean and Sub-Saharan African regions only.

Financial performance is measured as the agency's annual protected areas budget expressed on a per-square-kilometer basis. Foreign funds have been excluded from the agency budgets because of incomplete and inconsistent data. However, the analysis does note where foreign assistance is known to have been significant. The agency budgets include both operating expenditure and capital expenditure. However, few countries reported significant capital expenditures, so the comparisons are, in practice, reflective of annual operating expenses. The protected area budgets that pertain to a range of years in the mid-1990s have been standardized to 1996 U.S. dollars. The budgets have been converted to U.S. dollars in the budget year reported by the agency and scaled up to 1996 values with the U.S. dollar deflator. The foreign exchange conversion rates and the U.S. dollar deflator were taken from International Monetary Fund (IMF) (1997).

Basis of Comparison

The Caribbean and Sub-Saharan African regions are treated separately in the analysis. For each region, the parastatal agency budgets are compared with the government agency budgets on the basis of 1996 U.S. dollars per square kilometer protected. In each region, the budgets for each type of agency are aggregated, and a mean per-square-kilometer budget is compared. The Caribbean region is composed of seven parastatal agencies and seven government agencies. The African region contains four parastatals and eight government agencies.

The analysis compares parastatal and government agencies within these regions, taking account of differences in economic development and average protected area size. A recent WCMC study of global protected area budgets found significant economies of scale in protected area management (James et al. 1999). Small protected areas are relatively expensive to administer because of high fixed costs and a large perimeter to area ratio. As a result, budgets for small protected areas can be high when expressed on a per-square-kilometer basis. Economies of scale in management costs are particularly relevant in the Caribbean region where protected areas are fragmented and range in size from a few hectares (St. Lucia) to over one hundred square kilometers (Dominican Republic). To account for this variation, agency budgets in the Caribbean are compared based on three size classes: large (mean area greater than one hundred square kilometers), medium (mean area between ten and one hundred square kilometers), and small (mean area less than ten square kilometers).

In the African region, protected areas tend to be large, and differences in budgetary inputs are more closely correlated with the level of economic development and the availability of government resources (James et al.1999). In the regional analysis of African protected area budgets, countries are grouped on the basis of 1994 per capita income: lower income (below $150 per capita), intermediate income (between $150 and $500), and higher income ($500 to $3,000). The point of these group-ings is to hold constant differences in levels of economic development when com-paring parastatal and government budgets for protected areas within the region.

SURVEY RESULTS

Caribbean

The survey results for the Caribbean region are summarized in table 4.1. On av-erage, the parastatal protected areas in the Caribbean receive twice as much fund-ing, $1,886 per square kilometer, as the government-funded protected areas, $989 per square kilometer. In two out of the three comparative groups, the parastatals exhibit higher per-square-kilometer funding intensity than their government-funded counterparts. In all of the groups, the parastatals have more diverse funding sources.

The large size class has only two agencies for comparison: the Bahamas National Trust, a parastatal, and the Directorate of National Parks in the Dominican Repub-lic, a government-funded agency. The parastatal agency invested $324 per square kilometer, while the government agency invested $73 per square kilometer. The rela-tively lower per-square-kilometer conservation budgets for the Directorate of Na-tional Parks may be explained by the fact that it has larger protected areas on aver-age (504 square kilometers) and the Dominican Republic has a lower per capita income ($1,330) than the Bahamas ($11,800).

In the medium size class, the parastatal agencies are represented by two indepen-dently operated protected area systems on separate islands of the Netherlands Antilles, Bonaire and Saba. Five government protected area systems are included for com-parison: Turks and Caicos, Dominica, Jamaica, Trinidad and Tobago, and St. Kitts and Nevis. The control group countries have a mean per capita income of $3,568, compared with $8,956 in the parastatal. The mean area of the government-funded agencies is twenty-nine square kilometers, compared with eighteen square kilome-ters for the two parastatals.

In the medium size class, the parastatal administered protected areas received $10,828 per square kilometer on average, compared with $619 per square kilome-ter in the government-funded agencies. The parastatal agencies would be expected to have higher per-square-kilometer budgets due to their higher income levels and smaller mean areas, though these differences are not great enough to explain the parastatals' seventeen times higher rate of investment. Among the government-funded agencies, the highest budget is recorded for St. Kitts and Nevis at $4,441 per square kilometer, still well below the parastatals' budgets. Notably, St. Kitts and Nevis is also the most comparable government agency to the parastatals in terms of mean size and income.

Table 4.1

Protected Area Budgets for Caribbean Region, by Size Class

Type Country	Agency	Budget (1996 US$)	Protected Area (km²)	Budget (1996 US$/km²)	Mean Size of Protected Area (km²)	Per Capita Income
		Size Class: Large (more than 100 km²)				
Parastatal						
Bahamas	Bahamas National Trust	$ 405,531	1,253	$ 324	208.8	$ 11,800
Government						
Dominican Republic	Directorate of National Parks	741,036	10,086	73	504.3	1,330
		Size Class: Medium (10–100 km²)				
Parastatal						
Bonaire NA	Bonaire Marine Park	286,714	26	11,027	26.0	8,956
Saba NA	Saba Marine Park	103,090	10	10,309	10.0	8,956
Total or Mean		**$ 389,804**	**36**	**$ 10,828**	**18.0**	**$ 8,956**
Government						
Turks & Caicos	Dept of Environment & Coastal Resources	116,850	519	225	15.7	5,000
Dominica	Forestry & Wildlife Division	662,505	168	3,943	42.0	2,800

–continued–

Table 4.1 (continued)

Type Country	Agency	Budget (1996 US$)	Protected Area (km²)	Budget (1996 US$/km²)	Mean Size of Protected Area (km²)	Per Capita Income
Government (continued)		Size Class: **Medium** (continued)				
Jamaica	Natural Resources Conservation Authority	$ 191,830	803.0	$ 239	89.2	$ 1,540
Trinidad & Tobago	Wildlife Section (Forestry Division)	18,676	269.0	69	17.9	3,740
St. Kitts & Nevis	Conservation Commission	115,456	26.0	4,441	13.0	4,760
Total or Mean		**$ 1,105,317**	**1,785.0**	**$ 619**	**28.3**	**$ 3,568**
Parastatal		Size Class: **Small** (less than 10 km²)				
Antigua	National Parks Authority	962,963	24.0	40,123	4.0	6,770
Barbados	Folkestone Marine Park	135,352	2.7	50,130	2.7	6,560
Montserrat	Montserrat National Trust	43,847	8.4	5,220	2.1	3,900
St. Lucia	St. Lucia National Trust	560,752	0.3	1,869,173	0.1	3,130
Total or Mean		**$1,702,914**	**35.4**	**$ 48,105**	**2.5**	**$ 5,090**

–continued–

Table 4.1 (continued)

Type Country	Agency	Budget (1996 US$)	Protected Area (km²)	Budget (1996 US$/km²)	Mean Size of Protected Area (km²)	Per Capita Income
Size Class: Small (continued)						
Government						
Bermuda	Dept of Agriculture, Fisheries, and Parks	$ 10,007,420	111.0	$ 90,157	1.1	$ 17,790
Summary						
Parastatal Total or Mean		$ 2,498,249	1,324.4	$ 1,886	60.2	$ 7,153
Government Total or Mean		$11,853,773	11,982.0	$ 989	64.4	$ 5,280

Sources: Questionnaire responses (see note 1) and James, Green, and Paine (1999).

Notes: Budget figures represent an average for fiscal years 1995–1998; figures were converted to U.S. dollars at prevailing exchange rates, deflated to 1996 dollars, and rounded to nearest dollar.

The small size class is the only group where the government agency reports higher protected area investment than the parastatals. In the small size class, the average of the four parastatal agency budgets is $48,105 per square kilometer, compared with $90,157 square kilometer for the government parks department in Bermuda. Bermuda is a highly developed country with a per capita income of $17,790 and a highly fragmented system of small parks (111 protected areas averaging one square kilometer each). Unlike Bermuda, the parastatal countries have not attained developed country status, as their mean per capita income is $5,090. Also, the parastatal agencies each have a larger mean area under protection, with the exception of St. Lucia. Hence, protected area investment in the parastatal agencies is biased downward by their protected area size and per capita income.

Perhaps the most comparable parastatal agency to Bermuda in terms of mean area is the St. Lucia National Trust, which operates three protected areas totaling 0.33 square kilometer. The St. Lucia National Trust's protected area expenditures total $560,752 (equivalent to $1.87 million per square kilometer), well in excess of the government budget in Bermuda. The three other parastatals in the small size class have smaller budgets than Bermuda, but only one fell short by a major amount. The parastatals include Antigua ($40,123 per square kilometer), Barbados ($50,130 per square kilometer), and Montserrat ($5,220 per square kilometer).

Sub-Saharan Africa

Table 4.2 presents the results for Sub-Saharan Africa. In African protected area systems, parastatal investment averages $556 per square kilometer, compared with $38 per square kilometer in government-funded agencies. In each of the three comparative groups, the parastatals demonstrated both higher investment and more diverse funding sources.

In the lower income category, Tanzania's parastatal agency is compared with the government agencies in Ethiopia, Sudan, and Zaire. The Tanzania National Parks budget is $170 per square kilometer, compared with an average of only $16 per square kilometer for the group of government-funded agencies. Tanzania National Parks derives almost all of its budget from tourism revenues. Donations amount to the equivalent of $3 per square kilometer annually, and the agency receives no subsidy from the government. Instead the Tanzanian parastatal remits 50 percent of its annual surplus to the national treasury as a corporation tax.

In the intermediate income category, the Kenya Wildlife Service, a parastatal, is compared with Uganda, Zambia, and Malawi. Kenya's internally generated budget of $310 per square kilometer is more than ten times that of the government agency group, whose average investment is $29 per square kilometer. In addition to the internally generated funds, foreign assistance to the Kenyan Wildlife Service contributes another $160 per square kilometer in operating funds and a massive $739 per square kilometer in capital investment, for a total budget of $1,209 per square

Table 4.2
Protected Area Budgets, Sub-Saharan African Region

Type Country	Agency	Budget (1996 US$)	Protected Area (km²)	Budget (1996 US$/km²)	Mean Size of Protected Area (km²)	Per Capita Income
		Low Income (below $150 per capita)				
Parastatal						
Tanzania	Tanzania National Parks Association	$ 6,865,081	40,300	$ 170	3,358	$ 140
Government						
Ethiopia	Ethiopian Wildlife Conservation Organization	2,010,326	32,403	62	2,315	100
Zaire	Institute of Zairian Nature Conservation	439,451	100,262	4	5,898	NA
Sudan	Wildlife & National Park Forces	1,087,600	93,467	12	6,676	NA
Total or Mean		**$ 3,537,377**	226,132	$ 16	5,025	$ 100
		Intermediate Income ($150–$500 per capita)				
Parastatal						
Kenya	Kenya Wildlife Service	10,159,569	32,726	310	839	250

–continued–

Table 4.2 (continued)

Type Country	Agency	Budget (1995 US$)	Protected Area (km²)	Budget (1996 US$/km²)	Mean Size of Protected Area (km²)	Per Capita Income
		Intermediate Income (continued)				
Government						
Uganda	Uganda National Parks	$ 388,496	8,336	$ 47	1,389	$ 190
Malawi	Dept of National Parks, Wildlife & Tourism	730,684	10,585	69	1,176	170
Zambia	National Parks and Wildlife Service	1,818,198	80,740	23	1,468	350
Total or Mean		**$ 2,937,378**	**99,661**	**$ 29**	**1,424**	**$ 237**
		High Income ($500–$3,000 per capita)				
Parastatal						
South Africa	National Parks Board	46,275,329	34,244	1,351	2,140	3,040
Zimbabwe	Dept of National Parks & Wildlife Management	13,104,074	30,089	436	1,433	500
Total or Mean		**$ 59,379,403**	**64,333**	**$ 923**	**1,739**	**$ 1,770**

–continued–

Table 4.2 (continued)

Type Country	Agency	Budget (1996 US$)	Protected Area (km²)	Budget (1996 US$/km²)	Mean Size of Protected Area (km²)	Per Capita Income
		High Income (continued)				
Government						
Botswana	Dept of Wildlife & National Parks	5,590,133	100,250	56	11,139	2,800
Namibia	Ministry of Environment & Tourism	$ 8,562,095	112,159	$ 76	5,608	$ 1,970
Total or Mean		**$ 14,152,228**	**212,409**	**$ 67**	**7,324**	**$ 2,385**
		Summary				
Parastatal Total or Mean		$ 76,404,053	137,359	$ 556	1,561	$ 983
Government Total or Mean		$ 20,626,983	538,202	$ 38	3,738	$ 930

Sources: Questionnaire responses and James, Green, and Paine (1999).
Notes: Budget figures represent an average for fiscal years 1995–1998; figures were converted to U.S. dollars at prevailing exchange rates, deflated to 1996 dollars, and rounded to the nearest dollar.

kilometer. Kenya's total investment is very nearly equal to that of South Africa, a considerably more developed country with the highest protected areas budget in Africa.

In the higher income category, the National Parks Board of South Africa and the Department of Wildlife and National Parks in Zimbabwe, both parastatals, are compared with the government-funded conservation agencies in Botswana and Namibia. The parastatal agencies reported an average protected areas budget of $923 per square kilometer, compared with $67 per square kilometer in the government-funded areas. Part of the large discrepancy here (the parastatal budgets are fifteen times higher) may be due to the more intensive management needs and population pressures in the South Africa and Zimbabwe park systems. If so, the parastatal structure apparently has enabled these agencies to respond with greater financial inputs.

DISCUSSION

Caribbean

Diversification of revenue sources has enabled the higher parastatal funding of protected areas in the Caribbean region. The incentive created by revenue retention within the agencies has led to efforts to develop new sources of funds. These efforts have taken the form of more and better services offered, and new charges for formerly free services. All of these efforts represent a greater realization of the economic value of a country's environmental assets and the reinvestment of these values into conservation activities. The high volume of tourism to the Caribbean raises the marketable values of the protected areas, and the parastatal agencies appear to be well positioned to take advantage of this financial opportunity. This section briefly reviews the steps taken by the Caribbean parastatal agencies to increase and diversify their revenues.

The parastatal agency in the large size class, the Bahamas National Trust, receives only $11 per square kilometer from the government. By comparison, this allocation is only a fraction of the $73 per square kilometer received by the Dominican Republic's parks agency. The Bahamas National Trust adds another $313 to their conservation budget from revenues raised and retained in park operations. Subscriptions and donations also contribute a small amount.

In the medium size class, the parastatal agencies on the islands of Bonaire and Saba in the Netherlands Antilles are largely independently financed protected areas. Bonaire receives 3 percent of its annual budget from the government, and Saba receives nothing. Both earn the majority of their revenues from visitor fees, primarily from diving fees and boat moorings. Both actively seek donations from visitors and manage trust funds that make yearly contributions of interest income. In Bonaire, donations contributed $104 per square kilometer, and the trust fund income added $398 per square kilometer; Saba received the equivalent of $805 per square kilometer in donations and $186 per square kilometer in investment interest. Though contributing only a small proportion of the budgets in Bonaire and Saba, donations and trust fund income alone amount to a funding base roughly equivalent to the control group budgets ($619 per square kilometer).

Furthermore, both Bonaire and Saba are actively taking steps to increase their revenues from visitor services, their main source of funding. For example, Bonaire has proposed to the government that their diver fee be extended to cover all users of the marine park, including the yachters, windsurfers, and snorkelers who currently pay nothing. Additionally, they plan to begin charging an annual fee to the owners of private and commercial moorings in the park. Saba, unlike Bonaire, earns a significant proportion of its annual budget from souvenir sales (equivalent to 23 percent of operating funds) and plans to expand such sales. In both cases, the incentives provided by financial independence have resulted in the diversification of revenue sources and a greater capture of the financial value of their environmental assets.

Also in the medium size class is the Department of Environment and Coastal Resources (DECR) of the Turks and Caicos islands, a British dependency. The DECR is a government-funded agency struggling for greater financial independence. The government funded budget is only $225 per square kilometer, considerably below the $619 per square kilometer average for medium-sized government conservation agencies in the Caribbean. The DECR estimates that its current budget allows it to meet less than half of their stated conservation objectives. In response, the agency has taken steps to increase its self-sufficiency but notes, "At least ten proposals regarding self-financing in protected areas have been unsuccessfully presented to the government."[2] To provide extra funding for protected areas, the DECR has proposed implementing a diving fee, boat license fees, and an increase in the hotel accommodations tax. To date, only the boat license fees have been approved by government, but the revenues must be returned to the treasury. The agency notes that the government greatly opposes the "ring fencing" of park revenues, which it perceives as government funds.

In the small size class, St. Lucia is the only one of four parastatals that reported a larger budget than Bermuda's parks department. The St. Lucia National Trust budget is composed in nearly equal parts of a government grant and internally generated revenues; donations and subscriptions add only 1 percent to total budget. On the basis of revenues raised internally, the St. Lucia National Trust spends nearly $750,000 per square kilometer on protected areas, well in excess of the level of funding in Bermuda.

The other parastatals in the small size class have each taken steps to raise their revenue bases. For example, the Antigua National Parks Authority has developed a marketing plan "in order to sensitize and attract more visitors to the parks."[3] Antigua has recently upgraded its services to attract more visitors and has introduced an all-inclusive fee to the parks. In Barbados, fees for use of the protected areas have traditionally not been charged. However, the parastatal management currently has a proposal for the implementation of user fees before the government. This proposal would enable the Barbados National Conservation Commission to reduce its current dependence on government funds for about 90 percent of its budget.

Sub-Saharan Africa

Tourism revenues make a major contribution to the conservation budgets of the African parastatal agencies. Much of the funding advantage the parastatals have over their government-funded counterparts stems from the retention of revenue from visitor services and park entry fees. Here again, the incentive created by revenue retention appears to lead agencies to increase and diversify their funding sources. The African experience with parastatals shows that developing countries with substantial tourism can realize a greater proportion of the economic value of protected areas through the creation of parastatal agencies.

In the intermediate income category, the Kenya Wildlife Service has positioned itself to benefit from the country's large share of the region's tourism, much of which is attracted to the wildlife parks. The agency has successfully increased revenues through raising entry fees, improving the visitor services, and successfully promoting and marketing the parks. The parastatal has also been extremely effective in attracting foreign donors. Kenya is one of the best examples of successful institutional change, as the improved financial performance has been a direct result of the creation of the parastatal structure to manage the nation's protected area system.

By contrast, Zambia has modified the institutional structure of protected area resource management in a different direction. The Luangwa Integrated Resource Development Project (LIRDP) oversees the sustainable use of the wildlife resources around the country's most visited national parks in the Luangwa valley. In addition, sustainable use projects within nearby Game Management Areas have been initiated. The projects' objective are to achieve the sustainable utilization of wildlife in the region through transferring some of the property rights over the wildlife resources to the local communities (Lungu 1990). The LIRDP receives a substantial amount of foreign assistance from both bilateral and nongovernmental organization donors. Some of the revenues of the LIRDP are passed on to the national parks in the area. In 1993, LIRDP support added $41 per square kilometer to the budget of South Luangwa National Park and an adjacent game management area (Dublin, Milliken, and Barnes 1995). As a sustainable use project, the LIRDP may help reduce the poaching problem in the parks, but it is unlikely ever to produce the revenues needed to achieve adequate protected area conservation.

In the lower income category, Tanzania, like Kenya, receives a large share of the wildlife tourism in East Africa. However, its internally generated revenues are 50 percent less than the Kenya Wildlife Service. As a result, the achievement of conservation objectives, such as the control of poaching, is dependent on foreign funding to a greater extent in Tanzania than in Kenya (Dublin, Milliken, and Barnes 1995). The shortfall in its financial performance relative to Kenya suggests that the

Tanzania National Parks may not be fully taking advantage of the institutional incentives. This may relate to the informal institutions within the agency, such as a reluctance to raise park entry fees or to change other modes of operation. It is not possible to determine the reasons for the weaker financial performance without closer study, as informal institutions are subtle and not easily quantified.

In the higher income category, the South Africa National Parks Board's high level of financial resources is the result of a diversified revenue base. The annual government allocation to the parastatal is equivalent to $312 per square kilometer, only about 10 percent of the total budget. The National Parks Board takes a proactive approach to revenue generation by developing visitor services (68 percent of budget), generating investment income (8 percent of budget), and soliciting donations (1 percent of budget). The board is currently seeking $100 million in financial assistance from foreign and domestic sources to expand the country's network of protected areas.

The incentives provided by financial independence are also driving greater efficiency in the National Parks Board's operations. The agency management notes that certain "commercial operations which have been performed in house are being (or will be) outsourced to professional companies."[4] If a contractor can perform an operation more efficiently than the board, then outsourcing the operation will reduce the agency's total costs. The reduction in the board's operating costs increases the surplus available to fund conservation activities. Thus, the South Africa National Parks Board appears to be another example, along with Kenya, of a successful response to the incentives created by financial independence.

The Zimbabwe Department of National Parks and Wildlife Management (DNPWM) has recently been converted into a parastatal agency. Their internally generated budget of $302 per square kilometer is similar to that of Kenya. In addition, the government subvention is equivalent to $134 per square kilometer, and foreign assistance adds another $92 per square kilometer, for a total annual expenditure of $528 per square kilometer. Before the parastatal structure was created in Zimbabwe, the DNPWM had a budget of $144 per square kilometer (Martin 1993). Since the change, government support for protected areas in Zimbabwe has remained roughly constant, but the new infusion of funds from protected area operations has resulted in a tripling of the conservation budget. The management of the DNPWM notes that they are now "reviewing tariffs so that they are consistent with those on the market. Ours were much lower."[5] The agency is also taking steps to increase the range of services offered to visitors.

CONCLUSION

The results of this study suggest an asymmetry in the value of park revenues to protected area agencies and their value to national treasuries. The revenues arising from protected areas are quite small relative to national government budgets, but they can be very large relative to protected area budgets. The parastatal agencies reviewed here show that the retention of protected area revenues makes an enormous contribution to conservation budgets. Furthermore, this study has shown that control over the revenue stream creates an incentive to increase revenue generation and diversification, thereby maximizing the financial value of a country's protected areas. Conversely, government management of protected areas may fall short of fully realizing the potential financial values because of the insignificance of park revenues to the national treasury. Due to this asymmetry of values, a parastatal protected area agency can achieve major conservation benefits at little cost to governments.

The parastatal structure creates an "institutional incentive" to improve the financial performance of national protected area agencies. For such an institutional change to produce better results, however, the informal modes of operation with the agency must be compatible with the new incentives. This requires a willingness on the part of agency managers to take the steps necessary to raise revenues, reduce costs, and attract foreign support, while keeping biodiversity conservation as the primary objective. Not all agencies will have such conducive informal institutions. For example, the Tanzanian parastatal appears not to take full advantage of the opportunities provided by financial independence, which may be a reflection of organizational expectations and traditions. On the other hand, Kenya's experience shows that the creation of the parastatal agency can bring about a change in institutional behavior, as evidenced by the vigorous measures taken to improve both financial and conservation performance. The balance of the evidence presented in this study suggests that the creation of parastatal agencies does appear to improve financial performance.

An important variable not explicitly quantified in the analysis is tourism expenditure. Many countries in the Caribbean and Sub-Saharan Africa receive a substantial amount of foreign tourism, and it is probably not a coincidence that many of these countries also manage their protected areas through parastatal agencies. The quantity of tourism to a country can create a large financial advantage over relatively less visited countries that may distort the analysis presented here. However, it may still be true that a parastatal is better positioned to maximize the revenues received from tourism services, due to the incentive provided by financial independence. It remains an open question as to how much better a given country might do in attracting tourism if it turned its protected areas over to a parastatal agency. However, in a country that receives a substantial amount of foreign tourism, a parastatal structure is unlikely to hurt financial performance. The outcome depends on the extent to which the protected area managers take advantage of the incentives.

Tourism expenditures are usually distributed unevenly among a country's protected area system. Inevitably, in any country, some protected areas are more marketable than others. Conversely, some protected areas may be valuable as reserves for biodiversity conservation but not attractive to tourists. Hence, there is a case for treating the funding and management of national protected area networks as a single operating unit and redistributing funds among protected areas. A redistribution of funds can take place within a parastatal agency, if it had a mix of financially attractive and nonrevenue earning protected areas under its authority. Alternatively, a parastatal might manage the most marketable areas in a country and redistribute some of its surplus to government-managed areas. Either way, the pooling and redistribution of funds among protected areas within a system might be an objective of parastatal agencies to further a country's biodiversity conservation objectives.

While this study has concentrated on the performance of parastatal protected area agencies in the developing countries, the conclusions apply equally well to the advanced countries. In fact, the higher disposable incomes in the advanced countries suggest an even greater scope for protected area managers to capitalize on the financial incentives provided by the parastatal structure. Higher incomes engender a greater demand for environmental amenities as the rapid growth in tourism, and nature tourism in particular, illustrates. Instead of treating the increase in visitors as an environmental liability, a parastatal protected area agency would create the incentive for managers to channel funds from tourism into conservation activities. Instead of limiting access to parks, as has been done in some U.S. national parks, a parastatal agency would encourage managers to convert the value people place on parks into conservation funds.

NOTES

1. Responses to survey questionnaire are hereinafter referred to as "questionnaire response."

2. Questionnaire response, J. L. Garland, Department of Environment and Coastal Resources, Turks and Caicos Islands, British West Indies.

3. Questionnaire response, A. M. Martin, National Parks Authority, Antigua.

4. Questionnaire response, P. Fearnhead, National Parks Board, South Africa.

5. Questionnaire response, C. Machena, Department of National Parks and Wildlife Management, Zimbabwe.

REFERENCES

Bromley, Daniel. 1991. *Environment and Economy: Private Rights and Public Policy.* Cambridge, Mass.: Blackwell.

Dixon, J. A., and P. B. Sherman. 1990. *The Economics of Protected Areas: A New Look at Benefits and Costs.* Washington, D.C.: Island.

Dublin, H. T., T. Milliken, and R. F. W. Barnes. 1995. *Four Years after the CITES Ban: Illegal Killing of Elephants, Ivory Trade, and Stockpiles.* IUCN Species Survival Commission, African Elephant Specialist Group. Gland, Switzerland: IUCN.

International Monetary Fund. 1997. *International Financial Statistics Yearbook, 1997.* Washington, D.C.: Author.

International Union for the Conservation of Nature. 1992. *Protected Areas of the World: A Review of National Systems.* Vol. 3: *Afrotropical.* Gland, Switzerland: Author.

James, Stephanie Presber. 1996. "An Institutional Approach to Incentives for Conservation." Paper presented at the IUCN World Conservation Congress, Montreal, 17 October.

James, Alexander N., Michael J. B. Green, and J. R. Paine. 1999. "Global Review of Budgets and Staffing of Protected Areas." Cambridge: World Conservation Monitoring Center.

Leader-Williams, Nigel, and Steve Albon. 1986. "Allocation of Resources for Conservation." *Nature* 336: 533–35.

Lungu, F. 1990. "Luangwa Integrated Rural Development Project (LIRDP) and Administrative Design for Game Management Areas (AMADE)." In *Living with Wildlife: Wildlife Resource Management with Local Participation in Africa,* ed. Agnes Kiss. Washington, D.C.: World Bank.

Martin, Rowan B. 1993. "Should Wildlife Pay Its Way?" Keith Roby Address, Department of National Parks and Wildlife, Perth, Australia, 8 December, as cited in "Conserving Biodiversity; Resources for Our Future," by Stephen R. Edwards in *The True State of the Planet,* ed. Ronald Bailey. New York: Free Press, 223–24.

McNeeley, J. A., J. Harrison, and P. Dingwall, eds. 1994. *Protecting Nature: Regional Reviews of Protected Areas.* Gland, Switzerland: IUCN.

North, Douglass. 1990. *Institutions, Institutional Change, and Economic Performance.* Cambridge: Cambridge University Press.

United Nations Environment Program. 1996. "Sharing of Experiences on Incentive Measures for Conservation and Sustainable Use." Paper presented at the third Conference of the Parties to the Convention on Biological Diversity, Buenos Aires, Argentina, 4–15 November 1996. Document UNEP/CBD/COP/3/24.

5

Preserving Institutional and Ecological Diversity in Argentina's Protected Area System

Javier Beltrán, Alexander James, and Mariano L. Merino

Argentina's first national park was established in 1903. Since then, the protected area system has grown slowly and coverage has reached only 4.5 percent of the country's land area. This coverage is lower than average for South America (about 6.5 percent), and, as shown in table 5.1, Argentina has the sixth lowest percentage of land area under protection in the region (International Union for the Conservation of Nature [IUCN] 1998). Several of the thirteen ecoregions described for the country (Dinerstein et al. 1995) are underrepresented in the Argentine system, including the Pampas, the Argentine Espinal, and the Patagonian steppe (Administración de Parques Nacionales [APN; National Parks Administration] 1997).

Argentina's protected areas are managed within a two-tier national and provincial system. The national system of protected areas is composed of thirty-two units and covers thirty-three thousand square kilometers, or 1 percent of the land area, but not all provinces have national protected areas. For example, national protected areas cover 8,820 square kilometers, or 9.4 percent of Neuquen Province, though four provinces—Catamarca, Mendoza, Santa Fe, and Santiago del Estero—have no national protected areas in their jurisdictions (APN 1997).

The provincial system of protected areas is considerably larger and more diverse than the national system. The provinces administer 156 protected areas, covering around 94,000 square kilometers, or 2.7 percent of Argentina's land area. Considerable variation exists, however, even with provincial protected areas. San Juan Province, for example, has 19.5 percent of its land area in the provincial system; Entre Rios Province has none. Nonetheless, with its greater size and representativeness, the provincial protected area system makes a critical contribution to the conservation of Argentina's biological diversity.

During the 1990s, much consideration went into developing strategies for strengthening Argentina's system of protected areas. Though the strengthening of

Table 5.1
Protected Areas in Argentina and Other Latin American Countries

Country	Total Area (km²)	Number of Protected Areas	Total Area Protected (km²)	Percent of Total Area Protected (%)
El Salvador	21,395	2	52	0.2
Guyana	214,970	1	585	0.3
Uruguay	186,925	13	477	0.3
French Guiana	91,000	2	1,001	1.1
Paraguay	406,750	20	14,011	3.4
Argentina	*2,791,810*	*188*	*127,042*	*4.5*
Suriname	163,820	14	8,042	4.9
Peru	1,285,215	34	67,606	5.3
Brazil	8,511,965	581	526,106	6.2
Mexico	1,972,545	152	159,762	8.1
Colombia	1,138,915	94	93,655	8.2
Honduras	112,085	81	11,310	10.1
Nicaragua	148,000	70	16,375	11.1
Ecuador	461,475	23	69,221	15.0
Bolivia	1,098,575	37	178,187	16.2
Costa Rica	50,900	88	8,923	17.5

—continued—

Table 5.1 (continued)

Country	Total Area (km²)	Number of Protected Areas	Total Area Protected (km²)	Percent of Total Area Protected (%)
Chile	751,625	88	141,373	18.8
Panama	78,515	31	15,474	19.7
Guatemala	108,890	42	21,668	19.9
Belize	22,965	49	9,132	39.8
Venezuela	912,045	195	563,056	61.7
	20,530,385	1,862	2,031,259	9.9

Note: Coverage can be overestimated due to double counting of areas belonging to different but overlapping sites.

Source: APN (1997).

the provincial system presents an opportunity to improve conservation in Argentina, it is rightly recognized that institutional capacity at the provincial level is lacking. As a result, some proposals advocate the transfer of important provincial protected areas to the national system, and five priority areas totaling 3,400 square kilometers have recently been earmarked to receive protection at the national level.

Another proposal has been to strengthen provincial administrative capacity through the creation of a Federal Council of Natural Protected Areas (Consejo Federal de Areas Naturales Protegidas) composed of representatives from the national and provincial administrations. The objective of the council would be to transfer expertise to the provincial level and to coordinate conservation strategies. Part of this strategy would be to nationalize the administration of all units in the provincial protected area system under a national network (IUCN 1992).

This chapter will evaluate the role of the provincial conservation agencies in alternative strategies for strengthening Argentina's protected area system.

COMPARISON OF NATIONAL AND PROVINCIAL PROTECTED AREA MANAGEMENT

Under provisions of the 1853 constitution, partially reformed in 1994, both the national and provincial governments are entitled to create protected areas in their jurisdictions. We consider the relative strengths and weaknesses of the national and provincial protected area systems in Argentina in five respects: legal and administrative institutions, financial and human resources, public participation, private investment, and management performance. In general, the provincial protected area system is characterized by greater institutional and administrative diversity than the national system.

Legal and Administrative Institutions

The National Parks Law (no. 22.351, 1980) currently in effect provides for the creation of protected areas in national territory or in land passed on to national jurisdiction by the provinces. The National Parks Administration (APN), an autonomous body under the Secretariat for Natural Resources and Human Environment (SERNAH), is in charge of managing the system of national parks, national monuments, and national reserves. Four Technical Regional Delegations (Northeast, Northwest, Center, and Patagonia) have been created for the purpose of decentralizing administration and management of the national protected area system (APN 1997).

By comparison, the provincial system of protected areas contains considerable diversity in its legal institutions and management structures. Not all of the provinces have a law for the designation and management of a system of protected areas. In eleven provinces, individual sites are protected by means of provincial decrees (see table 5.2). Most provincial legislation includes provisions for the creation of protected areas by municipalities or universities. Also, privately owned protected areas can be added to the provincial system if they have met certain ecological and management criteria. More than thirty distinct legal designations are used throughout the system, reflecting a heterogeneous arrangement of protected areas subjected to different ownership, administrative, and management regimes.

Some provinces have established conservation agencies specifically to manage protected area systems. In others, responsibility for protected area management falls on less specific bodies such as a natural resource, environment, or tourism departments (see table 5.2). The institutional capacity of the provincial agencies varies considerably, as will be discussed.

Though the majority of the provincial protected areas are managed by government agencies, five are administered by municipalities, thirty-one by individuals, and nine by universities (table 5.3). Municipal management is often accomplished in conjunction with provincial departments (APN 1997). Protected areas on land owned by universities or technological institutes are also managed in agreement with the respective provincial administrative body (World Conservation Monitoring Center [WCMC] 1995). Privately owned protected areas may be managed independently or by provincial administration. Independent administration is often undertaken by nongovernmental organizations that either buy the land themselves or provide management advice to private landowners (IUCN 1992).

Financial and Human Resources

The national system is financed through a protected area fund consisting of a budgetary allocation from the national congress; fees, fines, levies, and concessions in the protected areas; and donations and other contributions. The fund can be used to create new protected areas, promote scientific studies, cover expenditures, salaries, investments, and any other activity foreseen in the legislation. The APN is in charge of administering the fund and of preparing annual financial statements that are audited by the national attorney general.

The fund for the APN reached $25 million in 1996, and the agency employed a total 725 people (APN 1997). In addition, the APN also receives considerable support from international donors. For example, a loan from the Global Environment Facility and the APN's own resources will allow it to spend $22.5 million over a five-year period, mainly on land purchases to expand the national system of protected areas (World Bank 1997).

Many of the provincial agencies have the legal authority to establish a protected area fund, though none has done so. Instead, funding for the provincial areas has been restricted to annual allocations, if any, from the budgets of provincial legislatures. Information on the provincial budgets for protected area conservation is difficult

Table 5.2
Argentina's Protected Area System

Jurisdiction	Law	Administrative Agency	Degree of Autonomy
National	National Parks Law 22351/80	APN	Full autonomy; under SERNAH
Buenos Aires	Natural Reserves & Parks Law 10907/93	Directorate for Natural Resources	Low; under Provincial Ministry for Farming Issues
Catamarca	None specific	Secretariat for the Environment	Unknown
Chaco	Natural Protected Areas Law 4358/96	Sub-Secretariat for Natural Resources & the Environment	Low; under Provincial Ministry for the Production
Chubut	None specific	Provincial Organization for Tourism	Unknown
Córdoba	Wildlands Law 6964/83	Service for Protected Areas	Full autonomy
Corrientes	Natural Protected Areas Law 4763/93	Directorate for Nature Parks & Reserves	Full autonomy; under Provincial Ministry for Ag., Cattle Raising, Industry & Commerce
Entre Rios	Natural Protected Areas Law 8967/95	Area of Flora and Fauna	Low; under Provincial Directorate for Vegetal Production & Renewable Resources
Formosa	None specific	Department for Fauna and Flora	Unknown
Jujuy	None specific	Directorate for Natural Renewable Resources	Unknown
La Pampa	Natural Protected Areas Law 1231/91	Sub-Secretariat for Ecology	Unknown
La Rioja	None specific	Directorate for the Environment	Unknown

–continued–

Table 5.2 (continued)

Jurisdiction	Law	Administrative Agency	Degree of Autonomy
Mendoza	Natural Protected Areas Law 6405/93	Council for Science & Technology	Full autonomy
Misiones	Natural Protected Areas Law 2932/92	Department for Nature Protected Areas	Low; under Provincial Ministry for Ecology & Natural Renewable Resources
Neuquén	None specific	Department for Fauna & Flora & Nature Protected Areas	Unknown
Río Negro	Natural Protected Areas Law 2669/93	Service Protected Areas	Low; under Provincial Ministry for Economy
Salta	None specific	Directorate for the Environment & Natural Resources	Unknown
San Juan	None specific	Directorate for Territorial Ordering & Environmental Management	Unknown
San Luis	None specific	Directorate for the Environment	Unknown
Santiago del Estero	None specific	Unknown	Unknown
Santa Cruz	None specific	Unknown	Unknown
Santa Fe	In draft	Directorate for Ecology & Fauna Protection	Low; under Provincial Ministry for Ag., Cattle Raising, Industry & Commerce
Tierra del Fuego	Environmental Law 55/92	General Directorate for Natural Resources	Unknown; under Provincial Secretariat of Development & Planning
Tucumán	None specific	Unknown	Unknown

Source: APN (1997) and Various (1980–1996).

Table 5.3
Management Regimes of Argentine Protected Areas

Jurisdiction	Total Land Area (km²)	APN			Provincial		
		A	B	C	A	B	C
Buenos Aires	307,757	1	30	0.0	9	707	0.2
Capital Federal	200	0	0	0.0	0	0	0.0
Catamarca	102,600	0	0	0.0	1	7,700	7.5
Chaco	99,633	2	150	0.2	4	242	0.2
Chubut	224,686	2	2,867	1.3	5	3,685	1.6
Cordoba	165,321	1	370	0.2	6	10,734	6.5
Corrientes	88,199	1	151	0.2	1	12,000	13.6
Entre Rios	78,781	2	109	0.1	0	0	0.0
Formosa	77,066	2	570	0.7	3	268	0.3
Jujuy	53,219	2	923	1.7	3	3,039	5.7
La Pampa	143,440	1	99	0.1	8	418	0.3
La Rioja	89,680	1	2,150	2.4	3	4,315	4.8
Mendoza	148,827	0	0	0.0	8	4,474	3.0
Misiones	29,801	2	682	2.3	13	1,350	4.5
Neuquen	94,078	4	8,822	9.4	6	667	0.7
Rio Negro	203,013	1	2,220	1.1	5	16,155	8.0
Salta	155,488	3	1,816	1.2	2	143	0.1
San Juan	89,651	1	740	0.8	2	9,229	10.3
San Luis	76,748	1	1,500	2.0	2	187	0.2
Santa Cruz	243,943	3	9,128	3.7	4	228	0.1
Santa Fe	133,007	0	0	0.0	3	68	0.1
Santiago del Estero	136,351	0	0	0.0	1	1,114	0.8
Tierra del Fuego	32,980	1	630	1.9	2	820	2.5
Tucuman	22,524	1	100	0.4	3	334	1.5
	2,796,993	32	33,057	1.2	94	77,877	2.7

Notes: Column A is the number of protected areas; column B is the protected area in square kilometers; column C is the percent of the total land area that is protected (rounded to the nearest tenth). Data listed under the "Other" regime pertain to protected

Table 5.3
(continued)

Jurisdiction	Private			Other			Total		
	A	B	C	A	B	C	A	B	C
Buenos Aires	2	50	0.0	7	230	0.0	19	1,018	0.3
Capital Federal	0	0	0.0	0	0	0.0	0	0	0.0
Catamarca	0	0	0.0	0	0	0.0	1	7,700	7.5
Chaco	1	17	0.0	0	0	0.0	7	409	0.4
Chubut	7	51	0.0	2	300	0.1	16	6,903	3.1
Cordoba	2	87	0.1	2	2	0.0	11	11,192	6.8
Corrientes	1	142	0.2	0	0	0.0	3	12,293	13.9
Entre Rios	0	0	0.0	0	0	0.0	2	109	0.1
Formosa	2	110	0.1	0	0	0.0	7	948	1.2
Jujuy	0	0	0.0	1	3,640	6.8	6	7,602	14.3
La Pampa	0	0	0.0	1	95	0.1	10	612	0.4
La Rioja	0	0	0.0	0	0	0.0	4	6,465	7.2
Mendoza	0	0	0.0	0	0	0.0	8	4,474	3.0
Misiones	10	129	0.4	5	2,270	7.6	34	4,431	14.9
Neuquen	0	0	0.0	0	0	0.0	10	9,489	10.1
Rio Negro	0	0	0.0	2	30	0.0	8	18,405	9.1
Salta	0	0	0.0	0	0	0.0	5	1,959	1.3
San Juan	0	0	0.0	3	8,360	9.3	6	18,329	20.4
San Luis	0	0	0.0	0	0	0.0	3	1,687	2.2
Santa Cruz	2	167	0.1	0	0	0.0	9	9,523	3.9
Santa Fe	3	152	0.1	3	116	0.1	9	336	0.3
Santiago del Estero	0	0	0.0	0	0	0.0	1	1,114	0.8
Tierra del Fuego	1	19	0.1	0	0	0.0	4	1,469	4.5
Tucuman	0	0	0.0	1	141	0.6	5	575	2.6
	31	924	0.03	31	15,184	0.5	188	127,042	4.5

areas managed by technological institutes and miscellaneous entities.

Source: APN (1997).

to obtain or simply not available. What data there are suggest that the provincial protected areas have less funding than the APN on a per-hectare basis. For example, Tierra del Fuego has $1.50 per hectare and Buenos Aires has $2.20 per hectare compared to the APN with $7.6 per hectare.

With regard to the number of wardens per hectare, however, the differences between the APN and provincial administrations are far less evident. Where data exist, they show that provincial agencies staff their protected areas at levels equivalent to the APN. In fact, Misiones Province staffs its protected areas at a level considerably higher than does the APN. Though the number of staff working for provincial administrations generally does not exceed ten, in many provinces personnel from departments such as fishing and hunting or forestry share responsibility for control and enforcement activities within protected areas.

Public Participation

The National Parks Law affords very little participation of civil society in either planning or managing the national system of protected areas. However, some preliminary actions to decentralize the decision-making process and involve communities have been initiated recently by the APN. The Directorate of Environmental Interpretation and Extension contains a multidisciplinary Human Settlements Department charged with resolving conflicts with human settlements surrounding protected areas. The Technical Regional Delegations are assisting cooperation among the APN, local communities, and provincial authorities.

In the provincial system, public involvement in protected area planning and management is increasingly encouraged. For example, Law 2669 of Rio Negro Province and Law 4358 of Chaco Province promote a complete decentralization of management through the creation of committees called Local Authorities for Conservation (ALC). These committees, which consist of honorary members proposed by the community, have advisory and deliberative roles and are called on to play an active part in the preparation and implementation of management plans.

Private Investment

The National Parks Law contains no provisions for protected areas on or extending into private land within the national system. As a result, the APN does not have any institutional incentive to involve private landowners in protected area conservation. Private properties are allowed in areas of national reserve that surround national parks, but their activities are restricted to 5 percent of the land.

By contrast, five provinces—Buenos Aires, Entre Rios, Córdoba, Misiones, and Rio Negro—officially recognize protected areas on privately owned land in their legislation (see table 5.2). Moreover, a total of ten provinces have incorporated private land into their protected area systems, covering an area of about one thousand square kilometers (see table 5.3).

The process whereby private property is included in the provincial system normally includes a field survey to be undertaken by the management body. If the estate is considered worthy of official protection and the proprietor accepts the designation, then certain financial incentives may apply. For example, Law 10907 of Buenos Aires Province exempts landowners from property tax while the estate is officially under protected status. The Buenos Aires Provincial Directorate for Natural Resources can subsidize maintenance and other costs of the property and can invite municipalities to waive local taxes. In the case of the Misiones Province, the property tax exemption reaches 60 percent, as long as the landowner has no outstanding debt with the province and the property has an approved conservation management plan that maintains at least 70 percent of the primary vegetation. Tax exemption can reach up to 80 percent when the property conserves its original vegetation cover and there are no plans for exploiting it.

Management Performance

The National Parks Law is clearly based on the principle of passive management, which is maintaining the natural character of the land by restricting human intervention. Coincidentally, the APN has invested significantly less resources in implementing management actions and evaluating its consequences than in programs of land purchasing, control, and surveillance.

The elaboration of conservation management plans for each protected area in the national system is mandatory under national legislation. In spite of these provisions, a relatively small number of such plans has been prepared and implemented in the national system. Management actions of any kind are carried out in only 30 percent of national protected areas (APN 1997).

The lack of management is further exacerbated by the fact that the national legislation specifies no clear targets for the assessment or monitoring of the effectiveness of protected area management. Instead, some qualitative assessments have been used in the past to classify management outcomes in protected areas of the national system. For example, Fourcade and Uribelarrea (1992) estimate that of the twenty national parks existing in 1992, about half were well managed, three were reasonably managed, and the rest were poorly managed.

Provincial agencies are also required by law to develop management plans for protected areas. The conservation management agencies are usually responsible for preparing these plans, although in some cases they can approve plans prepared by others. In general, the provincial agencies do not have the resources with which to implement minimum measures of control, enforcement, or management in most protected areas. Despite this lack of funds, conservation management activities of some kind were implemented in 44 percent of provincial protected areas, a higher ratio than for the national system (APN 1997).

ASSESSMENT OF THE PRESENT SYSTEM

The mix of protected areas in Argentina does not constitute a harmonic system of interconnected conservation units—both national and provincial—with complementary management purposes and regimes. To the contrary, there is a loose assemblage of twenty-four provincial protected area systems, with the national system prevailing over the others in terms of institutional stability, degree of autonomy, access to financial resources, and management capacity.

The national system evolved under a framework of legislation that has experienced very little change since its first version was passed in 1934. This original legislation did not foresee many aspects of modern conservation such as the need to preserve a representative sample of the country's biodiversity, the value in attracting private sector resources, and the opportunity to diversify management responsibility among the full range of stakeholders. As a result, APN has not had the institutional incentives to develop and implement these aspects of modern conservation management.

In addition, the APN receives a large proportion of the financial resources currently being dedicated to *in situ* conservation activities in Argentina. APN's protected area fund has grown consistently over the past decade and benefits further from the substantial resources of international donors (APN 1997). Despite the APN's considerable resources and administrative capacity developed over years of operation, the management of the national protected areas is widely perceived as inadequate. Many protected areas are left unmanaged, and the resources and energy of the private and nongovernmental sector have gone untapped. These shortcomings are attributable to the APN's institutional structure rather than to the efforts of its highly competent, professional, and well-resourced staff.

By contrast, the provincial protected areas have been starved of funds and administrative capacity for decades. In response, many provincial protected area agencies have diversified their administration and management structures to involve other interested individuals and groups. About half of the provincial agencies are governed by protected area legislation dating from 1983 onwards. This legislation is generally less restrictive with regard to human presence and promotes a more participatory approach to protected area planning, administration, and management. The remaining provinces have no legal instruments for long-term stability and management of protected areas.

The provincial system is institutionally diverse but fragmented. Because many provinces do not have protected area legislation or a specific conservation agency, coordination of a conservation strategy at the provincial level has not been feasible. The funding deficiencies have exacerbated this problem, especially by limiting the development of administrative capacity at the provincial level. However, these weaknesses may have engendered certain positive characteristics of provincial protected area management, such as the participation of the private sector and universities, the formation of local advisory bodies, and the evolution of different levels of sustainable use in the protected areas.

Proposals for institutional change in the provincial system should aim to build on these strengths. A successful institutional change would bring more funds to the provincial system and create an incentive to develop administrative capacity within the provinces, while allowing them to coordinate their institutionally diverse approaches to protected area management.

OPTIONS FOR INSTITUTIONAL CHANGE

Since 1984, several attempts have been made to unify protected area legislation across the country, but none has proceeded beyond draft form. The most consistently supported one, written by the APN, proposes the creation of a Federal Council of Natural Protected Areas composed of representatives from APN and each province, as the highest authority for implementation of a new protected areas law. The draft of the new law "states national conservation objectives and provides a legal framework for a coherent system, *consolidating both national and provincial protected areas*" (IUCN 1992, 175, emphasis added).

In 1986, the process of consolidating the provincial and national protected areas was begun on an informal basis (i.e., nonlegislative) with the creation of the National Network of Technical Cooperation in Protected Areas in Argentina (IUCN 1992). The National Network is composed of representatives of national and provincial agencies. Its provisional board of directors has representatives from the APN, eighteen of the twenty-three provinces, and the Federal Environmental Commission. The purpose of the National Network is to increase cooperation between the national and provincial agencies, coordinate a national biodiversity conservation strategy, and standardize protected area legal designations.

The strategy of consolidating protected areas at the national level further strengthens the APN over the provincial agencies. The consolidated sites would be transferred to the centralized APN system, permanently removing the diversity of management regimes that may be in place at the provincial level. In fact, this strategy expands the national institutions for protected area management when the provincial system offers much more diversity and flexibility. It would be more beneficial for the conservation of Argentina's biodiversity to promote a thriving and diverse provincial system of protected areas. The extension of the APN system, while logical given the national agency's superior funding and administrative capacity, overlooks the unique opportunity for conservation in Argentina that promotes and strengthens the diverse provincial system.

An alternative institutional structure would be to establish a provincial council, separate from the APN, that creates incentives for improving the provincial system of protected areas. A provincial council would require annual funding from the national congress for council administration and programs. The council would also require the authority to raise and retain revenues from diverse sources such as foreign donors and the private sector. Council decisions would be made by a body of representatives whose membership rotates on a regular basis through the provinces.

The core activities of the provincial council would include the coordination of a provincial conservation strategy in conjunction with the national system. The council would also work to develop administrative capacity within the provincial conservation agencies. Institutional capacity might be improved in areas such as best practice in conservation management or in negotiations with the private sector. Most important, perhaps, the council could coordinate the raising and distribution of additional funds to the agencies. Fund-raising efforts would be consolidated under the provincial council that would be able to present donors a coordinated provincial conservation strategy.

Under the provincial council, the provinces would maintain the ongoing management of their protected areas and with it the diversity of legal and management regimes. While overall conservation strategy would be negotiated at the council level, the provinces would retain a high degree of autonomy in implementation activities. For example, provinces could continue to draw on local organizations, nongovernmental organizations, or private individuals for protected area management. In this way, the institutional diversity of the country's protected area system could be maintained while conservation strategy, fund-raising, and administrative capacity building is coordinated at the national level.

The establishment of a provincial council represents an institutional change that would create self-sustaining incentives for the strengthening of the provincial system of protected areas. The access to donor funding and availability of administrative support from the provincial council would create an incentive for the provinces to build institutional capacity in their conservation programs. The many provinces without protected areas legislation or a conservation agency would have the incentive to implement these institutions to better access the resources available from the provincial council. The provincial council in time would emerge as a competing power base to the APN. This could only be beneficial given the institutional shortcomings within the national system.

CONCLUSION

The current proposals for a national council would further entrench APN's domination of protected area management in Argentina. The national council and the proposed new conservation law represent an extension of the centralized model of national park management in Argentina. A better strategy would be to build on strengths of the provincial system by creating instead a provincial council. A separate provincial council represents an opportunity to create management capacity in a second national-level conservation organization. This capacity would encourage the provincial agencies to preserve their diverse management styles and institutional configurations to the benefit of Argentina's biodiversity.

REFERENCES

Administración de Parques Nacionales. 1997. *Natural Protected Area System in Argentina: Status, Statistical Tables, and Priority Actions.* Buenos Aires: APN, World Commission on Protected Areas, and Network of Technical Cooperation of Food and Agriculture Organization of the United Nations.

Dinerstein, E., D. M. Olson, D. J. Graham, A. L. Webster, S. A. Primm, M. P. Bookbinder, and G. Ledec. 1995. *A Conservation Assessment of the Terrestrial Ecoregions of Latin America and the Caribbean.* Washington, D.C.: World Bank.

Fourcade, M. T., and D. S. Uribelarrea. 1992. "Protected Area Systems in Argentina." In *Spaces without Inhabitants? National Parks in South America*, ed. S. Amend and T. Amend. Caracas: IUCN and Nueva Sociedad, 12–17.

International Union for the Conservation of Nature. 1992. *Protected Areas of the World: A Review of National Systems.* Vol. 4: *Nearctic and Neotropical.* Gland, Switzerland: Author.

Various. 1980–1996. [National parks law and protected area legislation of the provinces of Buenos Aires, Chaco, Córdoba, Corrientes, Entre Rios, Formosa, Rio Negro, and Tierra del Fuego Provinces.]

World Bank. 1997. *Environment Matters at the World Bank: July 1996–June 1997.* Washington, D.C.: Author.

World Conservation Monitoring Center. 1995. "Environmental Profile: Argentine Cordillera." Unpublished manuscript.

Part III

Opportunities for Institutional Change

6

Contracting Out at Parks Canada: Employee Takeovers

Christopher Bruce

In response to the unprecedented growth in the size of its debt and deficit, the Canadian government began, in the early 1990s, to consider seriously the many alternative options it had for increasing efficiency. The first step was to reduce the size of the civil service by offering early retirement packages. Next, a set of incentives was put into place to encourage departments to implement cost-saving measures. For example, multiyear budgets were introduced, departments were allowed to retain some of the revenues they had raised, managers were permitted to apply a portion of the funds they received from sale of obsolete assets to the purchase of new assets, and departments were given greater control over spending decisions.[1] Finally, when it became clear that many efficiencies still remained untapped, the government began to look more closely at contracting out initiatives.

Parks Canada's "employee takeover" (ETO) process was one of the most ambitious of these initiatives. To provide its employees with the opportunity to bid for contracts on an equal footing with private firms, which had more business experience, the contracting-out process was designed to proceed in two stages. In the ETO stage, only employee groups were allowed to submit bids. In the second stage, once the employee-based groups had obtained experience operating businesses, the bidding was to be opened to all firms.

As the contracting of government services to the private sector is still in its infancy, many practical and theoretical questions about the ETO process remain unanswered. The purpose of this chapter is to use Parks Canada's experience with ETOs to provide evidence concerning some of those questions. To this end, the chapter is developed in three stages. First, it investigates the theoretical circumstances in which contracting out could be expected to improve the efficiency of government service delivery. Second, it employs the theory of public choice to analyze the political hindrances that might discourage the introduction of contracting out. Finally, the chapter employs Parks Canada's experience with ETOs to provide an empirical test of many public choice propositions.[2]

CONTRACTING OUT: THE THEORY

Traditionally, economists have analyzed "the government" as if it was a monolith. We speak of "government policy," for example, as though it had been conceived and implemented by a single entity with unique preferences. More recently, however, economists have recognized that the observed behavior of government agencies might best be described as the outcome of a competition among such interest groups as voters, consumers, politicians, and government employees. Some of the models that have developed from this recognition focus on the tension that arises between the goals of government employees and those of their political masters. These models suggest that it might be possible to improve government efficiency by encouraging competition among the providers of government services—through either intra-governmental or external competition. In this section, I first provide a brief summary of the literature concerning the behavior of government agencies and then analyze the circumstances in which external competition (contracting out) could be expected to improve efficiency.

The Economics of Bureaucracy

Modern economic models of the employer–employee relationship are based on what is known as "principal-agent" theory.[3] This theory builds on the observation that the goals of employers (principals) and employees (agents) will be inconsistent with one another unless institutions bring them into congruence. Whereas politicians might seek to maximize the probability of reelection, for example, government employees might attempt to maximize their incomes with as little effort as possible. This will create a conflict in which employees attempt to shirk in their duties while directing funds away from vote-producing expenditures toward employee compensation. Politician-employers can be expected to respond to this conflict by attempting to reward employees for behavior that is consistent with the politicians' goals.

But principal–agent theory further predicts that politicians will find this course difficult because they have less information about their employees' activities than do the employees themselves. (This situation is the so-called "asymmetrical information" problem.) In the federal governments of Canada and the United States, for example, most cabinet ministers have responsibility for agencies whose staffs number in the tens of thousands, many (if not most) of whom are experts in their fields.

Governments have traditionally responded to this problem by developing very broad guidelines for the behavior of civil servants. For example, limits have been set on civil servants' salaries, and departments have been prevented from making expenditures without prior approval from a central watchdog agency.[4] However, although these constraints may prevent some of the most egregious inefficiencies associated with the bureaucratic provision of services, they are of only limited effectiveness because of the lack of information possessed by politicians. Furthermore, they introduce numerous inefficiencies of their own. For example, it has been argued that the establishment of upper limits on civil servants' salaries acts to inhibit innovative behavior. If there is a cap on salaries and on the rate of salary progression, the "upside" to successful introduction of an innovative approach may be insufficient to compensate for the risk associated with failure. Aditionally, if all revenues have to be returned to a central fund to ensure that agencies do not have an incentive to overcharge users, then agencies have little or no incentive to raise revenues at all, even when it would be in the public interest to do so (see McKenzie 1997, 108).

Many of those who advance principal–agent theory have attempted to describe methods by which these sources of inefficiency could be avoided. Carmichael (1989), for example, describes a number of techniques used by employers to ensure that employees do not shirk. These include the use of efficiency wages,[5] rank-order-tournaments,[6] and nonvested pensions,[7] among others. Although these policies can also be applied to civil servants, the academic literature has concentrated on the possibility that governments could introduce competition into the "purchase" of their services. In this way, politicians would not have to determine whether their service providers were operating in an efficient manner. If the current providers were acting inefficiently, it would be in the interests of potential competitors to identify that inefficiency and offer to rectify it. Thus, the classic principal–agent problem, that employees are able to hide information about shirking and budgetary waste, would be minimized.

Two forms of such competition have been suggested. First, Landau (1969), Caves and Christensen (1980, 974), and Breton (1990) have all proposed that the government could encourage competition *among* its agencies. Charter schools are an example of such an innovation. Each charter school is funded by the ministry of education but is established specifically to offer an alternative to the public school system. Examples of this type of competition are rare, however, in part because diseconomies of scale often make it inappropriate to break government agencies into smaller units.[8] It does not seem likely, for example, that it would be efficient to have two or more competing agencies collecting taxes or providing armed forces.

More commonly, competition is fostered by seeking bids from the private sector. This can be accomplished either by contracting out the service or by selling it to private interests (privatizing). Provided that the market for the service is truly competitive, there will be a strong incentive to minimize costs, provide the level of service that consumers wish to obtain, and introduce innovative procedures.[9]

One method of introducing competition to the provision of government services would be to allow employee groups to bid against one another. Competition would be maintained in the long run by requiring that the employees who win the first

contract leave the civil service and operate as private contractors. At the conclusion
of the first contract, subsequent bids for the service would be opened to all private
firms.

The Economics of Contracting Out

For employee takeovers to improve the efficiency of governmental production,
three aspects of the contract must be addressed. (Each of these points will be discussed in more detail in the following sections.) First, firms that contract for the
production must not face external costs or benefits.

Second, if the bidding process operates in such a way that potential bidders are
discouraged from participating, either because they feel that they are inadequately
informed about the nature of the service to be provided or because they feel that
the process is biased against them, the competitive advantages of private markets will
be lost.

Third, the nature of the contract with the successful bidder must be such that
the potential for future competition is not diminished significantly. For example, if
the successful bidder for the provision of automobile repair services were given ownership of the only repair shop in the region, future potential bidders would have to
make substantial fixed investments to become legitimate competitors for a future
repair service contract.

External Costs

Private firms will not produce the desired level of output if they are not required
to pay for the full value of the costs that they impose on society. The socially optimal level of production is reached by expanding output only as long as the social
value of an incremental unit exceeds its social cost. A private firm, on the other hand,
will expand output as long as incremental *private* revenue exceeds incremental *private* cost. Thus, if the firm's private revenue equals the social value of its product,
but its private costs are less than social costs, it will expand output beyond the socially optimal level.

In the context of national parks, a simple example of this situation occurs when
visitors to a private campground hike in a nearby park. Whereas the campground is
able to charge a fee that reflects the value that its guests place on its services, it pays
none of the costs that hikers impose on the flora and fauna or on congestion of the
park. As a result, the campground operator has an incentive to encourage levels of
hiking and other activities in the park that are well in excess of the social optimum.[10]
One method of dealing with this problem may be to have a government parks agency
operate the campground, with the explicit directive that the benefits of increased
use of the campground are to be weighed against any costs that campers impose on
the park's environment. A corollary of this argument is that privatization and con-

tracting out of park services may not be in the public interest if the government cannot find a way to force private firms to take account of the environmental costs that their activities create.

Competitive Bidding Process

If the primary purpose of any contracting out process (including ETOs) is to break this monopoly power through the use of competitive bidding, it is important that the contracting process be organized in such a way that potential competitors are not discouraged from participating. Three areas of concern are particularly important. Bidders must not feel (1) that the process favors some applicants over others, (2) that they will discover sources of "hidden" costs only after they have won the contract, or (3) that the process is biased against the awarding of any contract at all (i.e., the process is biased in favor of leaving the provision of the service within the civil service). Furthermore, if the competitive process is to encourage bidders to offer innovative ideas, they must be offered as much leeway as possible in their methods of delivering the contracted service.

All Bidders Must Be Treated Equally

If it is anticipated that some bidders will receive preferential treatment over others, the nonpreferred bidders may refuse to participate, and the degree of competition will be reduced. This perception can be minimized, first, by providing all bidders with the same information concerning the service to be provided and, second, by ensuring that all members of the committee evaluating the bids are seen to be strictly impartial. Both issues are particularly problematic when one of the groups entering the bidding process is composed of individuals who are currently working in the service that is to be contracted out. Clearly, the current manager of a campground will have more information about the costs of operating that facility than will an outside bidder. In such case, it can be expected that more outside bids will be received and that all bidders will work more assiduously to provide the most competitive bids possible, if the campsite's accounts are made as transparent as possible to all potential applicants. In turn, this implies that the department itself must ensure that its accounts carefully record the full costs (and revenues, where applicable) of operation.

It will be particularly difficult to maintain the perception of impartiality if one of the applicants is currently working in the facility to be contracted out or if one of the applicants has connections to the political party that is in power. In either case, extreme care will have to be taken to ensure that the evaluation committee is composed of individuals who have no personal connection with any of the applicants. A corollary of this point is that the names and affiliations of all of the decision makers must be released to the bidders.

Ensure That All Requirements Are Clearly Identified

Potential bidders will be discouraged from participating if they anticipate that hidden costs will be revealed only after the contract has been awarded. This argues both for making the current cost information available to all bidders and for setting out the contract's requirements as clearly as possible in advance.

There Must Be No Bias against Awarding a Contract

If potential bidders believe that the current managers of the service will use their influence to bias the process against the awarding of a contract, they will be discouraged from participating. Three steps must be taken to ensure that the perception of impartiality is maintained. First, those managers who would be adversely affected by a decision to contract out must have no influence over that decision other than the right to make representations to the decision-making body. (Even in that case, the content of those representations must be made available to the bidders, and the latter must be offered the opportunity to rebut any adverse arguments.)

Second, if the bids are to be measured against a benchmark to determine whether they offer a significant gain in efficiency, the means by which the benchmark was established must be clear to all participants. If bidders anticipate that current managers will artificially manipulate the benchmark either by exaggerating the level of service that must be provided or by underestimating the costs that the government is currently incurring, they will be reluctant to enter the competition.

Finally, bidders will be reluctant to reveal innovative ideas to a government agency if they are concerned that their bids will be rejected on spurious grounds and the innovations appropriated by the agency. Two steps may help minimize this concern. First, the agency must make clear in advance how it would provide the relevant service if it rejected all bids. This way, all participants would be able to determine whether the agency had appropriated the suggestions of bidders. Second, if the agency rejected an outside bid but used some of the suggestions made in that bid, it could be required to award the bidder an amount equal to the costs that were saved.

Provide Bidders with as Much Flexibility as Possible

One of the criticisms of government agencies is that they are not innovative in the ways that they deliver their services. To encourage competitive bidders to suggest how that delivery might be improved, they must be given as much flexibility as possible when designing their delivery systems. Rather than specifying to the last detail what tasks are to be undertaken, by whom, and how, performance standards could be set that could be met by any method chosen by the applicant. For example, rather than requiring that a campground operator clean the shower stalls a certain number of times per day, provide a specified number of interpretive talks, and maintain picnic tables to a certain standard, surveys of campers could be taken to determine their level of satisfaction. As long as a benchmark level of satisfaction could be attained, the operator would be left to select the approach to be taken.

Optimal Contractual Terms

An important characteristic influencing the nature of this contract is the extent to which production of the service requires investment in capital goods that are specific to that service. If such capital is owned by the government but used by a private contractor, incentives must be provided to ensure that the contractor maintains the capital properly. Alternatively, if the capital is to be provided by the contractor, either some mechanism must be provided to ensure that the contractor is compensated for that investment at the end of the contract or the contract must be of sufficient duration to allow the contractor to recoup its investment. Also, Klein, Crawford, and Alchian (1978) have warned that when specific investments are made, the contract must protect both parties against opportunistic behavior by the other. The government must guard against the possibility that the contractor will use its position as sole supplier to drive up the contract price either during the contract or at the time of contract renewal. The contractor must guard against the possibility that the government will use its position as sole buyer to drive the contract price below long-run cost.[11]

In summary, the primary drawback to government production of public services is that the civil service is a monopoly provider of those services. This leads to all of the classic symptoms of monopoly production.

The contracting out of government services is intended to respond to these problems by introducing a strong competitive element to the production of these services. Hence, an essential element of any contracting-out process must be the maintenance of a competitive market for the service to be provided. The first requirement for such a market is that the bidding process must be fair; otherwise, potential bidders will be discouraged from participating. Where there is only a small number of firms in the private market, the government may be able to increase competition by allowing its own employees to bid for the contract.

At the same time, the government must be careful that it does not choose a contractual form that reduces competition. In particular, long-term contracts with the private sector offer few advantages over provision by the civil service if the government finds itself dealing with a monopoly supplier. This problem is particularly difficult to resolve when provision of the service requires significant investments in specific capital. In such cases, care must be taken to ensure, on the one hand, that the contract compensates the private firm adequately for its investments and, on the other hand, that compensation does not require that the government commit itself to a long-term contract with the private supplier.

Finally, cases in which it is difficult to specify the nature of the service create special problems for the contracting process. The government must take care to ensure that the successful bidder does not take advantage of ambiguities in the contract to provide a service of lesser quality than was anticipated. At the same time, the government must not discourage firms from bidding on future contracts by taking advantage of those same ambiguities to demand a higher quality or quantity of service than the contractor had anticipated.

Political Factors

The purpose of the preceding section was to analyze the circumstances in which the contracting out of government services might result in a net social gain. But just because a policy meets this requirement does not mean that the government will introduce it. If the policy imposes costs on a subset of voters, those individuals may attempt to use the political process to derail the policy. In the case of contracting out, one such group is composed of the civil servants in the affected agency. These individuals may lose their jobs or suffer reductions in wages and benefits and will definitely experience an increase in uncertainty. Hence, they will likely oppose the contracting out process.

The area of economics known as *public choice theory* helps explain this opposition.[12] The authors in this literature generally argue that civil servants can influence public policy by voting in public elections. Bush and Denzau (1977), Frey and Pommerehne (1982), and Bennett and Orzechowski (1983) all found, for example, that civil servants had a higher voting turnout than did the electorate as a whole. Rubinfeld (1977) concluded that schoolteachers were more likely to vote for increased local school expenditures than were other voters. Courant, Gramlich, and Rubinfeld (1980) found that public sector employees tended to favor lower reductions in state expenditures than did private sector employees. Also, Blais, and Dion (1991) found that civil servants had a tendency to vote for left-wing parties.

Employees can also leverage their voting power by appealing to other interest groups. Unionized civil servants, for example, may be able to convince the members of other unions to vote against a government that introduces policies (e.g., contracting out) that result in layoffs or reduced wages. Similarly, civil servants may be able to convince the consumers of the affected service that the quality of service will decline if it is contracted out. As consumers do not usually pay for the full cost of these services, they may not be swayed by the argument that the reduction in quality is offset by a reduction in the cost of delivery.

Furthermore, employees may be able to control information and the decision-making procedures to bias the contracting-out process against private bidders. For example, those who would be negatively affected by contracting out may use their influence to limit the number of services that are put out to tender or to raise the standards against which external bids are compared (Bruce 1997).

These arguments suggest that even if it can be shown that contracting out improves efficiency, it may not be introduced. If the government does not pay close attention to the interests of its employees before it begins a contracting-out process, it may find that insurmountable political pressures will block even the most carefully constructed plan.

THE EMPLOYEE TAKEOVER PROCESS AT PARKS CANADA

When the Canadian government set out to balance its budget in the mid-1990s, one of the first agencies to give serious consideration to the expansion of the contracting out process was Parks Canada.[13] In part, this was because many of Parks Canada's services, such as campground operation and road clearing, could easily be contracted to small, local companies. But just as important, Parks Canada perceived that in an era of shrinking budgets it would only be able to expand its services by entering into partnerships with local communities, businesses, and environmental groups. At first sight, it appeared that the contracting out of small services could both save money and provide closer links between the agency and its users.

Parks Canada recognized, however, that its unions would object strenuously if the contracting out process resulted in significant layoffs. Accordingly, it was decided to answer some of these objections by issuing the first set of contracts solely to current employees. This process was referred to as an *employee takeover*. In this process, the affected department was to identify a service or set of services that it believed would be appropriate for contracting out to the private sector. It was then to call for bids from current government employees who could form partnerships with organizations outside of government for contracts to provide the specified services.[14] If the bidders met a minimum set of criteria, the "best" bid was to be selected and the successful employees required to leave government employment to operate as private contractors. At the end of the initial contract, the service was then to be tendered on the open market. That is, the ETO process was designed to act as an intermediate stage in the evolution from pure government provision of the service to pure private provision—a stage that increased the chance that former employees would be able to bid successfully against existing private firms. The purpose of this section is to describe how this process operated in the Alberta Region of Parks Canada.[15]

The Official Process

In the spring of 1996, regional offices of Parks Canada were instructed to review their programs to identify candidate services for ETOs.[16] In each case, they were advised that the purpose of a takeover was to "create a more flexible and innovative program delivery environment and to deliver affordable, accessible and responsive services, while treating employees fairly and reasonably"(Treasury Board of Canada Secretariat 1996a, 1). Administrators were advised to take account of the following factors when determining whether a service was suitable for an ETO:[17]

1. *Was the necessary expertise available for delivery of the service?* Administrators were cautioned against accepting ETO proposals when the expertise required to provide the service was unique to the employees who were submitting the proposal. Clearly, the concern was to avoid the establishment of private monopoly suppliers of services.

2. *Would the ETO reduce pressure for other workforce adjustments?* Officially, at least, ETOs were not to be ends in themselves. Rather, they were designed to contribute to the broader problem facing Parks Canada—namely, that of minimizing the financial impact of employee layoffs during a period of significant budget cuts.[18]

3. *What was the existing level of competition in the private market?* The Employee Takeover Toolkit contained the following cautions to those who were evaluating current park programs:

> If the current supplier market consists of a few companies that have been in the business for many years, it may be difficult for the employee company to position itself to ever successfully compete against these companies. On the other hand, if the supplier market consists of many small young companies, it would be meaningful to know why the supplier market is not more mature. (Treasury Board of Canada Secretariat 1996b, chap. 4)

The latter caution appears to relate to the concern discussed earlier—that there is a risk that the ETO would become a monopoly supplier. The former caution, however, appears to have a more paternalistic basis—the concern that the ETO might eventually fail because it would not be able to compete (after the expiration of its contract) in the existing market.

4. *Was there potential for expansion into the existing private market?* Parks Canada anticipated that successful programs would have the ability to expand their customer bases beyond the contract to ensure the long-run viability of the companies. In markets with very few potential competitors, this criterion may have been designed to ensure that the ETO process would increase the degree of competition in the long run. In markets that already had numerous potential competitors, however, this criterion appears primarily to have been paternalistic.

Employing these criteria, the Alberta regional office identified a set of forty candidate programs for employee takeover. These programs included operation of campgrounds; maintenance of buildings, trails, and vehicles; plowing of roads; painting of signs; and operation of natural hot springs. In all cases, the contracts were for provision of services only. No construction of fixed investments were to be undertaken, nor were the contractors to receive a share of any revenues collected from users.

In July 1996, the Alberta Region issued an "Invitation for Expression of Interest," outlining the services to be provided in each of the forty programs and inviting employee groups to submit brief proposals called "expressions of interest." Each such proposal could refer to any one of the forty candidate programs, a combination of those programs, or programs not identified in the invitation. Following a brief review, seventy-four groups were invited to submit formal bids, none of which was for a program that was not included in the forty identified by Parks Canada.

At this stage, Parks Canada provided each bidding group with a "Request for Proposal" specific to the program for which the bid was being made. Each request provided an estimate of the costs of conducting the required services based on the 1995–96 fiscal year budget for that service and a detailed description of the duties that the successful contractor would be expected to perform. For example, the request for operation of the campgrounds in the Lake Louise area contained more than thirty pages of duties. Furthermore, those requests that dealt with services to the public required that the contractor satisfy a visitor satisfaction survey.

Recognizing that most civil servants would have very little experience preparing a business plan, Parks Canada provided bidders with a variety of sources of assistance. First, both the Request for Proposal and the Employee Takeover Toolkit contained detailed advice concerning the preparation of bids, and senior officials from Parks Canada were available with further information. Second, employees were eligible for as much as $12,000 in financial support to hire expert advice and up to fifteen days' leave with pay for each bid which they prepared.[19] Finally, the employee groups were allowed to enter into business relationships with individuals or companies from the private sector. The only requirement with respect to the last was that the employees must own at least 20 percent of the shares of any venture that was formed.

The Request for Proposal identified six criteria that were to be used to evaluate the proposals:

1. *Service delivery and stewardship*—This category measured the bidder's ability to meet the service standards set out in the request and identified whether any aspect of the proposed business plan conflicted with Parks Canada's mandate. Extra points could be awarded if the proponents included factors such as a plan to deal with peak and shoulder periods or a commitment to introduce flexible opening hours.

2. *Financial viability*—This component required that the proponents show that they could operate their company as a going concern and have sufficient funds to complete the start-up period successfully. Parks Canada was particularly concerned that the proponents not burden themselves with substantial long-term debt and that they demonstrate that they would have the financial resources to compete with the private sector once the initial contract had been completed.

3. *Savings to the Crown*—Bidders were told that they would have to demonstrate that their proposed contract price did not exceed a "ceiling price" and that their proposal would be more likely to be accepted the further their contract price was below the ceiling price. The ceiling price was not identified, however.

4. *Human strength of organization*—Proponents were asked to demonstrate that
    the management team possessed the appropriate background and experience
    and that the employee workforce had the right mix of skills and expertise to
    carry out the business plan.
5. *Risk and contingency planning*—Proponents had to demonstrate an understand-
    ing of the risks facing them and provide evidence that they had established
    contingency plans to minimize those risks.
6. *Realism and credibility of the business plan*—Parks Canada's primary concern
    in this category appears to have been that the business have a reasonable chance
    of success beyond the initial three-year contract. In particular, it was empha-
    sized to bidders that Parks Canada would be looking for "a vision for the busi-
    ness which extends beyond the life of the initial . . . contract" (Parks Canada
    n.d., 12).

Once the proposals were received in March 1997, they were submitted to independent panels. Each panel included a number of individuals with general expertise in the preparation of business plans and at least one person with expertise in
the service to be provided. Although the initial reviews appear to have been completed by the beginning of May, no proposal was complete enough to allow negotiations to begin immediately for provision of the service in the 1997 summer season. Instead, most proposals were rejected in the May round, and the remainder were
sent back to the proposers for further information. This led to a second round in
which most of the remaining proposals were also rejected. By the end of August,
Parks Canada officials were projecting that no more than three or four of the seventy-four proposals would be accepted and that those would be for services requiring relatively small budgets.

The Political Process

Operating in parallel with the official ETO process was an equally active but
unofficial, political process. At least five sets of players participated in this process:
the cabinet minister responsible for Parks Canada, senior administrators in the department, program managers, the unions, and employees of the affected programs.
Of these, the senior administrators and the unions made their positions abundantly
clear. The administrators, who had put forward the ETO proposal, were in favor of
the proposal and the unions, who stood to lose a significant portion of their membership, were opposed. Experience with contracting-out procedures in other government agencies suggests that the program managers would also have been opposed,
although they were not in a position to make their opinions public.

The loyalties of the affected employees were divided because Banff offers many
opportunities to earn profits from the tourist trade and the culture of the town is
highly entrepreneurial. In this culture, many park employees saw the ETO process
as an opportunity to become business owners. At the same time, however, it was

clear that those who did not obtain ETO contracts with the government might lose their jobs or, at least, suffer a significant reduction in wages. Even those who did obtain contracts could expect to suffer from a loss of job security. This division meant that the employees did not become a strong political force either for or against the ETOs.

The position of the cabinet minister was also unclear. On the one hand, the over-riding political goal of the government was to balance its budget. Hence, the minister responsible for Parks Canada was under considerable pressure from her cabinet colleagues to reduce spending. On the other hand, the civil service unions were able to organize a powerful coalition of lobby groups targeted at the minister personally. In this process, the unions were able to rely on two sources of influence. First, during the ETO process, the minister responsible for Parks Canada had to face reelection in a district containing a high percentage of union members, primarily steelworkers. The civil service unions campaigned actively in that election against her department's policy of contracting out. Second, the unions also appealed to Canada's powerful environmental lobby groups for support. They argued that contracting out would constitute "privatization of Canada's heritage." This slogan struck a sympathetic chord with environmentalists, perhaps because they were concerned that privatization would make it more difficult to exert political influence on Parks Canada's activities.

In addition, the unions were able to place some political pressure on Parks Canada's senior administrators. Although the contracting out of park services constituted one aspect of Parks Canada's vision for itself, its senior administrators had also become convinced that the department could better achieve its objectives if it could obtain a measure of independence from Canadian Heritage, the larger ministry in which it was situated. To this end, Parks Canada administrators had been lobbying the government to be designated as an "agency" that would remove it from the direct control of the ministry and provide it with greater flexibility in managing its budget. As this lobbying process may have been derailed had the affected unions objected to the introduction of an agency, the unions were offered an opportunity to obtain concessions in other areas. One of the conditions they set was that their opposition to the ETO process be resolved to their satisfaction.

Evaluation

There are three possible explanations for the failure of contracting out: (1) the procedures for obtaining ETOs were flawed, (2) seventy of the seventy-four proposals failed to suggest means by which efficiency could be improved, and (3) political pressures became so great that Parks Canada could not afford to provide the necessary support for the ETO process.

With respect to the first of these explanations, three general sets of criteria were proposed earlier in this chapter for evaluating ETO procedures. These were the degree of noncompetitive behavior that was permitted in the proposed contracts, the precautions that were taken to ensure that successful applicants did not impose costs on the environment, and the extent to which Parks Canada's bidding process was perceived as fair.

Three elements of the approach employed by Parks Canada ensured that there would be ongoing competitive markets for the contracted services. It maintained ownership of all of the capital assets that were site-specific, it accepted bids only on services that did not require unique expertise,[20] and it restricted contract duration to three years. The first of these ensured that the primary asset that potential future bidders would have to provide was management expertise. The second element ensured that it was only those management skills that were relatively abundant that would be offered. Hence, at the end of the first contract, a considerable number of firms would remain that might bid on the second contract. The fact that contracts were restricted to three years in length ensured that firms would have only limited monopoly power during the term of their contracts. Thus, it would have been largely superfluous to include any reference to the competitiveness of the product market in the criteria outlined in the requests.

Environmental impacts were taken into account at three different stages of the process. First, the "service delivery and stewardship" criterion used to evaluate the proposals explicitly rewarded business plans demonstrating that "operations will be carried out in a manner that respects environmental or commemorative objectives."[21] Second, the detailed standards that bidders were required to meet generally precluded most activities considered harmful to the environment. Finally, with contracts only three years in length, park administrators had considerable bargaining power when dealing with recalcitrant operators.[22]

Nevertheless, a number of administrators to whom I spoke remained concerned that the issuing of contracts to private firms would impede their ability to monitor environmental damage. In particular, it is their view that, once profit-seeking firms begin to operate facilities such as hot pools and campgrounds, those firms will agitate for expansion of those facilities—expansion that would intrude on natural settings and bring additional visitors to already overcrowded parks.

Parks Canada introduced a number of policies to ensure that the bidding process was as fair as possible and to encourage as many bidders to enter the competition as possible. Potential bidders were provided with financial support and with considerable assistance from senior Parks Canada staff to ensure that all bidders were well informed. Detailed expectations were set out for each proposal to assuage any concerns that unforeseen requirements might be introduced during the term of the contract. Independent expert panels were employed to assess the proposals to assure bidders that Parks Canada managers would not bias the selection procedure against them.

But these precautions alone proved to be insufficient. The biggest problem was that bidders were inadequately informed concerning the financial criteria against which their proposals were to be evaluated. Three factors were of particular importance. First, the financial information provided to bidders was for the 1995–96 fiscal year, but the data employed to calculate the "ceiling price" against which bids were evaluated were drawn from estimates for the 1997–98 fiscal year. In the preparation of those estimates, managers had been told to anticipate significant cutbacks. By failing to inform bidders that the target was moving, Parks Canada ignored a clear directive outlined in the toolkit:

> Not all of the information required for preparing the business case, especially information on the costs and revenues, is readily available. In some cases, assumptions must be made about the potential costs or savings. In such cases, *departments should make sure they clearly spell out the assumptions*, and that the rationale behind them is well documented. (Treasury Board of Canada Secretariat 1996b, chap. 3, emphasis added)

Second, because it was the managers of the affected programs who were asked to prepare the 1997–98 fiscal year budgets, the possibility of bias cannot be dismissed. It was clearly in the interests of managers, who would lose their departments if the ETO bids were successful, to submit budgets that were as low as possible. The limited information available suggests that such manipulation was an important factor in the failure of many ETO bids. In one case, for example, the 1997–98 fiscal year budget was 32 percent lower than the 1995–96 budget.

Finally, there was considerable confusion over the breakdown between fixed and variable costs—that is, between those costs for which the successful bidder would be responsible and those for which Parks Canada would be responsible. The financial information provided for most packages divided costs into four categories: direct, indirect, overhead, and other. It appears that some bidders overestimated their costs because they believed that they would be responsible for two or three of these categories, whereas Parks Canada had anticipated that it was only one (or possibly two) that would be borne by the contractor.

The result was that many bidders dramatically underestimated the price ceiling against which they were being evaluated, and their bids were rejected even though their proposals were fundamentally sound. These rejections did not arise because bidders had failed to identify potential efficiency gains, but because they had misunderstood the criteria against which their proposals were being judged.

It was well within Parks Canada's ability to have rectified these problems at any stage. The original intent had not been to deal with the ETO proposals on a "take it or leave it" basis. Rather, it had been anticipated that, once Parks Canada had determined that a proposal was worthy of consideration, the precise details of the agreement with the contractor would be subject to negotiation. Parks Canada's senior administrators could have resolved the problems identified earlier at this stage. The potential for local managers to bias the assessment procedure and the problems with data interpretation must have been clear as the process unfolded, yet nothing was done. Instead, the ETO process was allowed to die.

It is not possible to determine definitively why the ETOs were abandoned. The objective evidence suggests strongly, however, that the unions' lobbying efforts were successful. Resistance from environmental groups plus the serendipitous political opportunities presented by the minister's election and Parks Canada's application for agency status left the unions in a very strong position. Their resistance likely caused Parks Canada not to pursue the ETO process.

CONCLUSION

Politics seems to have led to the failure of Parks Canada's ETO process. Bidders were able to identify sources of efficiency gains, and deficiencies in the bidding process could have been rectified by Parks Canada during the bidding process. The primary cause of the breakdown was the strength of political opposition that the unions were able to mount.

Parks Canada's experience with ETOs suggests that it is not sufficient to devise and implement carefully structured procedures for operating contracting out processes. It is also necessary to recognize that, because contracting out can result in wage reductions or layoffs, strong opposition from employee groups is likely. These concerns must be addressed to ensure that employees do not use political pressures to derail a process that can improve efficiency.

NOTES

1. See Clark (1993).

2. In my analysis I will concentrate on economic factors. It should be noted, however, that the speed and vigor with which the ETO process was imposed on government employees, and the fact that virtually none of the proposals was accepted, produced a human relations nightmare.

3. The model presented here is a simplified version of that found in Bruce (1997).

4. For example, the Treasury Board in Canada and the General Accounting Office in the United States.

5. This is a policy of setting wages above market rates to provide a penalty for workers found shirking "after the fact."

6. In rank-order tournaments, workers compete with one another for promotions. Only the winner of the tournament is promoted. Rose-Ackerman (1986) advocates the use of such tournaments among government agencies.

7. If a worker's pension is not vested, he or she will lose the employer's contribution to the pension if he or she is fired. Hence, as long as the employer can determine, ex post, that the employee had been shirking, the threat of the loss of the nonvested portion of the pension can act as an incentive to adopt the employer's goals.

8. Nevertheless, this is an option that I believe should be given greater consideration. It is often the case, for example, that a single national park will have numerous campsites within its boundaries. These campsites could compete with one another for customers.

9. Numerous studies have concluded, in general, that significant cost savings result from contracting out. See especially McDavid and Clemens (1995) for Canadian examples; Dilger,

Moffett, and Struyk (1997) for U.S. examples; and Domberger and Hall (1996) for Australian examples.

10. Giving ownership of the park to the campground operator will not solve this problem. As long as flora and fauna have value to individuals other than visitors to the park, the campground operator will find it difficult to extract the full social benefit of any conservation activity yet he will have to bear the full social costs. This problem is particularly acute in developing countries where private individuals are allowed to profit from the sale of hunting licenses. Although these individuals have an incentive to protect major trophy animals, such as lions and elephants, they have little incentive to protect those species of flora and fauna that do not provide food for the trophy species.

11. Assume, following Klein, Crawford, and Alchian (1978), that the long-run costs of capital are $4,000 per year and that the annual operating costs are $1,500. No contract will be reached unless the contractor can be assured of an annual fee of at least $5,500. Once the contract has been signed, however, the government will be able to drive the price down to $1,500 per year if the contractor has no other use for the capital, which has been invested.

12. Roughly speaking, public choice theory deals with the influence that voting behavior has on government policy.

13. Like most government agencies, Parks Canada had always engaged in a limited amount of contracting out.

14. In most cases, these contracts were to be for three years, but the length was negotiable.

15. Alberta was chosen in part because seventy-four of the ninety-one bids received nationally came from Alberta and in part because information about Alberta was readily available.

16. Much of the information for this section was drawn from Treasury Board of Canada Secretariat (1996b), hereafter referred to as the toolkit.

17. The following list is adapted from the toolkit (Treasury Board of Canada Secretariat 1996b).

18. The federal civil service in Canada is heavily unionized. A Workforce Adjustment Directive, signed by all of the major unions (including those dealing with Parks Canada), requires that if employees are laid off due to downsizing, they will either be transferred to equivalent positions elsewhere in the civil service or be paid substantial layoff benefits.

19. To be eligible for the maximum entitlements to financial support and leave with pay, the contract for which the bid was being made had to have an estimated annual value of $5 million or more. The lowest entitlements, relating to contracts of $500,000 or less, were for $6,000 and five days' leave (figures are in Canadian dollars). Arrangements could also be made for leave without pay if necessary.

20. Note that this was not one of the criteria set out in Parks Canada's Requests for Proposals. It only appeared in the toolkit. Nevertheless, review of the forty packages identified by Parks Canada as suitable for proposals indicates that none required a unique set of skills. Furthermore, some of the packages for which unsolicited "expressions of interest" were submitted included proposals to provide interpretive programs—programs that may well require knowledge specific to the local area. All of the unsolicited proposals were rejected at the "expressions of interest" stage.

21. "Request for Proposal," Part IV, p. 4.

22. Furthermore, Parks Canada had mechanisms in the contract clauses to audit operations and terminate contracts if contractors did not fulfill the terms of the contract.

REFERENCES

Bennett, James, and William Orzechowski. 1983. "The Voting Behavior of Bureaucrats: Some Empirical Evidence." *Public Choice* 41: 271–83.

Blais, Andre, and Stephane Dion, eds. 1991. "Introduction." In *The Budget-Maximizing Bureaucrat: Appraisals and Evidence*. Pittsburgh: University of Pittsburgh Press.

Breton, Andre. 1990. "Centralization, Decentralization, and Intergovernmental Competition." *Reflections Paper* No. 4. Kingston: Institute for Intergovernmental Relations, Queen's University.

Bruce, Christopher. 1997. "Rethinking the Delivery of Government Services." In *A Government Reinvented*, ed. Christopher Bruce, Ronald Kneebone, and Kenneth McKenzie. Toronto: Oxford University Press, 421–55.

Bush, W., and A. Denzau. 1977. "The Voting Behavior of Bureaucrats and Public Sector Growth." In *Budgets and Bureaucrats*, ed. Thomas Borcherding. Durham, N.C.: Duke University Press.

Carmichael, Lorne. 1989. "Self-Enforcing Contracts, Shirking, and Life Cycle Incentives." *Journal of Economic Perspectives* 3, no. 4: 65–83.

Caves, Douglas, and Laurits Christensen. 1980. "The Relative Efficiency of Public and Private Firms in a Competitive Environment: The Case of Canadian Railways." *Journal of Political Economy* 88: 958–76.

Clark, I. D. 1993. *Getting the Incentives Right*. Ottawa: Treasury Board of Canada Secretariat.

Courant, Paul, Edward Gramlich, and Daniel Rubinfeld. 1980. "Why Voters Support Tax Limitation Amendments: The Michigan Case." *National Tax Journal* 33 (March): 1–20.

Dilger, Robert J., Randolph R. Moffett, and Linda Struyk. 1997. "Privatization of Municipal Services in America's Largest Population Cities." *Public Administration Review* 57 (January): 21–26.

Domberger, Simon, and Christine Hall. 1996. "Contracting for Public Services: A Review of Antipodean Experience." *Public Administration* 74 (Spring): 129–48.

Frey, Bruno, and Werner Pommerehne. 1982. "How Powerful Are Bureaucrats as Voters?" *Public Choice* 38, no. 3: 253–62.

Klein, Benjamin, Robert Crawford, and Armen Alchian. 1978. "Vertical Integration, Appropriable Rents, and the Competitive Contracting Process." *Journal of Law and Economics* 21, no. 2: 297–326.

Landau, Martin. 1969. "Redundancy, Rationality, and the Problem of Duplication and Overlap." *Public Administration Review* 29, no. 4: 346–58.

McDavid, James C., and Eric Clemens. 1995. "Contracting Out Local Government Services: The B.C. Experience." *Canadian Public Administration* 38, no. 2: 177–93.

McKenzie, Kenneth. 1997. "Institutional Design and Public Policy: A Microeconomic Perspective." In *A Government Reinvented*, ed. Christopher Bruce, Ronald Kneebone, and Kenneth McKenzie. Toronto: Oxford University Press, 77–123.

Parks Canada. N.d. *Evaluation Criteria for the Independent Panel Review of Employee Take-Over Proposals*. Ottawa: Author.

Parks Canada, Alberta Region. 1996. *Invitation for Expression of Interest*. Banff: Author.

Rose-Ackerman, Susan. 1986. "Reforming Public Bureaucracy through Economic Incentives?" *Law, Economics and Organization* 2, no. 1: 131–62.

Rubinfeld, Daniel. 1977. "Voting in a Local School Election: A Micro Analysis." *Review of Economics and Statistics* 59 (February): 30–42.

Treasury Board of Canada Secretariat. 1996a. *Employee Takeover Policy.* Ottawa: Author.

———. 1996b. *Employee Takeover Toolkit.* Ottawa: Author.

7

New Management Strategies for Kruger National Park

Michael J. 't Sas-Rolfes and Peter W. Fearnhead

The Kruger National Park ("Kruger") is South Africa's oldest and most famous national park. It is also by far the country's largest, covering some two million hectares. Over the years, Kruger has become an important national and cultural symbol to many South Africans and a major tourist attraction for domestic and foreign visitors. Kruger is widely regarded as one of the world's best-managed national parks, but this could change ('t Sas-Rolfes 1996).

South Africa's new political and economic environment is affecting conservation policy and park management. Recent changes such as the demise of the apartheid system, a move toward democracy, free trade, and market-oriented policies presage the end of fortress park management in South Africa. The past policies and practices of strict preservation of park resources are becoming obsolete, and, to survive, park managers must embrace new strategies of social inclusiveness and sustainable use.

Using Kruger as a case study, this chapter examines the historical reasons for existing park management policies, discusses the changing policy context, considers how this may influence management objectives, and then suggests possible directions for change.

HISTORY

The strong preservationist ethic in Kruger's management has a long history. An early influence on wildlife management stemmed from its original purpose of protecting

It should be noted that this chapter was first prepared in 1997 and therefore may not reflect all ongoing changes in the management of Kruger National Park. But given the rapidity of change in South Africa, it is impossible to keep up with all the new management policies.

a supply of wild game for hunters. The park evolved from game reserves established in the 1890s, as the Sabi Game Reserve, because hunters had eliminated most of the game in the region (Carruthers 1995). The area was selected mainly because endemic diseases made it inhospitable for livestock and because it acted as a natural buffer region between South Africa and neighboring Mozambique. It was not selected because it contained ecologically diverse habitat—this concept was recognized as an important conservation criterion much later on in the twentieth century.

At its inception, Kruger was run along paramilitary lines, consistent with worldwide park management practices at that time. Many early game wardens had a military or law enforcement background rather than one grounded in science. Early wardens were largely preoccupied with law enforcement and the eradication of predator species, which were regarded as vermin. The role of predators as natural components of the ecosystem was only recognized in later years.

Early biological scientists were mostly veterinarians who opposed conserving wildlife because of its potential to carry livestock disease. However, in the 1930s a new group of scientists became interested in studying natural systems and managing them "scientifically." This approach became part of park policy in the 1950s when the National Party encouraged young white Afrikaans-speaking zoology students to enter the park system under an affirmative action policy.

Under this new scientific regime, Kruger entered an era of "management by intervention," which involved substantial manipulation of the natural systems within the park. This strategy included introducing animals of certain species that had previously become extinct (e.g., the rhinoceros), removing animals of other species whose numbers were thought to have become too high (e.g., elephants), controlled bush burning, and artificially providing water. Over time, the entire park was fenced off from surrounding areas and thus managed as a relatively closed system (see Scholes 1995).

Not only did management involve manipulation of the park's habitat, but management policies (e.g., fire policy) were changed several times, so that such manipulation has been inconsistent over time. Today, although Kruger's land area consists of indigenous fauna and flora, its hydrological and species dispersal systems have been substantially modified. In this sense, Kruger's ecosystems may never again be regarded as truly "natural"; they will always be influenced by some form of human intervention.

Political influence has also contributed to the evolution of Kruger's management policies. In 1926, the South African parliament passed the National Parks Act, proclaiming Kruger as the country's first national park. The National Parks Act established the South African National Parks (SANP) as the management authority of the new park. The SANP is structured as a parastatal—a nominally independent organization governed by a board of trustees appointed by the Minister of Environmental Affairs and Tourism. This parastatal status allows the board wide discretionary powers in financial management; for example, the board is empowered to raise and retain its own revenues and may determine the allocation of its own expenditure.

During the era of National Party rule, the SANP received generous state subsidies and other backing and, in return, supported government policies. The park's management regime also developed certain characteristics under the influence of apartheid thinking and Afrikaner nationalism. These included the National Party government's lack of international cooperation and insular approach to policy formulation.

Black South Africans living on the periphery of Kruger benefited little from the park's existence (Carruthers 1995). As Kruger was expanded, local people were evicted from their homes and poorly compensated. Those that were not ousted were only allowed to continue living in the park if they provided labor or rent. Certain people had access to their former ancestral lands restricted, and their rights to hunt and harvest wild species (which constituted their traditional subsistence lifestyle) were usurped. Over time, local people became alienated from wildlife creating negative sentiments, first toward Kruger and then toward wildlife conservation in general. This situation did not improve during the apartheid era, and many black South Africans continue to perceive it as a symbol of white supremacy where animals are considered more important than people (Hanekom and Liebenberg n.d.).

The Changing Environment

South Africa's political environment has changed dramatically with the demise of the apartheid National Party government. Under the African National Congress (ANC), government has initiated sweeping reforms, which include measures of economic liberalization such as the removal of trade barriers and reduction of some state subsidies. The new government faces the challenge of redressing past injustices and uplifting the country's poor by creating jobs and directing resources toward sectors such as education, primary health care, and housing. With economic development as such a high priority, the relative importance of conventional wildlife conservation appears to have diminished.

The implications for the management of Kruger include greater financial independence and a mandate to serve a broader constituency. Government expects all South African institutions to make a contribution to its Growth, Employment, and Redistribution Strategy (GEAR), and the SANP is no exception. The SANP will increasingly have to justify the large areas of scarce land that have been set aside, which are perceived by some to be used inefficiently for the benefit of only a few people. Specifically, the government regards the SANP as having the potential to make a significant contribution to growth in the tourism industry, one of the central themes of GEAR. In addition, there is a widely perceived need for local communities, which in some cases were evicted from the land where parks were proclaimed, to benefit from these areas and become involved in the decision-making processes that affect them.

The South African government is also reallocating its financial resources to reflect its accountability to a broader electorate, and the level of subsidies granted to the SANP is declining in real terms. Currently, the government provides approximately 17 percent of the SANP's total budget in the form of a state subsidy; the remainder is generated through entrance fees, provision of accommodation, restaurants, shops, and game activities such as night drives and walking safaris. Tourism generates an operating surplus that is used to cover the costs of administering the SANP's conservation activities. Kruger, as the largest and most popular national park, generates 78 percent of the SANP's income from tourism. It also carries the highest conservation costs, including a large component of professional scientific staff. Overall, Kruger's nonsubsidy income exceeds expenditure by a small margin. The SANP manages several other parks that are considered ecologically important but relatively unattractive as tourist destinations, and these parks depend on state subsidies to a much greater extent.

In the past, the SANP received government grants to build infrastructures such as roads and tourist camps. More recently, it has had to rely on its own sources of finance generated from commercial operations to fund very limited improvements. A current application for commercial loan finance for park fencing, roads, and the upgrading of various tourism facilities has presented the organization with some challenges in satisfying the bank's requirements for security. Government is not prepared to guarantee the loan, yet legislation does not allow the ceding of moveable assets as collateral. In the future, the SANP will likely have to leverage the private sector for capital investment in parks by allowing them to perform certain functions.

The SANP is eager to continue expanding its portfolio of parks. Certain key habitat types and ecosystems in South Africa are considered to be inadequately represented within existing parks. To achieve the goal of conserving biodiversity, the SANP has earmarked several new areas for acquisition. Most of this land is in the form of privately owned farms, the sizes of which are based on what was considered to be viable agricultural units. Sustained protection of the agricultural sector, one of the National Party's key support strategies, has led to inflated land prices. Park development through land purchase is therefore a costly process. However, since the SANP does not have sufficient funds to acquire these areas, it is increasingly having to consider entering into innovative contractual arrangements with third parties (private sector, nongovernmental organizations, and local communities) to secure such areas for conservation. Two new national parks have recently been proclaimed, and numerous expansions have been made to others, making use of these mechanisms.

The SANP must also contend with an international lobby in the form of animal rights and animal welfare groups. With the South African government's new emphasis on international cooperation, transparency, and participation, animal welfare groups have become more vociferous and active in trying to influence policy. These groups are essentially opposed to sustainable use unless it takes the form of nonconsumptive uses such as wildlife tourism. Animal welfare groups enter into fierce debates with proponents of consumptive sustainable use in forums such as the Convention on International Trade in Endangered Species (CITES), but they also tackle issues such as the SANP's elephant culling policy in Kruger. The SANP thus finds itself at the center of some very heated policy debates.

The changing environment therefore presents the SANP with two principal challenges. In deciding on future management strategies for Kruger, the SANP must ensure that (1) the park becomes relevant to and accepted by a broader political constituency in South Africa by offering greater benefits to previously disenfranchised people and (2) its operations remain financially sustainable and increasingly less dependent on state subsidies.

KRUGER MANAGEMENT RESPONSE

In meeting the challenges of a changing environment, the SANP has taken some steps to break away from its past policies, but more progress is required. This section will review the current status of management issues in three areas: social inclusiveness, financial resources, and environmental management.

Social Inclusiveness

Kruger is now open to all races, and the number of black South Africans visiting the park is continually increasing. However, a lack of flexibility in marketing and pricing policies means that the SANP is not efficient in satisfying different market segments: visiting the park is expensive for the average black South African, but a relative bargain for the average foreign tourist. At current levels, fees are insufficiently low to make the park readily affordable for most South African blacks, and it is therefore debatable to what extent current pricing policy achieves the political objective of equity. Furthermore, accommodation prices have increased substantially in recent years.

The SANP is employing other tactics to ensure that black South Africans benefit from Kruger. The most obvious of these is a new affirmative action employment policy that favors black South Africans for all new and vacant posts. Other measures include special rates for local black tour operators and the formation of communication forums to initiate dialogue with rural people living adjacent to the park. The SANP has also formulated an economic empowerment policy that aims to ensure that the procurement of goods and services in parks are provided by small, medium, and microenterprises (SMMEs), particularly from neighboring communities. In the case of Kruger, the portion of procurement provided by SMMEs has grown to 18 percent of the total procurement. Similarly, at the organizational level, economic empowerment is an important criterion in the awarding of all tenders. Because many of these measures require radical changes in the attitudes of neighboring communities and are also dependent on the pace of the national economic transformation, they will take considerable time and effort to become effective.

Financial Resources

The SANP must balance the need to make parks such as Kruger readily accessible to all South Africans by keeping park entrance and accommodation fees as low as possible, while generating enough funds to pay for conservation activities. The reduction in the government subsidy has resulted in the need to increase fees to balance the budget. As a result, Kruger needs to implement mechanisms to capture more of the value created by parks to fund noncommercial conservation activities.

At present, most commercial visitor services in Kruger are provided by SANP staff and management. In providing private visitor hospitality services such as lodging, food, and retail, the SANP is likely to be far less economically efficient than competing commercial operators. Unionized labor and the typical public sector work ethic increase the cost of delivery and lower the quality of service. The consequences of SANP performing the tourism function are (1) a high cost of delivery, particularly the human resources element, which is sometimes twice that of the private sector; (2) prices that have been escalated in isolation of market forces, normally in an attempt to cover operational costs; (3) the squeezing out of the traditional domestic market, with only 56 percent of visitors being South African; (4) a lack of product differentiation and market segmentation, with continued emphasis on the traditional self-driven, self-catering product designed for the domestic market despite the increase in foreign visitors; and (5) a low service ethic compounded by inefficient policies and procedures.

Furthermore, the previous underpricing of access and especially accommodation has had side effects that adversely affect private sector conservation initiatives. The capital costs of most of Kruger's camps and infrastructure have been subsidized (directly paid for) by central government, and the SANP does not need to recoup the commercial cost of capital. Conversely, most private wildlife reserves and operations are privately financed and therefore need to recoup their capital costs to be financially viable. The SANP thus has an advantage over the private sector, which enables it to undercut market prices and out compete private operators. Unfortunately, by so doing, the SANP has discouraged further development of the private wildlife tourism industry. Not only does this approach stifle potential economic development and job creation, but it also indirectly discourages wildlife conservation on private land.

In recent years, the SANP has started to provide guided walking trails and organized night drives; it has also built a few smaller exclusive camps and offers a wider choice and better quality of food and provisions in its shops. However all lodging, food and retail functions continue to be provided and managed by the SANP itself, with relatively limited regard to specific consumer preferences. Despite this, Kruger remains a popular tourist destination, because of the quality of the wildlife and wilderness experience. This suggests that considerable economies are to be gained from increasing the participation of the private sector in the provision of visitor services. The challenge for the SANP is to involve the private sector on terms in which Kruger can earn enough revenue to manage the park and provide other public services related to its conservation and social objectives.

Environmental Management

In recent years, the SANP has revised several of its environmental management practices in Kruger. Whereas Kruger was previously fenced off from neighboring private game reserves, these fences have now been removed, thereby allowing wild animals to traverse freely across the park boundaries. In the future, the SANP may remove fences on Kruger's eastern boundary to create a larger area that extends into Mozambique.

The SANP faces substantial challenges in managing Kruger's water resources. Previously five perennial rivers flowed through the park. Today four of those rivers have become seasonal; they have been depleted and polluted by upstream usage for forestry, agriculture, industry, and household consumption. Since the 1940s, the SANP has had a water provision policy in Kruger, and by 1980 about seventy dams and weirs had been built, and almost four hundred boreholes drilled. This policy has been widely criticized on grounds that it has been responsible for loss of biological diversity in the park. For example, the artificial water provision policy is thought to have contributed to a series of changes in species composition that led to the near extinction of one species, the roan antelope.

The SANP has amended its burning and fire control policy several times during Kruger's history. Ironically the policy has almost done a full circle. Early fire policy was aimed at preventing the spread of fires into the park from outside with a laissez-faire approach to internal fires; then a "no-fire" policy was adopted that saw the introduction of fire breaks; and recently a more or less nonintervention policy has been adopted, subject to certain precautionary limits.

Previously, the SANP has also culled large herbivores, such as buffalo and elephant, to prevent damage from overgrazing by these species and possible losses in biological diversity. After protests from animal welfare groups, the SANP sought alternatives to elephant culling. One of these was to move live animals to new areas, but such areas are limited in supply, and the costs of translocation are very high. Other options include artificial birth control or the reduction of artificial water provision to induce higher calf mortality in times of drought. None of these options is costless, however, and economic considerations may ultimately determine the SANP's long-term policy on elephant management in Kruger.

THREE NEW STRATEGIES

How can the SANP address these management issues in a way that is consistent with its new objectives? We suggest three broad approaches, which we call "democratization," "commercialization," and "diversification." Democratization entails a more participative approach to decision making and wider distribution of all the benefits and costs associated with Kruger's existence. Commercialization entails the use of business principles and practices to improve operational efficiency. Diversification implies a wider range of management policies and practices; as a concept, it has many potential applications.

Certain synergies exist among these three approaches. For example, democratization will be greatly enhanced through both commercialization (by generating additional overall benefits) and diversification (by providing services that cater to a greater number of diverse people).

Democratization

As discussed earlier, the SANP has already made some tentative steps toward gaining greater political acceptability in the new South Africa. However, some of these measures (e.g., keeping park fees low and employing noncommercial employment practices) are economically inefficient and only benefit a select group of people. There are other ways to spread the benefits of the park's existence to a broader constituency without compromising economic efficiency and financial viability. The following are three specific examples:

- Instead of offering a fairly uniform, low-priced visitor experience, the SANP could cross-subsidize visits for educational purposes by offering better and more exclusive recreational experiences to affluent visitors (e.g., foreign tourists) and charging far more for these.
- Instead of simply providing a few additional jobs for selected internal staff members, the SANP could create economic opportunities for local entrepreneurs by allowing contractual private concessions for commercial activity within the park, by replacing inefficient state-run operations, and by creating additional enterprises.
- Decisions on environmental management policy could be made in a transparent way after obtaining input from external scientific experts and any interested members of the public.

Commercialization

At present, nearly all activities within the boundaries of Kruger are performed by SANP staff regardless of whether they have a private or public orientation. With regard to lodging, food, and retail services, Kruger runs twenty-three rest camps with a total of approximately forty-two hundred beds, ten restaurants, fourteen shops, and a number of filling stations. The SANP could probably achieve significant improvements in efficiency by "outsourcing" many of its visitor services.

The delegation of noncore activities to outside experts would allow SANP management and employees to focus on those activities for which they are considered to have the greatest expertise, such as scientific management services. Outsourcing would therefore result in a change of SANP emphasis from actually performing certain functions to monitoring and managing relationships with private operators.

What is the most appropriate way for the SANP to initiate a process of commercialization? There are two important criteria:

• Outsourcing must provide gains in economic efficiency, improving both the standard of visitor services and the financial returns they provide to the SANP.

• Outsourcing should not undermine the SANP's core conservation objectives in any way.

To ensure that these criteria are satisfied, all outsourcing must take place through commercial contracts, which are awarded through a transparent and competitive bidding system (auction or open tender). Contracts would specify the rights and responsibilities of both parties and include termination clauses for noncompliance. These measures are necessary to ensure that no monopolies or rent-seeking opportunities are created, as this would undermine the objective of efficiency. To ensure compatibility with its conservation objectives, the SANP could include certain minimum environmental performance standards as a contractual obligation, with any breach of these subject to a termination clause.

Diversification

The principle of diversification can be applied in several different ways in developing new management strategies for Kruger to achieve political, economic, and conservation goals. To achieve Kruger's new objectives, park management should be diversified along three lines: land use, visitor services, and educational outreach.

With regard to land use, zoning could form the cornerstone of a range of new management strategies for Kruger. In a park management context, zoning provides a useful tool for diversification by designating different areas for different uses and management techniques. Under a system of different use zones within the park, managers can adopt a range of approaches simultaneously.

The SANP already zones different parts of Kruger according to the intensity of use. Previously tourists were denied access to large areas within the park, which were designated "wilderness" zones. The SANP now considers that limited human use in a sensitive manner poses no threat to either the biodiversity or atmosphere of such areas, and in the future all parts of the park may be opened to at least some form of visitor access. Future zoning is therefore likely to be based on providing different intensities of wilderness experience.

Not only can the SANP provide for a diversity of visitors, rates, services, and intensity of visitor experience, but it can use the principle of diversification to achieve multiple conservation goals. To some extent, it already does this. For example, at least one area within the park is maintained as a predator exclusion zone to breed the rare Lichtenstein's hartebeest. However, most previous management of water, fire, and population control has been uniformly applied throughout Kruger.

In the future, the intensity and type of management could be varied between areas; for example, elephant populations could be allowed to expand without any control in some areas (to allow evolutionary processes to take place), whereas other areas could serve as dispersal zones where removals could take place (to maintain stasis and conserve other species such as baobabs). The SANP is currently considering a new system that will allow for such a diversity of approaches to burning, artificial water provision, and elephant population management.

Second, to diversify the product range available to visitors in Kruger, the SANP could consider measures such as:

- providing new and different types of accommodation (e.g., bush lodges, tented camps, tree houses, water bungalows, overnight hides) in camps of varying sizes;
- offering a wider choice of visitor experiences (e.g., guided open-vehicle drives, off-road drives, short walks, canoeing, mountain biking and horseback riding);
- varying the standard of accommodation, food, and other visitor services between different camps and charging accordingly varied rates, to provide for all different market sectors, from low-budget (large scale) to luxury (exclusive); and
- adopting more flexible pricing policies (charging higher rates for peak holiday periods and weekends; offering strategic concessions during off-peak periods).

Third, the SANP could further diversify the range of educational and recreational services that it offers to the public. This would achieve two worthwhile goals:

- It would allow more South Africans to benefit meaningfully from the park's existence.
- It would provide a more efficient way of tapping market demand, thereby greatly enhancing potential financial returns.

Achieving these two goals, in turn, would help secure the future of Kruger by ensuring that a larger number of people have a vested interest in enjoying the benefits of the park and by ensuring that park operations remain financially sustainable.

CONCLUSION

The new South African political agenda presents SANP with fresh challenges and opportunities. To adapt to the changing political and socioeconomic environment, the SANP must reconsider its management policies and practices for Kruger National Park. The decisions made by the SANP in the next few years will determine whether Kruger remains one of the world's leading national parks.

The SANP must strive to make Kruger more meaningful to a wider spectrum of South Africans and less dependent on state funding. The SANP must improve on its past legacy of social exclusion, economically inefficient visitor services, and inconsistent environmental management practices.

In pursuing new management strategies, the SANP could be guided by the principles of democratization, commercialization, and diversification, as discussed in this chapter. In particular, all future dealings should be subjected to the forces of competition and public scrutiny, especially those involving the commercialization and privatization of public assets.

Before proceeding with new policies and strategies, the SANP should engage the public in far more discussion and debate than it has in the past. To ensure the future success of Kruger, the SANP should encourage and consider a full range of ideas, both conventional and radical. This chapter represents only a small step in that direction.

REFERENCES

Carruthers, Jane. 1995. *The Kruger National Park: A Social and Political History.* Pietermaritzburg: University of Natal Press.

Hanekom, Derek, and Louis Liebenberg. N.d. "Utilization of National Parks with Special Reference to the Costs and Benefits to Communities." Discussion document, mimeograph. Copy available from the authors; contact M. 't Sas-Rolfes at afreco@global.co.za or Postnet Suite 340, Private Bag X1005, Claremont 7735, South Africa.

Scholes, R. J. 1995. *The Kruger National Park: Wonders of an African Eden.* London: New Holland.

't Sas-Rolfes, Michael. 1996. "The Kruger National Park: A Heritage for All South Africans?" Working paper. Harare, Zimbabwe: Africa Resources Trust.

8

A Trust Approach to the Grand Staircase–Escalante National Monument

Terry L. Anderson and Holly Lippke Fretwell

The Grand Staircase–Escalante National Monument is a dramatically scenic 1.9 million-acre area at the southern border of Utah. It features the Grand Staircase, a series of benches and cliffs that form a set of natural steps, and the Escalante Canyons, a maze of connected canyons cut through by the Escalante River.

The area is biologically diverse and archaeologically rich. Pictographs painted on the face of sandstone cliffs, rock shelters, and pit-house village sites go back at least eight thousand years. The region is increasingly popular for hiking and climbing and is also used for livestock grazing, alabaster mining, and oil production.

In 1996, President Clinton designated the area as a national monument. This designation was extraordinary for several reasons:

- The size of this monument dwarfs all other monuments in the lower forty-eight states. The mass of land is larger than Utah's five national parks combined and larger than Delaware and Rhode Island.[1]
- The proclamation was made without consultation with Utah's congressional delegation or its governor, who have almost uniformly opposed treating the site as a protected area. They feared (correctly, it appears) that setting it aside might curtail or limit production of coal, natural gas, and oil as well as grazing.
- President Clinton's announcement took place at the Grand Canyon in Arizona. While avoiding Utah because of opposition to the monument designation, Clinton won the approval of many environmentalists around the country.

Thus, the Grand Staircase–Escalante National Monument was born in the midst of controversy. It is likely to remain in this quagmire unless the management structure

---

This chapter was previously published as *PERC Policy Series*, PS-16 (September 1999). Copyright © Political Economy Research Center.

can be taken out of politics and made more responsive to the land's potential for multiple uses. It is time to consider how this large expanse of land within the federal estate can be managed in a way that reconciles environmental and economic goals.

This chapter argues that the Grand Staircase–Escalante National Monument should be managed as a trust. By a trust, we mean that a board of trustees should be established with the explicit responsibility of maintaining the unique recreational, archaeological, and environmental values of the area and that maintenance should be funded out of revenues from commodities and recreation. Such a trust could provide funds for conservation while also allowing the continuation of traditional uses of the land, including grazing, oil production, and coal mining. Such an arrangement would give monument managers incentives to choose the most appropriate use for each land segment while taking into account the overall objectives established for the monument.

Trusts are widely used to protect and manage private and public lands, so our proposal is not revolutionary. This chapter will explain the nature of trusts, including some of the problems they face, and show how a trust could manage a national monument more effectively than a government agency can. We will propose a specific plan for Grand Staircase–Escalante and, based on an inventory of the monument's assets, show how we can have our environmental cake and eat it too. If this can work for the Grand Staircase–Escalante, such a trust approach has promise for other federal lands as well.

PROBLEMS WITH THE PARKS

The president's proclamation establishing the Grand Staircase–Escalante monument placed it under the direction of the Bureau of Land Management (BLM), which is guided by the multiple-use principles outlined in the Federal Land Policy Management Act. According to the bureau, traditional uses such as "commodity extraction and grazing" can exist alongside "the public's newer demand for more recreation" (BLM 1996, vii). Thus, in contrast to monuments managed by the National Park Service, which does not allow production of commodities, this trust would be free to maintain at least some traditional commercial uses.

The opportunity to marry commodity and amenity production comes at a time when Congress is searching for new ways to finance and manage federal lands, including parks. This congressional search reflects concern about federal deficits as well as increasing awareness of problems with the current management by the National Park Service.

The National Park Service, which oversees most other national monuments, has increasingly visible problems. From potholes in Yellowstone's roads to excessive sewage discharge at Kings Canyon, California, the infrastructure of the National Park Service is crumbling. Park Service officials estimate that the agency needs at least $5 billion to repair the system. Visitor services are not what they ought to be, either. For example, a *Consumer Reports* (1997, 12) survey found that the most frequent complaints of visitors to Yellowstone National Park were about inadequate visitor facilities and lack of traffic control. Even the preservation of wildlife habitat is often poor. In 1995, a group of prominent wildlife biologists reported that "animal abundance and diversity are declining in many parks" (Wagner et al. 1995, 62). The group stated that "the government's own analyses stress a bewildering array of problems affecting the attainment of natural-resources goals" (91).

Even though congressional appropriations have risen faster than inflation, many parks are poorly maintained. With most of the budget coming from Congress, there is no incentive for Park Service managers to increase revenues from visitors or to keep costs down to make ends meet (see Leal and Fretwell 1997). As a result, in 1995, only Arches National Park in Utah had revenues greater than its operating budget (National Park Service 1995). The majority of the Park Service budget is paid by general taxes. Only 10 percent of its budget is covered by entrance fees, special use permits, and concession royalties.[2]

Because Congress holds the purse strings, demands of congressmen often hold sway. For example, Montana's three-member congressional delegation succeeded in earmarking $6 million to renovate a backcountry chalet system in Glacier National Park—even though it is used by fewer than 1 percent of park visitors, and even though the park's roads and visitor centers are in serious need of repair (Pound 1997).

In other cases, Park Service officials show poor judgment. For example, a two-hole outhouse without running water cost the Park Service $333,000 at Delaware Water Gap National Recreation Area. Construction of employee housing units at Grand Canyon and Yosemite National Parks cost an average of $390,000 and $584,000, respectively. That is more than $300 per square foot; the average American home, in contrast, is built for $63 per square foot (*Billings Gazette*, 21 August 1997). According to the Interior Department inspector general, these single-family homes did little to alleviate the employee housing problem (Paige 1998, 14). Such distorted incentives can be found throughout the National Park Service (Leal and Fretwell 1997).

Park managers are not foolish or ill-intended people. Rather, their ability to manage environmental assets is severely constrained because they are not free to consider the benefits that might come from shifting both budget priorities and uses of some park land. Using a small portion of park land for commodity production and applying the revenues to enhance preservation of other parts of the park could raise substantial funds in some cases. However, producing commodities in the parks is generally illegal.[3] Park managers are forced to rely on Congress, where special interests often produce inefficient and sometimes environmentally destructive results.

A TRUST FOR THE GRAND STAIRCASE–ESCALANTE

Mismanagement of public lands generally results from improper incentives (Leal 1995; Leal and Fretwell 1997). For example, forest land managers often receive a share of logging receipts but nothing from recreational visitors, giving them an incentive to favor logging over recreation. As we have seen, park managers rely on Congress, not visitors, for their budgets. This leads to failure to realize potential revenues and to poor cost control.

In addition to depending on Congress for their budgets, park managers often have budgets tied to the number of visitors. This gives them an incentive to expand visitation beyond the carrying capacity allowed by existing infrastructure.

A trust for the Grand Staircase–Escalante monument could change these incentives, reducing the impact of politics and obtaining more funds for preservation. At its simplest, a trust is a legal assignment of certain powers to one or more persons, called *trustees,* who manage assets for the benefit of another. The trustees have a fiduciary or legal obligation to manage the assets within the constraints of the trust agreement.

Trusts are widely used. Many people establish them to give assets to heirs but to constrain their use while the heirs are minors, or an individual may create a charitable trust that will be used for specific purposes designated by the donor. Other charitable trusts are formed to achieve the wishes of a diverse population that cannot be expected to act jointly on all actions; a land trust to preserve habitat or open space is an example. In all these cases, the trustees must keep a watchful eye on how the assets are used.

While the trustees are responsible for carrying out the wishes of the creator of the trust, a potential problem persists: How will trustees be held responsible and accountable? With a money trust—that is, a trust whose goal is to earn money for the beneficiary—the goals are clear and performance is relatively easy to measure. The trustee is charged with maximizing the return on investments, subject to consideration of risks from investing. A trustee who is obviously earning subpar returns can usually be replaced with someone more competent.

Measuring the performance of trusts established for other purposes, however, is more difficult. If the goal is vague, performance will be especially difficult to measure. If the beneficiaries are not clearly specified, trustees may pursue their own goals rather than those of the beneficiaries.

To make sure that the trustee acts in the interest of the principal and carries out the mission of the trust, the mission must be stated clearly, and performance must be measured against this mission. Economists Michael Jensen and William Meckling (1976) recommended three ways in which the trustee can be made more accountable:

- specifying ways of measuring and monitoring the trustees' performance,
- compensating the trustees for acting in ways that correlate with the beneficiary's welfare, and
- enforcing specific behavioral rules or policies.

Accordingly, it is important to give clear directions to trustees in the trust document. The mission should include specific objectives that are easily measured and communicated to the beneficiaries. So, an organization such as the Nature Conservancy has a goal of preserving "plants, animals and natural communities . . . by protecting the lands and waters they need to survive" (Nature Conservancy 1999). In addition, the organization produces periodic reports on its activities highlighting the benefits for its supporters. Smaller land trusts that depend on voluntary contributions often provide specific, identifiable services such as trail construction, historic preservation, or open space preservation that have visible results.

We propose a trust that would manage Grand Staircase–Escalante for the benefit of the general public. The goal of the trust would be the one already established for the monument: "to protect a spectacular array of scientific, historic, biological, geological, paleontological, and archaeological objects" (BLM 1998, 1.1). The trust we propose would be required to cover all costs either from revenues generated from the assets in the monument or from private contributions of funds, property, or services by individuals, corporations, or charitable foundations.

The trust would have a board appointed by the president of the United States, with staggered terms to overlap presidential elections, thus eliminating the possibility that a president would immediately appoint a new set of trustees. To ensure that the board of trustees would carefully balance multiple uses in the monument and consider the fiscal implications of its decisions, trustees would be nominated from interest groups. The interests represented would include environmental, recreational, wildlife, Indian, ranching, mining, oil and gas, and state and local government.

Carefully structuring the mission and board of the trust would keep the trust committed to its objective and its beneficiaries. The trust would specifically define the monument's environmental, recreational, and archaeological assets and establish criteria for judging management and measuring trustee performance. In addition, financial self-sufficiency with revenues generated primarily from monument assets would provide an indicator that the trust was achieving its objectives. Staggering terms and requiring that specific interest groups be represented on the board would force the trust to consider the multiple uses required by the presidential proclamation.[4]

PRECEDENTS FOR THIS TRUST

A trust approach to federal land management was proposed by economist Richard Stroup and political scientist John Baden in 1982. They recommended establishing "wilderness endowment boards" that would be bound by the common-law doctrine of trust to manage and preserve wilderness areas. These boards would cover the costs of maintaining wilderness areas out of revenues earned.

Just as an art museum board is responsible for preserving art values, wilderness endowment boards would be responsible for preserving and enhancing wilderness values. Just as an art museum board might sell an Impressionist painting to acquire an Old Master or a modern abstract painting, the wilderness endowment board might allow carefully managed oil exploration and development to enable the board to acquire additional lands to be preserved. To ensure a bias in favor of enhancing wilderness values, Stroup and Baden (1982) proposed that board members be nominated by environmental groups.

Stroup (1985) also applied this idea to managing national parks or portions of parks through the creation of park endowment boards. He recommended that the tracts of land managed by endowment boards (or trusts) have a clearly stated mission. He noted that the members of each board should be selected for their dedication to the mission of the park. The trustees would have a legal responsibility to carry out the stated mission.

Private Trusts

While Stroup and Baden's proposal was unusual because it would have applied to the federal government, land trusts are common in both the private and public sectors. Indeed, most environmental organizations are trusts. The way that the National Audubon Society, an environmental trust, manages the Rainey Wildlife Sanctuary in Louisiana illustrates how a trust can be more effective than the government in achieving its goals of protecting birds and other wildlife (see Baden and Stroup 1981; Snyder and Shaw 1995).

The Rainey Preserve, a refuge for snow geese, wading birds, ducks, and other wildlife, also has natural gas wells operating on its property. These wells have earned Audubon about $25 million in royalties since the early 1950s. By requiring special exploration and extraction techniques, Audubon is able to ensure protection of wildlife habitat while producing natural gas and earning significant revenues. Writing in *Audubon* magazine, Mitchell (1981, 16) noted that sanctuary manager David Reed "liked the idea of cooperating with industry in a situation where it was likely there would be no adverse impact on the biotic community."

There appears to be minimal impact from the drilling. However, if there were greater impact, the additional revenues provide funds that can be used to offset these impacts. Clearly, the additional revenues provide funds that can be invested in more wildlife habitat elsewhere or in addressing other environmental problems. In other words, economically productive activity on Rainey provides the wherewithal to pay for habitat enhancement and other environmental goals, which can be costly.

This kind of win-win solution rarely occurs in the governmental arena. Indeed, while Audubon peacefully obtains revenues from its natural resources on Rainey, it adamantly opposes drilling for oil on the Alaska National Wildlife Refuge (ANWR). While the areas obviously differ, the trade-offs are similar: If Audubon owned ANWR it would have an incentive to negotiate with oil companies to allow drilling but also to make sure that wildlife on the tundra was not disturbed. Since ANWR is government owned, Audubon has no incentive to favor drilling because it has no stake in revenues and no control over how the drilling is done. Thus, the result is out-spoken opposition (Flicker 1995).

Other examples of private land trusts created specifically to protect environmental values abound. The Nature Conservancy is the largest and best known, but the number of local land trusts is growing. A recent estimate indicates that over 1,200 locally based trusts exist in the United States, managing five million acres. An additional ten million acres are protected by large trusts such as the Nature Conservancy (Land Trust Alliance 1999).

School Trust Lands

While many trusts are private, state school trust lands are a widespread example of government land trusts (see Souder and Fairfax 1996). When most western territories became states, they were granted land to benefit the public schools and other endowed institutions.[5] These school trust lands are managed with a clear mandate to generate sustained revenues for public schools. In essence, school officials, teachers, parents, and other interest groups concerned about the funding of public schools are the beneficiaries, and they have a clear incentive to monitor the management of the school trust lands.

Under such watchdogs, trust lands are generally well-managed. Costs are kept down and revenues are substantial. Leal (1995), who studied state versus federal timberland management in Montana, found that on average the state forests generated approximately $2 for every dollar spent while federal forests lost money, generating only $0.50 for every dollar spent. This contrast occurred even though state and national forests are adjacent to one another and similar in timber-growing potential. Leal concluded that because the Forest Service has no requirement to generate income for national forests, it has little incentive to operate with the same efficiencies as its nonfederal counterparts.

Cost-effective management of state lands did not lead to environmental deterioration, Leal found. An independent audit team of professional foresters and environmental representatives that was authorized by the Montana legislature found that the watersheds on state lands were better protected than on federal lands. The state forests had healthier stands of trees and were ecologically healthier, too (Schultz 1992, 4). Indeed, recent studies of the nation's forests indicate that many national forests are one spark away from disaster. Thirty-nine million acres of national forest are at risk of devastating wildfires, and another six million are dead or dying due to insect infestations (Fretwell 1999).

Revenues from well-managed properties can supply the means to protect the environment, providing protection that is often missing on federal lands. One study compared Big Bend National Park in Texas with nearby Big Bend Ranch State Park (Leal and Fretwell 1997, 20–25; see also this volume, chapter 3). The national park faces serious deterioration of facilities and trails, yet no deliberate effort is made to control where visitors go to limit their impact on the park trails (Big Bend National Park 1996, 7). In contrast, Big Bend Ranch State Park is divided into zones in which the number of visitors at any given time is strictly controlled. Environmentally sensitive areas are monitored to assess the effects of public use, and visitors can be rerouted to minimize harmful human impacts (Texas Parks and Wildlife Department 1994, 21).

The superintendent of Big Bend Ranch notes that revenues enabled him to spend money that would not otherwise have been available on improvements such as repairs, new materials for the visitor lodge, a pickup truck, and radios to facilitate communication (Leal and Fretwell 1997, 25; see also this volume's chapter 3). In other words, obtaining more revenues from visitors can enhance the ability of park officials to manage the park. This benefits both visitors and the park environment.

The Presidio

The Presidio in San Francisco provides a rare example of the trust approach adopted on the federal level. In the Omnibus Parks and Public Lands Management Act of 1996, Congress created a trust to manage the Presidio, a former military post on a promontory overlooking San Francisco's Golden Gate Bridge. The Presidio was the oldest continually operated military post in the nation. When it was decommissioned as an Army post, it was transferred to the National Park Service and became part of the Golden Gate National Recreation Area.

The Presidio contains 1,480 acres and 510 historic buildings with over seven million square feet of space. While small in size for a national park, its location in a strikingly beautiful setting in a major city makes it prime real estate and a subject of great interest. An annual budget estimated to be as much as $38 million a year would have made the Presidio the most costly park in the federal system. An additional $274 million is required for capital investments (Governor's Office of Planning and Research 1998). Under fiscal constraints, Congress was forced to examine alternative funding methods to retain control of the Presidio. Creativity and congressional debate produced the Presidio Trust. Its goals are to preserve and enhance the Presidio as a national park and achieve financial self-sufficiency by fiscal year 2013 (Presidio Trust 1998, 3).

A general management plan was developed for the Presidio based on the principle of *environmental sustainability,* a term defined as meeting the needs of the present without compromising the ability to meet the needs of the future. The plan blends the use of natural, cultural, and recreational resources with the development of centers for education and research. The Presidio is to serve as a place to study and improve the natural environment and humans' interaction with it.

The trust is responsible for managing the assets of the Presidio in a way that will minimize costs to the U.S. Treasury and make efficient use of the land and buildings. Trust goals include finding tenants and establishing programs to preserve the natural, historic, and cultural resources, while providing educational and recreational opportunities. The Presidio can be a community that promotes the ecological integrity of the site, socioeconomic diversity, and economic viability. The trust board of directors includes a designee of the secretary of the interior and six presidential appointees.

Unlike the managers of traditional parks, the Presidio board has a fiduciary obligation to generate revenues by leasing its buildings and using its property in ways that will eventually cover all operating expenses. The board may use the revenues for administration, preservation, restoration, operation and maintenance, improvement, repair, and related expenses.

The Presidio was not, however, forced to become financially self-sufficient immediately but was given a budget of up to $25 million per year for as long as fifteen years. If the self-sufficiency goal is not attained after fifteen years, all property under jurisdiction of the trust will be offered for sale to other federal agencies, public bodies, or private enterprises (in that order).

This approach is certainly not a perfect way of getting the incentives right for managers. Making $25 million per year available discourages financial independence at least for the fifteen years for which this amount has been allocated. In addition, the enabling legislation gives the trust a loophole: The trustees may transfer any portion of the property that they consider "surplus" to the secretary of the interior. This provision means that the board can shift unprofitable buildings or areas to the Park Service, increasing the profitability of the trust but sinking the Park Service further in the red.

Nonetheless, the Presidio Trust does force trustees to consider using lands in ways that will generate revenues and to use those revenues to preserve and enhance the urban park. The requirement of self-sufficiency forces trustees to choose land and resource uses that will cover costs.

Currently, the Presidio Trust has designed a conference facility, museum and visitor center, a scientific research and education complex, and residential housing. Since these structures will be adjacent to recreation facilities, open space, coastal bluffs, beaches, and woodlands as well as within the city limits of San Francisco, the Presidio can undoubtedly obtain revenues to cover its cost. Indeed, it should easily obtain funds to enhance the environmental conditions of the property. By 2013, leasing and other activities are expected to generate $37 million each year, making the Presidio financially self-sufficient (Presidio Trust 1998, 17). At the same time, the trust will have increased open space, restored natural areas, preserved historic buildings, and hosted visitors from around the world.

The Baca Ranch

The Presidio model was proposed in 1998 as a way of managing the Baca Ranch in New Mexico, a large private ranch that the federal government contemplated acquiring. Covering ninety-five thousand acres, the Baca Ranch is an island of private land surrounded by national forests. The ranch covers the Valles Caldera, a collapsed volcanic dome whose meadows hold elk herds, trout streams, and steaming pools—resembling a small Yellowstone National Park. While the deal to acquire the Baca Ranch fell through, the Valles Caldera Preservation Act, introduced in the Senate in October 1998, shows what a governmental trust could look like.

The bill would have created the Valles Caldera Trust to acquire and manage the Baca Land and Cattle Company. The bill would have allowed the trust to "solicit and accept donations of funds, property, supplies, or services from individuals, foundations, corporations and other private or public entities for the purposes of carrying out its duties."[6] In other words, it would not have to rely on taxpayer funding.

The act outlined the organization of the staff and the appointment of voting trustees, who would have been federal officials, including the supervisor of the Santa Fe National Forest and the superintendent of the Bandolier National Monument (lands surrounding the ranch), and seven individuals with expertise in such areas as livestock management, game management, forestry, conservation, cultural and natural history, and local government. The trust would have had responsibility for administration, preservation, and development of the preserve; interpretation and management of public use; and maintenance, repair, and improvement of the property. It would have continued operations as a working ranch while protecting the resource values and open space. Over time, the trust was to reach financial self-sufficiency.

These elements of the Valles Caldera Trust go a long way toward meeting the requirements for an effective trust. They provide criteria for judging management and measuring and monitoring trustee performance. For example, financial self-sufficiency—covering costs—is an indicator of performance, showing that visitors are being satisfied. Also, by appointing trustees with a variety of interests and expertise, the trust would have had some competition among trustees, and a variety of values would have been considered.

However, there was a glaring omission in the enabling legislation; it contained no provision for charging, retaining, and investing fees for use on the Baca Ranch. While the trust was expected to earn money for the federal government, the funds, it appears, would have gone to the U.S. Treasury. The experience of our national parks indicates that this would create a perverse incentive, discouraging managers from taking steps to increase revenues. Managers would receive little direct benefit from satisfying park visitors. As a result, the wishes of visitors, whatever the fees they paid, would have little impact on the actual management of the land. Had the Baca Ranch been purchased by the federal government, it might well have ended up, like other national parks, relying on Congress for its financial support.

THE PROPOSED TRUST

The Presidio Trust and the contemplated Valles Caldera Trust indicate that officials in the federal government are willing to experiment with a trust approach, and the

Grand Staircase–Escalante Monument Trust could be the next step. This experiment is timely for several reasons:

- Because the area is in the hands of the Bureau of Land Management, National Park Service restrictions will not apply. There is room for innovation.
- Congress is appropriating about $6.4 million per year for the monument during the planning process. While this is about four times the previous budget for the area, obtaining this amount of money through a trust is far from an insurmountable challenge.
- Historically, the Grand Staircase–Escalante area has been used for many purposes, from recreation to commodity production. Therefore, multiple use under a trust structure has precedents.

As already noted, the Grand Staircase–Escalante National Monument was created to "protect a spectacular array of scientific, historic, biological, geological, paleontological, and archaeological objects" (BLM 1998, 1.1). To achieve these goals, managers would have the opportunity to raise and retain revenues from the use of the land. While initial federal appropriations would be required for a few years, data indicate that the monument could become self-sufficient quickly, given its many assets.

In addition to spectacular canyons and impressive Anasazi archaeological sites, the Grand Staircase–Escalante National Monument includes coal, oil, and natural gas reserves. As a trust, Grand Staircase–Escalante would be able to obtain revenues from recreation, pure preservation, and natural resource development, including mining. The commodity production could take place where it would not abuse amenities or distract visitors. Revenues could be used to pay for reclamation and help preserve recreational and archaeological resources, especially where collecting fees may be difficult.

There is, however, an obstacle to this scenario. In establishing the new monument, President Clinton placed a restriction on multiple use. His proclamation states that "the land will remain open for multiple uses including hunting, fishing, hiking, camping and grazing," but it goes on to exclude mining. In his announcement, Clinton said:

> While the Grand Staircase–Escalante will be open for many activities, I am concerned about a large coal mine proposed for the area. Mining jobs are good jobs and mining is important for our national security. But we can't mine everywhere, and we shouldn't have mines that threaten our national treasures. (Office of the Press Secretary 1996, 3)

While the president's statement does not have the force of law, his decision to exclude mining has been accepted—both by the monument planning team and by the companies that would otherwise be executing the mining claims. The president's statement led Andalex Resources to stop its proposed coal mine on the Kaiparowits Plateau, the harsh and isolated land in the center of the monument. This is the site of one of the largest coal fields in the West, where Andalex had spent $8 million in mine research and development.

Although the presidential proclamation reduced the planning team's options by disallowing coal mining, that decision should be reconsidered. The reason is not simply because coal mining can produce revenues to support and maintain the monument but because mining can be done with little harm to the natural amenities of the area. The proposed Andalex mine, for example, would disturb only forty acres of surface area if underground mining techniques are used. This is a minute portion of the 1.9 million acres in the monument. No new road construction would be required, although twenty miles of existing roadways would be upgraded.

A trust structure would not mandate mining, but it would allow the trustees to weigh the revenue benefits from mining against the possible harmful effects. If commodity production can take place with little or no impact on amenity values as at Audubon's Rainey Preserve, trust managers could earn profits from commodity production and reinvest those profits in protecting the environment of the monument, including its archaeological sites. Whatever the environmental impact of mining, there is no reason that the effects could not be minimized, especially with the revenues that would result from the leases.

Even if mining is not allowed, the Grand Staircase–Escalante has the potential to be self-sufficient simply by requiring recreational visitors to pay their way. Hikers and mountain bikers could pay for access, as could visitors to the monument's archaeological sites. The fees could cover the costs of providing and preserving these amenities. If these costs are low, as is often argued, the fees for recreation and sightseeing could be relatively modest.

Elsewhere on federal lands, new visitor fees are giving agencies an enormous boost. The Fee Demonstration Program, which began in 1996, allows up to one hundred units in each federal land management agency (Bureau of Land Management, Fish and Wildlife Service, Forest Service, and National Park Service) to retain receipts for use within the area where they are collected.[7] These experiments provide managers with an incentive to raise fees to more realistic levels and to respond to visitor demands. With these revenues, facilities have been upgraded, and damaged resources are under repair. For example, at Natural Bridges National Monument, also in southern Utah, the new fees have allowed the reconstruction of five thousand feet of trails that were crumbling from overuse and wind and water erosion.[8]

Visitors overwhelmingly agree that higher fees are acceptable as long as the receipts are used to benefit the area visited (General Accounting Office [GAO] 1998, 80). If each visitor to a national park had paid a $5 fee in 1995, revenues for the national park system would have been greater than congressional appropriations for operating expenses (National Park Service 1995, NPS-24).[9]

Unfortunately, so far no effort has been made by planning officials even to consider alternative funding mechanisms for Grand Staircase–Escalante. The interim planning board, a diverse group of experts, has proposed a variety of activities and goals for the monument. These include preservation of landscapes, land forms, ecosystems, and historical sites; provision of facilities for camping and picnicking; interpretive signs; development of trails for automobiles, bicycles, hikers, horses, and off-road vehicles; and the establishment of scientific study sites for biological, paleontological, and archaeological sites. Yet the potential for revenues has not been addressed. Indeed, we can expect the managers to demand gradually larger appropriations than the current $6.4 million budget because the current management structure does not provide an incentive for restraint or consideration of revenue-generating opportunities. Taxpayers who will never see the monument are expected to foot the bill for another politically driven agency.

A FINANCIAL PLAN FOR THE TRUST

In contrast, our proposal for Grand Staircase–Escalante would raise money for the taxpayer, not drain it. And it would provide funds to protect the environment of the monument. Based on numerous official appraisals of the size and location and value of resource reserves within the monument, we perceive significant sources of potential revenue (see table 8.1).

Current Revenues

Current revenues, which come from oil, grazing, and recreation, total $465,750 per year.

Oil and Natural Gas

Drilling for oil and natural gas on Grand Staircase–Escalante lands is nothing new. As many as sixty companies have drilled for oil on the land. Leases for oil and gas exploration cover 190,000 acres within the monument. The Upper Valley oil field has five active wells producing about 250,000 barrels of oil per year. At an average price of $20 per barrel and a royalty payment to the federal government of 12.5 percent (split evenly with the state), annual federal royalties on the monument amount to $312,500. These wells could continue producing for twenty years, if monument regulations allowed them to operate profitably.

Grazing

Nearly all the 1.9 million acres of the monument are used for livestock forage. About eighty-four operators have permits for seventy-five thousand active animal unit months (AUMs). With an average grazing fee of $1.35 per AUM, grazing within the monument generates more than $101,000 per year.[10]

Recreation

About forty special and commercial recreation permits are issued each year to outfitters and guides and for wilderness training. The revenue from these permits is

Table 8.1
How the Grand Staircase-Escalante Could Cover its Costs

Actual Federal Revenues FY 1996

Oil	250,000 barrels @ $20/barrel x 6.25% royalty	$ 312,500
Grazing	75,000 active AUMs @ $1.35/AUM	101,250
Special Recreation Permits	3% of gross revenue from monument use	52,000
Total Current Revenues		$ 465,750

Potential Annual Federal Revenues

Conoco Oil	7.5 million barrels/year @ $20/barrel x 10% estimated success rate x 6.25% royalty	937,500
Andalex Coal	2.5 million tons/year @ $19.50/ton x 4% royalty	1,950,000
Visitor Fee	$5/person x 850,000 visitors/year (1998 actual)	4,250,000
Total Potential Revenues		7,137,500

Actual and Potential Annual Federal Revenues | | $ 7,603,250

Sources: Grazing: Dennis Pope, Biological Team Leader, GSE, e-mail correspondence, 3 February 1999; Recreation visits: Barbara Sharrow, Visitor Services Team Leader, GSE, telephone conversation, 10 September 1998, and e-mail correspondence, 26 January 1999; Commodities: Lee Allison, State Geologist, Utah Geological Survey, telephone conversation, 19 August 1997.

$52,000 a year. There is currently no charge or permit required for other recreation such as camping, hunting, and hiking. These activities are much more common in the Grand Staircase and Escalante regions on each end of the monument than on the massive Kaiparowits plateau.[11]

Potential Revenues

Revenues generated from commodity production and recreation could easily off-set the costs of operating and maintaining the monument. We estimate potential additional revenues from the monument to be over $7.1 million annually, well above the current $6.4 million appropriation.

Coal

The coal field on the Kaiparowits Plateau in the center of the monument encompasses 1,600 square miles, or 54 percent of the total acreage. The monument contains an estimated sixty-two billion tons of coal (compared with twenty-two billion tons of coal throughout the rest of Utah). Eighteen percent of the coal is thought to be recoverable.

Andalex Resources, Inc., was granted a coal lease for the Smoky Hollow Mine in 1985 covering 26,400 acres on the southern end of the plateau. Andalex withdrew its application to mine coal in January 1997, after the president's proclamation prohibiting coal mining. However, the mine could produce an estimated 2.5 million tons of coal each year. With an average price of $19.50 per ton, the mine would generate $1.95 million annually in royalty payments to the federal government.[12]

Andalex holds an additional seventeen leases covering nearly thirty-five thousand acres on which the company suspended mining. The acreage is part of a designated Wilderness Study Area (WSA), and mining might not ever be allowed on it. Since these leases were already held by Andalex, the monument designation order allows these lands to be exchanged for lease rights outside the monument. PacifiCorp also had a coal lease on the northern end of the plateau covering nearly forty thousand acres. Because this land was also in WSA status, PacifiCorp agreed to a land exchange with the federal government a few days before the presidential proclamation.

Oil

In addition to the oil fields that are currently producing oil, the monument has an estimated 447 million barrels of oil in the west flank of the Circle Cliffs tar sands deposit. Conoco holds a portion of fifty-nine leases covering 108,000 acres inside the monument, and in April 1997, the company was granted permission to drill an exploratory well. Conoco believes that up to fifty exploration prospects are adjacent to and within the monument, each capable of holding at least one hundred million barrels.

One of Conoco's prospective drill sites could theoretically produce another 150 million barrels of oil (Conoco 1997).[13] Assuming this oil is pumped over a twenty-year span, these wells could generate another $9.3 million annually for the monument. However, most experts estimate only a 10 percent probability of success.[14] Thus, the estimated value of untapped oil revenue in the monument is $937,500 annually.

Recreation

Special recreational use permits currently generate $52,000 per year. To augment these revenues, sightseers using the Hole in the Wall Road and the Burr Trail could be charged an entrance fee, and hikers, campers, off-road vehicle users, and other recreationists could be required to purchase a $5 permit. In 1998, nearly 850,00 visitors entered the monument.[15] If each paid a fee of $5, another $4.25 million would be available for monument operation.[16]

Under the trust model, managers would have to decide whether to forgo the $2.9 million annually from commodity production ($937,500 from the expected value of Conoco oil plus $1.95 million from Andalex coal). This revenue could be used to achieve the conservation goals of the monument. Estimated tourism receipts alone of $4.25 million would cover the bulk of the $6.4 million annual government allocation. Indeed, if recreation receipts were fully captured—that is, if recreational opportunities were increased and fees charged for them, rather than just for access— they could eliminate the need for commodity production within the monument. They could also eliminate any need for the monument to rely on government funds (and the political controls that often accompany such funds) during a transition period such as the fifteen years granted to the Presidio Trust.

CONCLUSION

Clearly, the opportunity exists for a trust that would preserve and enhance the ecological and archaeological amenities of Grand Staircase–Escalante without burdening the taxpayer or distorting managers' incentives, as occurs regularly now in the National Park Service. Implementing a trust arrangement would require congressional legislation that would provide the specifics of the trust, as the Baca Ranch legislation did.

Creating a trust to manage the Grand Staircase–Escalante National Monument would benefit the public, taxpayers, and residents of Utah. The key element of the trust would be to give the trustees the responsibility for funding the management of the monument and the ability to make decisions about how to do so. A trust that obtains its operating funds from revenues would give managers an incentive to look carefully at ways to use the land to obtain funds that can fulfill the mission of the monument. A well-drawn trust document would clarify the goals and the steps that the trustees could take to achieve those goals.

The Grand Staircase–Escalante is a unique national monument for many reasons. It is uniquely beautiful; it is uniquely large; it is uniquely endowed with marketable commodities; and it is uniquely managed as a national monument by the Bureau of Land Management. This combination gives the Grand Staircase–Escalante planning team all the more reason to make it unique in another respect—by managing it as a trust.

NOTES

1. Beginning with Theodore Roosevelt's establishment of the Devil's Tower National Monument, national monument acreage has grown to cover twenty-one million acres, an area nearly the size of Indiana, managed under the authority of the National Park Service (NPS). Until 1996, the largest of these outside Alaska was the Grand Canyon with 806,400 acres designated in 1908 (BLM 1999).

2. Special use fees and 15 percent of fee collections remain within the park in which they are collected, as does a portion of revenues collected from units participating in the Fee Demonstration Program of 1996. For a more complete discussion, see Fretwell (1998). Other revenues collected go to the general treasury, from which Congress reappropriates them.

3. The National Park Service cannot restrict access to mining claimants with valid existing rights, but it has the authority to regulate development to control the impact on park, recreational, and wilderness values.

4. The details of the trust arrangement could be further refined by examining how other conservation and environmental trusts operate.

5. Beneficiaries of these trusts usually include common schools, legislative, executive and judicial buildings, state hospitals, penal institutions, agricultural and mechanical colleges, military institutes, universities, and schools for the deaf and blind.

6. 6. S. 2621, sec. 106(g), 105th U.S. Congress, 1998.

7. Eighty percent of user fees in participating units remain within the unit; 20 percent are spent under agency discretion for units unable to generate receipts sufficient to cover costs (Public Law 104-134, title III, section 315, as amended, 104th Congress, 1996).

8. Written communication from Keith Stegall, SEUG trails coordinator, Canyon Lands National Park, Moab, Utah, 18 December 1998.

9. This estimate assumes an inelastic demand curve, which has been shown for the majority of parks participating in the Fee Demonstration Program. Fees have often as much as doubled with little change in visitation numbers.

10. Federal grazing receipts are minuscule compared to state trust lands (see Fretwell 1998). Data provided through e-mail correspondence from Dennis Pope, biological team leader, Grand Staircase–Escalante National Monument, 3 February 1999.

11. Data provided by Barbara Sharrow, visitor services team leader, Grand Staircase–Escalante National Monument, telephone conversation, 10 September 1998.

12. Public Law 105-335 (105th Congress, October 1998) transferred, through exchange, all Utah School and Institutional Trust Lands Administration lands and mineral interests

inside the Grand Staircase–Escalante to the federal government. The state and federal governments split an 8 percent coal royalty on federal lands. Thus, the state of Utah would also receive an amount of $1.95 million annually if mining were allowed. Data provided by Lee Allison, state geologist, Utah Geological Survey, telephone conversation, 19 August 1997.

13. This is a conservative estimate based on only one of eight possible drilling sites Conoco has identified within the monument.

14. The average success rate for finding commercial quantities of oil from exploratory wells is 10 percent (Allison telephone conversation, 19 August 1997).

15. Data provided by e-mail correspondence from Barbara Sharrow, 26 January 1999.

16. Again, as stated in note 9, this calculation assumes an inelastic demand curve, which has been shown in most Fee Demonstration Program parks.

REFERENCES

Baden, John, and Richard Stroup. 1981. "Saving the Wilderness: A Radical Proposal." *Reason* (July): 28–36.

Big Bend National Park. 1996. *State of the Park Report: Big Bend National Park Rio Grande Wild and Scenic River.* Big Bend National Park, Tex.: Author.

Bureau of Land Management. 1996. *Public Land Statistics.* Washington, D.C.: U.S. Department of the Interior.

———.1998. "Grand Staircase–Escalante National Monument Draft Management Plan, Draft Environmental Impact Statement." Cedar City, Utah: Author.

———. 1999. "Monuments Established by Presidential Proclamation (February)." Available: http://www.blm.gov/nhp/news/alerts/monuments.html.

Conoco, Inc. 1997. "Estimates Show Huge Revenue Potential for Federal, State, and Local Entities." Houston, Tex.: Author.

Consumer Reports. 1997. "Rating the Parks." June, 10–17.

Flicker, John. 1995. "Don't Desecrate the Arctic Refuge." *Wall Street Journal* (letter), 18 September.

Fretwell, Holly Lippke. 1998. *The Price We Pay.* Public Lands Report No. 1. Bozeman, Mont.: Political Economy Research Center.

———. 1999. *Forests: Do We Get What We Pay For?* Public Lands Report No. 2. Bozeman, Mont.: Political Economy Research Center.

General Accounting Office. 1998. "Recreation Fees: Demonstration Fee Program Successful in Raising Revenues But Could Be Improved." GAO\RCED-99-7. Washington, D.C.: U.S. Government Printing Office.

Governor's Office of Planning and Research. 1998. *California Military Base Closures and Realignments: Current Status of Reuse Efforts.* September. Available: http://www.cedar.ca.gov/military/current_reuse/98sep/presidio.htm.

Jensen, Michael C., and William H. Meckling. 1976. "Theory of the Firm: Managerial Behavior, Agency Costs, and Ownership Structure." *Journal of Financial Economics* 3, no. 4: 305–60.

Land Trust Alliance. 1999. *1990s Brings Surge in Land Conservation as Regional, Local Land Trusts Attract 1 Million Supporters* (1 July). Available: http://www.lta.org/newscen.html.

Leal, Donald R. 1995. "Turning a Profit on Public Forests." *PERC Policy Series*, PS-4. Bozeman, Mont.: Political Economy Research Center.

Leal, Donald R., and Holly Lippke Fretwell. 1997. "Back to the Future to Save Our Parks." *PERC Policy Series*, PS-10. Bozeman, Mont.: Political Economy Research Center. (Reprinted in this volume as chapter 3.)

Mitchell, John G. 1981. "The Oil Below." *Audubon Magazine* (May).

National Park Service. 1995. *Budget Justifications, FY1997*. Washington, D.C.: U.S. Department of the Interior.

Nature Conservancy. 1999. *The Nature Conservancy* (10 June). Available: http://www.tnc.org/welcome/about/about.htm.

Office of the Press Secretary. 1996. "Remarks by the President on Making Environment Announcement." Press release dated 18 September. Washington, D.C.: White House.

Paige, Sean. 1998. Managing the Great Outdoors. *Insight*, May 18, 12–14.

Presidio Trust. 1998. *The Presidio Trust Financial Management Program*. Report to Congress, San Francisco, 8 July.

Pound, Edward T. 1997. "Costly Outhouses Monuments to Red Tape." *USA Today*, 15 December.

Schultz, Bill. 1992. *Forestry Best Management Practices Implementation Monitoring*. Missoula: Montana Department of State Lands.

Snyder, Pamela, and Jane S. Shaw. 1995. "PC Drilling in a Wildlife Refuge." *Wall Street Journal*, 7 September.

Souder, Jon A., and Sally K. Fairfax. 1996. *State Trust Lands: History, Management, & Sustainable Use*. Lawrence: University Press of Kansas.

Stroup, Richard. 1985. "Rescuing Yellowstone from Politics: Expanding Parks While Reducing Conflict." In *The Yellowstone Primer*, ed. John A. Baden and Donald Leal. San Francisco: Pacific Research Institute for Public Policy, 169–84.

Stroup, Richard, and John Baden. 1982. "Endowment Areas: A Clearing in the Policy Wilderness?" *Cato Journal* 2 (Winter): 91–108.

Texas Parks and Wildlife Department. 1994. *Big Bend Ranch State Natural Area Management Plan*. Austin: Author.

Wagner, Frederic H., Ronald Foresta, R. Bruce Gill, Dale R. McCullough, Michael R. Pelton, William F. Porter, and Hal Salwasser. 1995. *Wildlife Policies in the U.S. National Parks*. Washington, D.C.: Island.

9

Parks Are for People—But *Which* People?

Karl Hess Jr.

Yellowstone National Park is literally and figuratively a fountain of nature's extravagance. It is the best show in northwestern Wyoming, if not in all of the intermountain West. But it is not the vignette of presettlement America proposed by the 1963 Leopold Report on wildlife management in the national parks. Less than extraordinary in its range of life (Kay 1997), Yellowstone is nonetheless unique and special. In part, its charm and its claim to fame rests on its transcendent values—its significance to an array of staunch friends and ardent supporters. It is, to some, a fitting monument to a vision of nature properly purified of human contagion (omitting, of course, the anomaly of three million visitors a year and an annual operating budget of just under $20 million). Indeed, Yellowstone has provided the model for management policy in protected areas worldwide. By the sheer might of its scientific prestige and popular acclaim, Yellowstone has shaped and molded a century of preservation and conservation thinking, propelling nations, rich and poor alike, down a road that has not always proven beneficial to either humankind or untrammeled nature.

THE MISANTHROPIC PARK

The U.S. National Park Service holds as a matter of faith and principle the dictum that "Parks are for People," but it begs the essential question of *which* people are parks for, and it conveniently obscures a persistent and unsettling antagonism to humans. The dictum relies on the metaphor, if not the guns, of John Muir's famous antidote to human trespass of nature: armed soldiers behind every tree. This dictum is the essence of Yellowstone National Park, and it is the conceptual foundation and template for a worldwide parks movement.

159

Yellowstone's foundations, like the foundations of other parks formed in its image, are revealing. Though created for sundry reasons—some as "pleasuring grounds" and others for causes more attuned to preservation—few national parks were carved from pristine wilderness. The creation of Yellowstone entailed the expulsion of indigenous people, ranging from small bands of Shoshone who lived year-round on the Yellowstone Plateau to Crow and Blackfeet who used the plateau for summer hunting. To the south at Jackson Hole—later to become the Jackson Hole National Monument and then the Grand Teton National Park—the consensus of historians is that "until shortly after 1800, Jackson Hole truly belonged to the Indians" (Kemf 1993).

Parks worldwide have joined Yellowstone in wielding the conservation tool of expulsion. In Latin America, 86 percent of all protected areas were formerly inhabited. In Sub-Saharan Africa the percentage is even higher. Indeed, in places such as the Nyika Plateau and, to the south, at Vwaza Marsh—both protected areas on the western edge of the Rift Valley in northern Malawi and both typical of the southern African experience—the task of making parks in the Yellowstone mold translated into state expropriation of customary tribal lands, the dismantling of villages, and the exiling of hundreds of families from ancestral grounds. In the case of the people of Nyika, the forced move proved unusually costly. Formerly isolated by high-elevation climate from the anopheles mosquito and for that reason physically unadapted to its unique malady, they bore the heavy toll of first-time exposure to an excessively malarial environment that had, a century earlier, driven Livingston from the shore of Lake Nyasa to the protected perch of present-day Livingstonia (Kemf 1993).

The foundations of Yellowstone, Nyika, and Vwaza Marsh national parks and many of the world's twenty-five thousand protected areas totaling 5 percent of the globe (an area roughly equivalent to the size of India) are alarmingly similar. They were established and sold as "Parks for People," yet in the balance, a minority of the people, usually comprising the poorest, the politically weakest, and the most proximate to the park's boundary, paid the price. The benefits flowed elsewhere, distributed in theory to all the people but concentrated in fact to government agencies formed to manage new parks and to the few visitors wealthy enough to visit them.

Yellowstone and its modern progeny have done more than redistribute resources from poor to rich. Contrary to their stated purpose, they have enforced and reinforced a new and decisive dichotomy between people and nature. By state decree, nature is out of bounds for things expressly human, and people within or on the boundaries of parks often are excluded from management decisions. Political control of parks is taken as the necessary condition for their existence on the assumption that no other entity would have the foresight, the will, and the resources to preserve them. Moreover, the state is assumed to escape the clutches of greed and leap beyond base economics to basic ecology. At the heart of this chapter is the question of whether parks live up to these assumptions.

ROCKY TIMES AND THE MOPANI BLUES

Park misanthropy and all its attendant state trappings of centralized control, political management, national community, and abeyance to the greater public interest might well be a bearable price to pay for nature preservation if the Yellowstone model worked as well as its reputation suggests it should. Unfortunately, it does not. In developed countries and most notably in the United States, the Yellowstone model is faltering for both political and biological reasons; America's national parks are simply not living up to their ecological expectations. In developing countries from the Americas to Africa to Asia, the Yellowstone model is a problem for the people who live near parks, for managers who steward parks, and for national treasuries that must pay for them.

We are learning that political management of protected areas is a double-edged sword, one edge being the security and predictability of a centralized protection regime and the other edge being the perverse incentives and even more perverse outcomes that attend that same regime. For example, while the natural resources staff at Grand Canyon National Park begs for outside funding to supplement a paltry federal science budget, tens of millions of dollars are appropriated by Congress on the making of inconsequential parks such as Steamtown, a park devoted to maintaining a collection of mostly Canadian steam locomotives. At the Presidio in San Francisco, the Park Service is prepared to spend up to $40 million a year just for operating expenses—a sum just slightly greater than the operating budgets of Grand Canyon, Yosemite, and Yellowstone combined. Increasingly, Park Service expenditures, at congressional bequest, are aimed more at creating public works projects for constituent employment than attending to the business of protecting and preserving the nation's crown jewels (Ridenour 1994).

Yet the problem is more than just "park barrel" politics; the Park Service itself is heavily bloated and fiscally ineffective. In 1995, for example, U.S. parks had about $670 million for total operations and maintenance and another $180 million for construction. At the same time, the total Park Service budget was in excess of $1.4 billion, meaning that more than $550 million, or 40 percent, never made it to the parks. Moreover, of the money that did make it to the parks, much was spent ineffectively. Agency housing cost four times that of equivalent private sector homes, and park visitor centers cost nearly three times that of similar structures designed and assembled by local architects and engineers (O'Toole 1997).

But the problem gets worse the closer we peer into the National Park Service's fiscal black hole. Park budgets are not based on fee revenues; they are dependent on congressional appropriations, which, in turn, are mostly driven by numbers of visitors. As a result, park administrators have a compelling interest in the expansion of park visitation. Rather than invest funds in natural resource programs that are hidden to most pass-through visitors, park managers invest funds in projects that enhance the volume of visitation. Park managers have little or no incentive to diversify and enhance the quality of park visitation beyond ensuring the usual grand attractions such as abundant elk and bison. To change this incentive, park managers would have to be allowed to charge and retain fees for a range of differential services, but they cannot. Although some parks now enjoy limited flexibility in charging entry fees, the bulk of fees still go to Congress, leaving parks and their administrators to the whims of political fortune (Hess and O'Toole 1995).

Biological problems, many of which are closely linked to the fiscal incentives that drive American parks, are also on the rise. Under the scientific guise of "natural regulation," park managers are treating their wildlife populations and wildlife habitat as if the two were truly natural. In so doing, they are extending the Yellowstone model of fortress nature to its logical conclusion: to the miscalculation that even fragmented islands can function as self-sustaining systems. But the ecological state of park lands delivers a much different verdict. In Yellowstone, Rocky Mountain, Mount Rainier, Glacier, and Grand Canyon, naturally unregulated wildlife has taken its toll on both fauna and flora (Wagner et al. 1995). On the northern range of Yellowstone, willows, aspen, and beaver are literally disappearing from the landscape under mounting grazing pressure from unnaturally large herds of elk (Kay 1990). At Rocky Mountain National Park, the devastation to winter range vegetation caused by skyrocketing elk numbers makes the overgrazing by livestock on surrounding national forest lands appear benign in comparison (Hess 1993).

Parks in developing nations fare no better under the protective shadow of the Yellowstone model. Parks in Zimbabwe, for example, face many of the same problems of Yellowstone and Rocky Mountain. In Hwange National Park, where large mammal populations are maintained for tourism by artificial water supply, elephants are rapidly outpacing the ecological carrying capacity of their protected habitat. Expanding elephant numbers together with fire are reducing acacia and mopani woodland to thickets and coppice scrublands and selectively removing critical species (Conybeare 1992). More often than not, however, the plague of parks in the developing world is the acrimony that exists between protected areas and the people who reside at, beyond, or even within their borders. Severed by state-drawn boundaries from the land and wildlife that had been theirs by customary if not statutory right, villagers now look upon parks and their bounty of resources as fair prey in an ongoing struggle for survival.

The incentives of these people are twofold. On the one hand, bare necessity compels them to develop land right up to the boundary of protected areas, through the use of either domestic livestock or cultivation of subsistence or commercial crops. As a result, wildlife loses habitat. In the many areas of east-central and southern Africa where half or more of most major grazing and browsing animals still live outside protected areas, the loss of nonpark habitat can and does carry serious ecological ramifications (Western and Pearl 1989; McNeely, Harrison, and Dingwald 1994). Indeed, in places such as Hwange, where human pressure on former elephant range concentrates elephants in an ever-increasing constricted space and, as a result, worsens vegetation conditions, the environmental costs are real and substantial.

On the other hand, rational calculations by shrewd border residents make poaching on forbidden park lands an attractive alternative. It is far better than putting up with crop losses from marauding elephants or passively watching land that could be used to grow food for their families squandered on protected wildlife that offers no material benefit if left alive. Because these sentiments are often shared among village residents, would-be poachers have a strong incentive and even stronger local support to poach as much as they can as soon as they can. Exploitation, not conservation, is the compelling interest of park neighbors as they contemplate and determine the fate of animal and plant resources that could be nutritional and economic supplements to an otherwise harsh and marginal existence. The tragedy of the commons is too often the fate of fortress parks that presume state-enforced boundaries are sufficient for protection.

But there are other, equally persuasive reasons that the Yellowstone model is ill suited to the protection needs of developing nations. Although protected areas have grown by 50 percent or more in many areas of the world, the discouraging fact is that over 85 percent of them are little more than paper creations (McNeely et al. 1994). They exist in law, they are listed in the ever-expanding repertoire of world parks and preserves, but their conservation status is more fantasy than fact. In Indonesia, for example, 17 percent of its tropical forest park lands have been logged illegally. In Costa Rica's Corcovado National Park, gold miners have invaded its interior, scarring parts of its landscape. In Thailand, national parks are being developed for golf courses, second homes, and hotels. In Chile's Alerce Andino National Park, ancient and towering coastal cypress trees, one of several signature species of the park, are being logged in public view (Hinchman and Hinchman 1995).

A large part of the problem is fiscal. It is easy and relatively painless for a developing nation to designate a protected area to appease western environmental interests. When it comes to footing the costs of parks, however, few developing nations have the financial resources (Child 1995). Western-style park conservation is simply too expensive.

Cost constraints carry a further implication for parks in developing countries, especially when viewed in the context of rural hostility to state-imposed preserves. Policing is neither a practical nor a realistic solution. Waging war against bordering communities may be the logical and correct extension of fortress park thinking, but it is not a strategy that promises long-term protection. Park managers who understand this are placed in a quandary. If they do not police their borders, park resources will be exploited. If they do, the stakes for park protection will simply be raised, escalating conflict with nearby villages and heightening the hostility that contributed to trespass and poaching from the start.

Seen in the context of an actual park, the dilemma and disincentives of management are striking. At Nyika National Park in Malawi, for example, poaching is chronic, and the patrol resources needed to even put a dent in it are woefully inadequate. As a result, Nyika burns every year as poachers set fires to enhance their poaching opportunities. The fires, in turn, diminish the cover and health of one of southern Africa's few remaining examples of high-elevation montane forest patches. Villagers, many of whom were relocated from the peripheries of the park to make way for Nyika's expansion, have no stake in preserving the park; their immediate interest is all that matters, and that interest is to harvest the dwindling populations of eland and roan antelope that still graze the park's extensive shortgrass veld.

At the same time, Nyika's managers have minimal enthusiasm for protecting their charge. The fight against poachers is futile, and the rewards for defending the park are virtually nil. The fact that Nyika National Park is one of the more spectacular montane parks in southern Africa and one that is increasingly targeted by European tourists does not alter the calculus of Nyika's embattled caretakers. Clearly, the disappearance of wildlife on the Nyika Plateau will undermine the tourist business. But because the salaries and the operating budgets of the park's staff are linked neither to wildlife nor to tourism, the loss of one or the other is not economically devastating. Moreover, given the lack of a linkage between wildlife, tourist dollars, and park operations, management has little incentive to stick its neck out to battle poachers in what is perceived as a losing battle.

American parks face similar threats from the communities that touch their boundaries and that exercise control over their physical and fiscal well-being. The Everglades, for example, are choking to death on the residue of phosphate fertilizers resulting from decades of high sugar tariffs and subsidized assistance to sugar growers by the U.S. Army Corps of Engineers. Neighboring farmers are the immediate source of the problem, but the deeper source is Congress where the purse strings that control both the Everglades and the sugar farmers are drawn and opened according to political expediency.

At Rocky Mountain, park managers are unwilling to acknowledge and act on the environmental damage being done by growing numbers of elk. They are fearful of offending a spectrum of communities, including the nearly three million visitors per year who have been told for decades that massive herds of elk are only natural, the animal rights groups, the gateway town of Estes Park, and the Colorado congressional delegation that can threaten to cut appropriations if park management is not in line with public expectations. Like their counterparts at Nyika and elsewhere in the developing world, the constituent communities of Rocky Mountain National Park have shallow stakes in the continued health of the park. Loss of aspen, willows, and beaver to ravenous elk and simplification of forest biota due to fire suppression are hidden costs, obscured by the beauty of the mountains and easily passed from generation to generation. The communities that surround Rocky Mountain, physically and fiscally, have other interests. Their prime incentive is to capture what benefits they can. The point is that no matter what happens to Rocky Mountain, people who capture benefits from the park never bear all the costs and often bear none (Hess 1993).

Because of this situation, the tendency has been to build barriers around national parks aimed at insulating them from assaults by interest groups trying to capture a share of the benefits. In many cases, and especially in developing countries, barriers have severed the link between self-interest and costs for stakeholders, be they park managers, neighboring communities, or more distant special interest groups. These barriers make park managers more attuned and responsive to political change and debate than to the subtler signs of the natural, social, and economic environment. It is not the survival of parks that determines agency careers but adaptation to the political world. Barriers can also induce bordering communities to exploit resources for short-term gain. Subsistence farmers living on the edge of Nyika exploit the park for food and hide, and middle-class residents along Rocky Mountain's edge exploit it for the visual spectacle of massive herds of elk. Finally, barriers can prevent distant interest groups from playing a more decisive role in park protection. Due to various bureaucratic rules, their stake is limited so they do what they can within the rules and ignore that which is beyond their control. In the end, these barriers neither protect nature nor serve humankind; rather, they create inappropriate institutions and even more inappropriate incentives.

SPANNING THE GREAT PARK RIFT

Political top-down management accounts for the rift that now divides protected areas from an assortment of human communities. This has weakened and displaced the ties that could bind people to their physical environments and that could promote coexistence. Reassembling a more harmonious whole is the challenge.

The solution begins with seeing ecology anew—understanding that political boundaries drawn even for the best of intentions are not natural, complete, or sustainable. To this end, we must ask two basic questions. First, should parks be managed as islands in a sea of encroaching humanity? Answering that question will reveal the expectations we hold for parks and the values we hope to pursue through them. Second, can parks be sustained as fragmented islands? This is the more interesting question, for in its answer lies the litmus test against which our value choices must ultimately be judged.

Answering the first question depends on how we see and interpret the mission of parks. For those who answer yes, the Yellowstone model is the appropriate path. It provides stability and constancy, the requisite ingredients for managing nature as a museum. This is a park of tourism and recreation.

However, we have a good reason to say no to the island vision of national parks, especially if we consider values other than tourism and recreation. In particular, for those who embrace a vision of nature that transcends boundaries and that encompasses biodiversity, islands are decidedly a disadvantage.

Attending to biodiversity cannot be achieved through the mechanism of island parks and their attendant top-down, highly centralized, political regimentation. Conservation of biodiversity, whether in developed or developing nations, calls for a root change in the park concept—a transformation from the Yellowstone model to an institutional environment where incentives and markets rather than politics and bureaucracy compel people to care for parks.

Such a transformation means changing the basic orientation of the park mission, shifting its perspective, management, and governance from one of introspection to one of community participation and governance. It means reestablishing substantive links among parks, nature, and people rather than relying on political boundaries.

Practical ecology and sound ecological principles back up this vision of parks for people. From the moment the world's first park was carved from the Yellowstone Plateau to the more recent flurry of park formations in Latin America, Africa, and Asia, the human hand has played a decisive role. The rural villages so characteristic of developing nations have transformed many parks with their wildlife poaching, tree cutting, and wildland fires. Park administrators, bound by budgetary lifelines, have molded and shaped their parks to fit economic and political demands. Many other interest groups are tied to national parks by voluntary choice, but they lack the control and accountability that would help harmonize their interests with those of parks and surrounding communities.

Ecological principles support the contention that island parks are not biologically viable systems. As our understanding of ecology has evolved from models of static equilibrium to models of process, disturbance, indeterminacy, chaos, and spontaneous ordering, the theoretical foundation for the Yellowstone model has eroded. We have learned that ecosystems are not discrete things, that their boundaries are artifacts of human organization, and that transcending those boundaries are the overlapping, entwined, and invisible processes of energy flow, nutrient cycling, and genetic exchange. It is these processes that mock the very concept of island parks.

Parks that make ecological sense, then, must be parks that have no boundaries but rather meld and mix in some way with the human communities that touch them physically, fiscally, and affectionately. Doing so means abandoning the barriers of the Yellowstone model. It means dismantling the institutional and political barriers that can impede essential processes or otherwise isolate reserves in a manner that diminishes species richness and complexity, whether from island biogeographic effects or human assaults. Such parks must be especially mindful of the essential role of nonpark lands. "The parks and reserves," notes David Western, "help to conserve a less altered, more confined nature, and the regions beyond help to conserve a more altered, less confined nature." For too long, he argues, "conservationists have ignored the non-park areas in favor of saving nature by segregating it from humanity" (Western and Pearl 1989, 158). That mind-set is no longer acceptable; parks, park management, and park governance must reach out to the human communities that encircle them and to the lands on which people live and forge their livelihoods.

The task is not simple; it requires much more than building multiple-use buffer zones around park islands or declaring this or that amalgam of parks, public lands, and private lands a greater ecosystem. Buffer zones are riddled with problems, both practical and theoretical. Certainly, they are a step toward reconciling the ecological nature of community with the artificial constraints of man-made parks. Buffer zones rightfully acknowledge that natural and human communities are not so easily segregated. But they do so hesitantly and only in piecemeal fashion. Further, buffer zones do not resolve the deeper issues of who the parks are for or how parks for people can be translated into a landscape of interacting, symbiotic human and land communities.

Institutional arrangements such as the network of organizations assembled under the umbrella of the Greater Yellowstone Ecosystem (GYE) make motions in this direction, but they, too, ultimately fail. The Greater Yellowstone Coalition (GYC), for example, has facilitated communications between various groups, providing input into Yellowstone management that was not there previously. Still, the GYC falls short of integrating the multiplicity of groups that impinge on Yellowstone. It does not provide an ecologically satisfying solution to the lingering rift between the communities of administration, place, and interest. It leaves unanswered the questions of where precisely people fit into the schemata of parks and how human and natural communities can coalesce and harmoniously coexist.

LESSONS FROM THE BUSH: COMMUNITY-BASED CONSERVATION

Community-based conservation (CBC) is a relatively recent development in the field of conservation biology, one that has focused almost exclusively on the conservation of natural resources in developing countries. It stems from two observations: (1) biological diversity is most threatened in the developing countries of the tropical and subtropical belts; and (2) indigenous peoples of those regions, many of whom live at a bare subsistence level, are unlikely to embrace resource conservation when it entails only costs. In application, CBC marries the concerns of land and resource conservation with the needs of rural people through institutional arrangements that make conservation a paying asset for communities.

Most often, CBC has been applied to communal lands where lack of resource ownership and control has encouraged resource exploitation among competing villages and, at times, among competing households. And because many communal lands lie adjacent to or overlap protected areas, CBC has had a profound impact on the status and state of biodiversity across a broad range of land types and land designations. In all cases, its objective has been to make conservation pay either directly through resource harvest or indirectly through various incentive programs. Its success, however, has been greatest when the flow of benefits to local communities comes directly from the activities of the people themselves and from the harvest, use, and marketing of the resources targeted for conservation. In this way, the self-interests of communities and individuals are directly hitched to the conservation of plant and animal resources.

It is important to note that CBC does not exist within a sterile vacuum; it has precedents that show the efficacy of self-interest and that argue strongly that local communities within more traditional societies have practiced and continue to practice resource conservation. This is particularly true when such communities are able to exercise governance over local resources and, at the same time, capture the full benefits of those resources as well as to bear the full costs of their misuse. The inland delta of the Niger River of Mali is a prime example. The entire delta is divided into thirty herding territories, within which are found hunting and fishing domains that are several hundred years old. Water priests from local villages hold the right to exclude outsiders and to allocate access to resources between village household heads. This system has provided an effective institutional arrangement under which common resources have been both governed and protected (International Institute for Environment ad Development [IIED] 1994).

The most celebrated modern example of CBC is the Communal Areas Management Program for Indigenous Resources (CAMPFIRE) in Zimbabwe. There, wildlife conservation in communal lands surrounding parks has been fostered by giving local villages well-defined hunting quotas in marketable game animals such as elephants, Cape buffalo, and antelope. The villages, in turn, market those quotas to safari companies who pay premium prices. So far the results have been promising. CAMPFIRE has helped transform wildlife from just a cost (measured in lost crops and lost human lives) into an asset that is worthy of conservation (Child 1995; Hess 1997).

Other CBC initiatives stress benefit flows from a variety of resources, including thatch grass, ecotourism, wrapping leaves, and butterflies (IIED 1994). The essential point to all of these efforts and the reason for their relative successes is that participating communities are integrated into, rather than segregated from, the affected lands and resources. When communities have valuable and secure rights in communal and protected areas, incentives for conservation are strong and CBC is effective. Where CBC fails is where the connection between the resource and the community is weak or economically insignificant. In the words of one participant in a failed CBC project at the Montagne d'Ambre National Park in Madagascar, "they [project officials] ask us only to protect forests, but for whose benefit they don't say" (IIED 1994, 29).

To date there has been no systematic application of CBC to national parks. Where it does occur, it has been determined more by accident that by design. Yet the few examples that do exist are instructive and suggest that the principles behind CBC hold lessons for park management.

Approximately 2,500 of Nepal's twenty thousand Sherpa people live in the Sagarmatha National Park. It is a park nestled squarely in the Himalaya Mountains and includes the Khumbu area, famous for Mount Everest. Prior to the influx of tourism and mountaineering, the Sherpas effectively managed and utilized forest resources under a strict system of social and community controls. Only with the establishment of a national park system and the opening of the area to outsiders in 1950 did the pressure for firewood from mountain expeditions increase (on average about thirty thousand kilograms of wood per expedition). Under these pressures, traditional Sherpa conservation practices broke down and forest depletion became a serious problem (MacKinnon et al. 1986). Returning control over park resources to Sherpa communities is a CBC initiative that could restore traditional community conservation.

A more promising example comes from Mauritania in West Africa, where indigenous people continue to live within the borders of the Banc d'Arguin National Park. The park, which is one of the five largest in Africa, stretches 180 kilometers along the country's coast and is divided equally between coastal waters and inland mud flats, mangrove swamps, marshes, islands, dunes and expansive desert. Long before the arrival of Portuguese settlers in the fifteenth century, the Imraguen people—their name meaning "the one who gathers life"—had been making a living from fishing the coastal waters in what now constitutes the Banc d'Arguin. During that time, they conserved both the fisheries and the inland marshes and desert. Aware of the Imraguen's historic conservation role, the government of Mauritania formally recognized the rights of the Imraguen to harvest and benefit from the park's resources. Not only has the creation of secure property rights in the park's resources encouraged a strong sense of stewardship and responsibility among the local people, but it has been the principal barrier against invasion of Banc d'Arguin waters by uncontrolled numbers of competing fishery groups (Kemf 1993).

The Wasur National Park in eastern Indonesia is still another example of the principles of CBC in action inside a park. About 2,550 people from thirteen villages live within Wasur's boundaries. Each clan and family has traditional use sites called *dusans*—predefined by past generations—for hunting, gardening, and spiritual events. Interestingly, the *dusans* cover the entire 413,810 hectares of the park, leaving not one acre of Wasur unclaimed. The result of this unusual institutional arrangement is that the lands and resources of Wasur National Park were being protected long before its legal creation; not surprisingly, they continue to be protected (Kemf 1993).

There are a few other supporting examples of indigenous people and parks coexisting to their mutual benefit. Along Nicaragua's Miskito Coast, communities are actively involved in the conservation of a newly established marine reserve (Kemf 1993). In Venezuela, local fishing villages are cooperating with that country's leading conservation nongovernmental organization (NGO) in the management of the Cuare Wildlife Refuge (Kemf 1993).

These cases make the point that long before the theories of CBC emerged, the practice of CBC was entrenched in some of the world's most cherished land- and seascapes. The relevant question is whether the concepts of CBC have application beyond the confines of traditional societies.

A number of conservationists have argued that CBC principles may be appropriate to developing nations, but they are not appropriate to Western-based societies where the rule of law and procedure provide adequate protection of park resources. Moreover, they fear that the principle of CBC—that people can and should be motivated to conserve through self-interest—is a precedent that has been tried on American public lands in the West, failed miserably, and should be avoided (Hinchman and Hinchman 1995).

This criticism, however, misses the point of why resource extraction on U.S. public lands did not result in conservation. What failed on America's federal estate were not individual ranchers and loggers with secure property rights but the top-down institutions devised by the national government to govern and allocate common resources. Those institutions, unlike the ones proposed under CBC initiatives, simply failed to establish a system of rights and responsibilities capable of fostering range and forest conservation. In contrast, prior to federal intervention on western public lands, communities of ranchers were actually engaged in effective CBC that prevented overgrazing until government intervention undermined it (Hess 1992).

Western affluence does not invalidate the principles of CBC. The failure of top-down regulation of national parks is a failure in governance and a failure in the systems of incentives and institutions that shape and influence the self-interests of park users and park managers. For this reason, CBC principles are clearly part of the solution to the future of parks everywhere.

Before us is a simple choice: Do we choose the path of John Muir with armed wardens behind every tree, or do we choose the path of incentives, self-governance, and institutions that support park management as if both people and ecosystems matter?

COMMUNITY AND PARK GOVERNANCE

Applied to parks, the CBC model is direct and simple: governance and the use of protected area resources (whether for physical consumption or metaphysical contemplation) must reflect the interests and incorporate the composition of communities that have a stake in protected areas, whether because of employment in their management, nearness to their borders, or fondness for their existence. In this regard, I do not differentiate between the spectrum of possible uses to which park resource can be applied. Passive contemplation of scenic or wildlife values can have an impact on park ecosystems that is as dramatic as the effect of illicit poaching of animals or the deliberate setting of wildland fires. Similarly, as CAMPFIRE illustrates, exploitive uses of protected area resources can yield advantages for biodiversity conservation that are as profound as those that might emerge from more hands-off management.

The model that I envision for parks and that I detail here does two things. First, it provides a direct channel for people to engage themselves in park affairs, through either usufruct interests in park resources or direct involvement in general park governance. Second, it provides a continuum in institutional arrangements that meet the historical and cultural circumstances of specific parks within developed or developing societies.

My model presumes three basic stakeholder types: the park's employees and managers (communities of administration), the people in close physical proximity to park boundaries (communities of place), and the individuals and NGOs distant from park boundaries yet intimately close to the values and issues that circumscribe (communities of interest). In most instances, these interest groups exist side by side. However, communities of place are generally more important in developing nations, while communities of interest are generally more conspicuous and influential in developed countries. In the former, networks of families rooted in place impinge most heavily on park management; in the latter, autonomous visitors, organizations, and distant park friends outnumber and outinfluence the park's physical neighbors. Moreover, not all parks are of equal significance. Some parks have global significance, encompassing a broad range of near and distant communities of interest. Other parks only have a national, regional, or local significance. These parks encompass more limited communities of interest, and, in the case of developing societies, they may be of importance almost exclusively to communities of place.

The CBC model applied to parks incorporates a private sector role that extends beyond the provision of park concessions, a role whose focal point lies in neither communities of interest (which most often embrace concessionaires) nor communities of place. I believe a robust and substantial private role is uniquely suited to parks in which communities of both place and interest are absent, are poorly represented, or lack the resources to adequately govern and protect.

I present a CBC approach using four parks or protected areas: Vwaza Marsh Wildlife Reserve as a *community park*, Nyika National Park as a *shared governance park*, Rocky Mountain National Park as a *trust park*, and Yellowstone National Park and the Greater Yellowstone Ecosystem as an *extended trust park*. After providing background information on individual park environment, history, and management (detailed earlier in the case of Yellowstone), I present a park-specific proposal for institutional reform.

Vwaza Marsh Wildlife Reserve: A Community Park

Vwaza Marsh Wildlife Reserve is a 984-square-kilometer protected area in northern Malawi, bordered on the west by Zambia and on the north, east, and south by agricultural lands devoted to subsistence agriculture and tobacco plantations.

Background

The reserve was created in 1978 for wildlife and watershed protection and is managed as a national park by the Malawi Department of National Parks and Wildlife. Major environmental features of the park include Lake Kazuni in the south; extensive brachystegia woodlands in the hills and uplands of the east, south, and central regions; dambo grasslands and mopani woodlands in the central and western regions; and an extensive marsh in the north, after which the park is named. Major wildlife species include elephant, Cape buffalo, hippopotamus, eland, kudu, impala, and hyena.

Vwaza Marsh is an isolated park with poor highway access and few outstanding values to attract large numbers of international visitors. Nationally, the reserve is important primarily to the scientific and natural resource management community for its biological diversity; tourism by Malawi nationals is virtually nonexistent. At the local level, though, the reserve is extremely important. Historically, it has provided water, meat, skins, and plant materials to village residents. However, following park designation, village access to the park and its resources was stopped.

Vwaza Marsh is currently threatened on a number of fronts. Its creation in 1978 entailed the forced removal and relocation of families from the park's core. Resentment resulting from that move has turned many border residents against the park and the Malawi Department of National Parks and Wildlife (DNPW). Moreover, population density around the park is extremely high, living standards are low (annual family income is under $200), and cultivation extends up to the park's boundary. These physical and economic conditions, combined with crop depredation and threats to human life from elephant and buffalo, have fostered wildlife poaching, illegal fires, and trespass fishing. In addition, the boundaries for the park were poorly planned at park conception; they included nonessential bottomlands and excluded critical areas of the Vwaza Marsh watershed. Concern exists that if poaching and fires continue and if siltation of Vwaza Marsh is not controlled, all major wildlife species of the park may be lost. Already, wildlife resources in the park have been reduced to the point where significant economic use is unlikely for years to come. Lake Kazuni, which is a major tourist attraction, is also facing an uncertain future; it is being impacted by agricultural development throughout the entire South Rukuru catchment.

Historically, park management has been top-down, boundaries have been patrolled, and local villagers have been prohibited from entering the park. However, as it became apparent in the 1990s that park management was failing, the Malawi DNPW initiated a CBC program of resource utilization in which local residents are allowed to harvest thatch grass, reed grasses, mushrooms, medicinal plants, fish, caterpillars, and termites from the park's core. Big game is currently not included in the CBC resource utilization program, but a change in policy is under discussion. Because the CBC program is recent, no definitive conclusions on its effectiveness are possible. However, anecdotal information suggests that the CBC program has improved relations between local villages and Malawi DNPW.

External fiscal and political problems cloud the future of the CBC program and the ability of Malawi DNPW to perform minimal management functions. Political pressure is mounting nationwide to open the nation's parks (about 21 percent of Malawi's total land surface area) to cultivation and settlement. Furthermore, operating funds for DNPW are growing more scarce. Basic management and patrol functions of park management can no longer be fulfilled.

Proposal

Vwaza Marsh is a park principally of local community interest. Primary stakeholder communities are management and border villages. In addition, a small number of ecologists and naturalists have an ongoing interest in the park's welfare. I propose that Vwaza Marsh be designated a community park. Under this proposal, secure and permanent usufruct rights in park plants and wildlife would be granted to local community institutions (traditional authorities and/or elected governing boards) for conservation, harvest, and allocation. Governance of the park would be jointly held and exercised by Malawi DNPW and traditional village authorities, as well as an advisory member representing the scientific and naturalist community. All management decisions would be by consensus of the parties. In those cases where consensus is not reached, parties would be subject to binding arbitration by a party jointly selected.

Funding for the park would occur in two stages. Stage 1 would be a transition period in which external funds, from either Malawian or foreign sources, would be required to maintain a park staff at approximately 25 percent of its current level. Many park management duties would be assumed by villagers. Stage 2, starting when the park's wildlife capital is restored, would move Vwaza Marsh into a self-sustaining economy. Minimal necessary park management operations would be paid from a percentage of tourist and safari hunting fees. Several advantages flow from this proposal:

- Secure usufruct rights for sustainable harvest of specified park resources would give villagers a vested interest in park conservation, resulting in reduction of all illegal, uncontrolled, and therefore nonsustainable activities.
- Bottom-up governance would provide an effective tool to villagers in deciding how park resources are used, further fostering their interest in park conservation.
- Greater village participation in park management would alleviate current fiscal problems by reducing staff overhead.
- Stage 2 economic self-sufficiency would reduce political interference from outside the park and strengthen local accountability for management decisions.
- Employee allegiance to the park and its wildlife interests would be strengthened by economic dependency on sustainable sport hunting and community resource harvest.

Nyika National Park: A Shared Governance Park

Nyika National Park is a 3,134-square-kilometer protected area in northern Malawi, bordered on the west by Zambia and on the north, east, and south by agricultural lands devoted to subsistence agriculture and coffee plantations.

Background

The park, designated in 1965 as Malawi's first national park, occupies most of the Nyika Plateau, a high-elevation ecosystem (1,800 to 2,600 meters) lying to the west of the Rift Valley escarpment and characterized by extensive low grasslands and montane forest patches in the higher-elevation center and brachystegia woodlands at the lower elevations. Principal reasons for creating, and later extending, the park were unique ecological values, including rare montane plant communities, a large leopard population, robust herds of roan and other antelope, and watershed values.

Nyika is an isolated park with extremely poor road access. In contrast to Vwaza Marsh, however, Nyika enjoys spectacular scenic and wildlife values that potentially could attract large numbers of international visitors. The park is also important nationally and internationally for the unique landscape and ecology it encompasses. As a result, a broad range of communities have an interest in the park. Local villages on the periphery historically relied on Nyika for food, fiber, and minerals. Today, however, their access to the park is prohibited by law. Other communities that share an interest in the park include a private safari operator, Malawi Wildlife Society, scientists, international NGOs, and park administration.

Nyika park is currently threatened on a number of environmental, economic, and political fronts. Its expansion in 1975 forced the relocation of families from the newly acquired park areas. Resentment resulting from the forced move has turned many border residents against the park and Malawi DNPW. Moreover, population density at some points around the park is extremely high and living standards are low (annual family income is under $200). These physical and economic conditions, combined with anger over past relocation, have fostered wildlife poaching, vandalism, and extensive and environmentally destructive human-set fires. Although definitive data are lacking, anecdotal information suggests that montane vegetation and eland and roan herds are bearing the brunt of the illicit activities. Concern exists that unless poaching and fire are brought under control, the primary ecological values of Nyika will be destroyed.

The history of park management in Nyika is similar to Vwaza Marsh; top-down management, protection by patrols, and local villager exclusion. Again, in the mid-1990s the failure of this approach led to a CBC program of resource utilization in which local residents can harvest thatch grass, reed grasses, mushrooms, medicinal plants, honey, masuku fruit, and caterpillars from the park's core. Big game is not being considered in the CBC resource utilization program. Because the CBC program is just beginning, no information exists to evaluate the potential success of the program. The one exception is the beekeeping project initiated in the early 1990s. It has benefited the few members of the surrounding community who participate in the program, but has had negligible effect on the attitudes and economic status of the majority of border residents.

Again, like Vwaza Marsh, fiscal and political problems make it impossible for the CBC program to work effectively. Also, the political pressure to open the park to cultivation and settlement makes ecosystem destruction a certainty.

Proposal

Nyika is a park of international, national, and local interest. Primary stakeholder communities are villagers, management, naturalist and scientific groups (in particular the Wildlife Society of Malawi), international NGOs, and a resident private concessionaire. I propose that Nyika be designated a shared governance park. Under this proposal, secure and permanent usufruct rights in selected park plants and wildlife would be granted to traditional authorities and/or elected community governing boards. Furthermore, secure and permanent usufruct rights in selected park resources would be sold to the resident concessionaire. All usufruct rights, communal and private, would be fully transferable. Governance of the park would be jointly held and exercised by Malawi DNPW, traditional village authorities, the resident concessionaire, and an elected representative of the park's national and international supporters (see my later trust proposal for Rocky Mountain National Park). All management decisions would be by consensus of the parties. In those cases where consensus is not reached within a reasonable time, a two-thirds majority voting rule will determine decisions.

Funding for the park would occur in two stages. Stage 1 would be a transition period in which funds, primarily from supporting international organizations, would be required to maintain a park staff at approximately 25 percent of its current level. A majority of park management duties would be assumed by villagers, the resident concessionaire, and members of the international scientific and environmental community. Stage 2 would move Nyika to self-sufficiency with operation expenses paid from a percentage of tourist and concessionaire fees.

Several advantages of this approach are worth noting:

- Secure usufruct rights for sustainable harvest of specified park resources would give villagers a vested interest in park conservation, resulting in reduction of all illegal, uncontrolled, and therefore nonsustainable activities.
- Secure usufruct rights for sustainable tourism would give the resident concessionaire a vested interest in park conservation.
- Bottom-up governance would provide an effective tool to villagers, the concessionaire, and national and international interests in deciding how park resources are used, fostering a broad interest in park conservation.
- Broader stakeholder participation in park management would alleviate current fiscal problems by reducing staff overhead.
- Stage 2 economic self-sufficiency would reduce political interference from outside the park and strengthen accountability for management decisions.

• Park economic self-sufficiency would link staff interests to the well-being of the park as defined by the health and functioning of wildlife, grassland, and forest patch components.

Rocky Mountain National Park: A Trust Park

Rocky Mountain National Park is located in north central Colorado along the Rocky Mountain front range, where it extends east and west across the continental divide. Established in 1915, the park covers 265,000 acres spanning an elevation range of 7,800 feet to over 14,000 feet. The park is bordered on the east by the town of Estes Park and a developing urban corridor stretching east and south to Denver. National forest lands border Rocky Mountain on the north and west. Park vegetation is zonated along an elevation gradient from lower montane to alpine: east of the continental divide, ponderosa pine woodlands and open grasslands merge with lodgepole pine forests that merge with spruce fir forests and alpine grasslands at the highest elevations; west of the divide, lodgepole pine dominates uplands, wet meadows and willows occupy bottomlands, and a spine of alpine peaks form the park's western boundary. Large mammals in the park include elk, bighorn sheep, black bear, mule deer, moose, and mountain lion. In recognition of the park's role as a prime example of the central Rocky Mountain ecosystem type, it was designated a biosphere reserve in 1976.

Background

Rocky Mountain is rapidly becoming an urban park with excellent air and highway access from the greater Denver metropolitan area. In contrast to both Nyika and Vwaza Marsh, the park's outstanding scenic and ecological values attract approximately 2.8 million national and international visitors each year. Because of the park's global standing and recognition, many stakeholders are not local. In addition, many of the people living along the periphery of the park are seasonal or part-time residents. Nonetheless, a small but significant community of residents rely on the park for both tourist-based income and general environmental amenities. Only one private concession exists within the park.

Rocky Mountain faces a number of serious environmental and management problems. Elk herds within the park's winter range now exceed carrying capacity by 300 to 400 percent, which is causing destruction of wetland, aspen, and alpine willow sites. Wildlife (particularly beaver and ptarmigan) are also being adversely affected. Although the park's own research confirms these ecological trends, park managers have resisted taking action because of the political sensitivity of the elk issue to some groups.

In addition, a long history of fire suppression has significantly altered the park's vegetation and left its eastern flank highly susceptible to a catastrophic fire on the scale of the Yellowstone burn of 1988. As with elk, the political sensitivity of the fire issue has constrained park management from taking action.

Complicating both the elk and fire issue is the pattern of residential and farm development along the park's boundary and eastward. Urban growth and intensive agriculture on the high plains has blocked historic winter elk migration out of the park (fostering overgrazing and overbrowsing in the park) and elevated public concern over park management fire policy. Besides pressing ecological concerns, park management is also faced with park overcrowding—an issue that joins the ranks of elk and fire in political sensitivity.

Again, park management is top-down (stakeholder communities influence park management primarily through congressional lobbying), governance structure is highly bureaucratic, the congressional appropriation process strongly influences park policy and management, and park boundaries continue to be based on assumptions of "naturalness" that are reinforced through official National Park Service policy. Indeed, while park managers do acknowledge the external pressures building on the park's eastern boundary, they appear unwilling to change or adapt in a way that would effectively acknowledge the increasingly unnatural circumstances of Rocky Mountain.

Not surprisingly, Rocky Mountain's future is clouded by the increasing inability of park management to respond to a series of rapidly developing crises. Strong control of park management by bureaucratic and political forces emanating from Washington, D.C., will likely reinforce management hesitancy and paralysis. Furthermore, no serious effort has been made by park management to inform or educate the park's considerable visiting public on the nature or the seriousness of the problems facing Rocky Mountain. Yet, unless the public is given adequate information, there is every reason to believe that it will continue to presume that Rocky Mountain is healthy.

Proposal

Rocky Mountain is a park of principally international and national constituent communities; local stakeholders exist, but they are, in terms of numbers, a minor subset to the park's 2.8 million annual visiting public. I propose that Rocky Mountain be designated a trust park. Under this proposal, public ownership of the park would continue; there would be no allocation of real or usufruct rights to communities of place or to private parties operating concessions apart from those created and allocated subsequently by the trust. Governance of the park, though, would be transferred from Congress and the National Park Service to a board of trustees who would have full discretion in the setting of park policy and management and in the hiring or firing of the park's superintendent. Board members would be elected by a self-selecting membership—in essence, a Friends of Rocky Mountain National Park Association. Membership in the association would be open to any individual willing to pay a nominal annual fee (in addition to entrance fees) or donate some amount of their time to park projects. In addition, the trust would finance park operations and salaries entirely from trust memberships, entrance fees, and other service and concession revenues. Economic analysis indicates Rocky Mountain could become economically self-sufficient immediately (Hess and O'Toole 1995).

The advantages of this proposal are as follows:

- Bottom-up governance by a membership-elected trust would significantly increase interested public awareness and knowledge of essential park issues.
- Local governance would shift responsibility and accountability for park resources from bureaucratic and political centers of power to constituencies (communities of interest and place) who have the greatest stake in the future of the park.
- Self-financing of the park by the trust would remove park management and operations from the control of an appropriation process that has no link of accountability to the park and its ecological components.
- Exclusive self-financing by membership and user fees would provide a market-driven mechanism by which all park users—not just park trust members—could influence park management and operations.
- Park management and science staff would have fewer obstacles impeding effective response to the current crises that plague the park.

Yellowstone National Park and the Greater Yellowstone Ecosystem: An Extended Trust Park

Vwaza Marsh, Nyika Plateau, and Rocky Mountain highlight our concerns for (1) the conservation of biological diversity, (2) the use of core parks as catalysts for extending biodiversity conservation to adjacent land ownerships, and (3) the closing of gaps between benefits and accountability. I believe that markets, when linked to secure and robust forms of participatory and decentralized governance, can provide a road map to sustainability that is largely lacking in most state-dominated models of protected area management. I further believe that the principles we have put forward are not confined to parks; they have applicability to other public lands that may occur in close physical or ecological proximity to protected areas. To make this point, I consider both Yellowstone National Park and the lands that constitute its extended ecosystem, the Greater Yellowstone Ecosystem (GYE).

Background

Yellowstone National Park shares many of the attributes and problems of Rocky Mountain National Park, although on a substantially greater scale and without the density and proximity of intensive urban development. It is a park of high geological and scenic diversity and moderate biological diversity. Historically, it served as the source for reconstituting herds of native bison, repopulating large areas of the Rockies with elk, and sustaining a small but important population of grizzly bears.

In addition, its geothermal environment is source to new and socially significant species of microfauna and microflora. Despite these attributes, Yellowstone is a fragment of a much larger bioregion. In recognition of this fact, land managers, scientists, and environmental groups pushed for and helped establish the managerial unit known as the Greater Yellowstone Ecosystem. Intended to promote sound land management, the 7.3 million–hectare GYE (almost as large as the country of Malawi) includes Yellowstone and Grand Teton National Parks; Gallatin, Custer, Shoshone, Bridger Teton, Caribou, Targhee and Beaverhead National Forests; Grays Lake and Red Rock Lakes National Wildlife Refuges; a national elk refuge; part of the Wind River Indian Reservation; state and local government lands; and private lands. Significantly, however, over three-quarters of the GYE is under the administrative control of the Park Service and the U.S. Forest Service. The Greater Yellowstone Coalition (GYC) represents a broad array of citizens interested in the GYE.

Proposal

I believe Yellowstone National Park and its greater ecosystem should be managed as an extended trust park. This would entail two levels of management: (1) control of immediate park affairs by a trust similar to the one recommended for Rocky Mountain National Park and (2) shared control of broader ecosystem affairs by a federation of GYE trusts, private property owners, and communities of interest (through GYC or some equivalent NGO or alliance of NGOs).

National forests in the GYE present a management challenge. They are politically managed, with decisions regarding use and allocation of resources made through a broad national process of political appropriations and competing political constituencies. Biological diversity has been threatened by politically driven forestry practices. In addition, public forests have not contributed positively to conservation initiatives on surrounding land ownerships. More significantly, the gaps between benefits and accountability have widened rather than narrowed under federal control. For these reasons, I believe a modified form of trust organization should be adopted for the national forests and integrated into the management of the GYE.

I propose the creation of formal and fully marketable usufruct rights for enumerated timber and range resources allocated as long-term leases. A governing trust, predicated on open membership and popular election of a board of trustees, would control, steward, and allocate all resources not otherwise transferred as range or timber use rights. This would maintain public ownership of the renewable and nonrenewable resource base and the nonmarketable facets of forest biodiversity and associated ecological processes and services. In effect, each national forest would enjoy shared governance between lawful holders of approved use rights and the public members of formally constituted governing trusts. As in the instance of national parks, forest service employees would continue in their function as managers, but they would be subject to direct control and supervision by citizen groups. (The recent forest management victory of the Quincy Library Group and the ongoing effort by the National Wildlife Federation, Defenders of Wildlife, and timber interests to forge a citizens' plan and oversight board for grizzly bear recovery in the Selway-Bitterroot region of Idaho and Montana are political developments suggestive of and favorable to the forest trust idea.)

Management of the larger GYE—specifically, policymaking and the raising of revenues—would be the responsibility of a federation of park and forest trusts, the GYC (or equivalent NGO), and other minor parties, including private property owners and federal, state, and local governments.

CONCLUSION

My analysis of the Yellowstone model and my sketch of what might supplant it is admittedly biased against state involvement. I intend by this view no criticism or disparagement of the men and women who have dedicated their lives to the management and protection of the world's national parks. They are creative and thoughtful scientists and natural resource managers, but their ability to function as they see fit has been compromised by institutional structures.

My criticism, therefore, is aimed exclusively at the historic assumption that nature protection and the operation of national parks must be the ward and obligation of the state. I object on numerous grounds, some historical, some political, and some ecological. I believe the historical record is clear: governments have not done the sterling job of park protection that popular opinion assumes. I also believe that political governance of parks is fraught with dangers, pitfalls, and catastrophic implications. Lastly, I believe that state control of parks is neither ecologically sound nor ecologically sustainable. Apart from their national and cultural content, national parks are fragments of extended communities that include very specific human constituencies. These constituencies are not the public interest; they are not society writ large. Rather, they are communities who by choice or circumstance have elected to join the natural communities of protected areas. This, I believe, is an important distinction central to my argument, my model, and expectations for future conservation of biological diversity.

I recognize, of course, that state involvement in national parks will likely continue at some level. I believe that whatever the role of the state in park management, it should be modest, nonobtrusive, and most of all respectful of the governance rights of stakeholder communities. If this can occur, we will have made an enormous stride forward. We will have answered the haunting question "*Which* people are the parks for?" We will have resolved, quite simply, that they belong to those communities that have the greatest stake in them and the greatest ability to manage them from the bottom up.

REFERENCES

Child, Graham. 1995. *Wildlife and People: The Zimbabwe Success.* New York: Wisdom Foundation.

Conybeare, A. M. 1992. "Elephant Occupancy and Vegetation Change in Relation to Artificial Water Points in a Kalahari Sand Area of Hwange National Park." Ph.D. dissertation, University of Zimbabwe, Harare.

Hess, Karl. 1992. *Visions upon the Land: Man and Nature on the Western Range.* Covelo, Calif.: Island.

———. 1993. *Rocky Times in Rocky Mountain National Park: An Unnatural History.* Niwot: University Press of Colorado.

———. 1997. "Wild Success." *Reason* 29 (October): 32–41.

Hess, Karl, and Randal O'Toole. 1995. "Tarnished Jewels: The Case for Reforming the Park Service." *Different Drummer* 2, no. 1.

Hinchman, Lewis P., and Sandra K. Hinchman. 1995. "Nature Preservation in the Global South: A Survey and Assessment." In *Law, Values, and the Environment: A Reader and Selective Bibliography,* ed. Robert N. Wells. Lanham, Md.: Scarecrow, 357–93.

International Institute for Environment and Development. 1994. *Whose Eden? An Overview of Community Approaches to Wildlife Management.* Nottingham, U.K.: Russell.

Kay, Charles E. 1997. "Yellowstone: Ecological Malpractice." *PERC Reports* 15, no. 2.

———. 1990. "Yellowstone's Northern Elk Herd." Ph.D. dissertation, Utah State University, Logan.

Kemf, Elizabeth, ed. 1993. *The Law of the Mother.* San Francisco: Sierra Club Books.

MacKinnon, John, Kathy MacKinnon, Graham Child, and Jim Thorsell. 1986. *Managing Protected Areas in the Tropics.* Gland, Switzerland: International Union for the Conservation of Nature.

McNeely, J. A., J. Harrison, and P. Dingwald, eds. 1994. *Protecting Nature: Regional Reviews of Protected Areas.* Gland, Switzerland: International Union for the Conservation of Nature.

O'Toole, Randal. 1997. "Saving the National Parks." *Different Drummer* 3, no. 4: 41–44.

Ridenour, James M. 1994. *The National Parks Compromised.* Merrillville, Ind.: ICS.

Wagner, Frederic, Ronald Forester, R. Bruce Gill, Dale R. McCullough, Michael R. Pelton, William F. Carter, and Hal Salwasser. 1995. *Wildlife Policies in the U.S. National Parks.* Covelo, Calif.: Island.

Western, David, and Mary Pearl. 1989. *Conservation for the Twenty-First Century.* New York: Oxford University Press.

Index

About the Contributors

Terry L. Anderson is executive director of the Political Economy Research Center in Bozeman, Montana; senior fellow at the Hoover Institution, Stanford University; and professor of economics (retired) at Montana State University. His work has helped launch the idea of free market environmentalism and has prompted public debate over the balance between markets and government in managing natural resources. Anderson has published widely in both professional journals and the popular press and is author or editor of twenty-one books, including *Political Environmentalism* and *Enviro-Capitalists: Doing Good While Doing Well*, the latter coauthored with Donald Leal. Anderson received his Ph.D. in economics from the University of Washington and has been a visiting scholar at Oxford University, the University of Basel, and Cornell University Law School. He was awarded a Fulbright Research Fellowship to Canterbury University and was a national fellow at the Hoover Institution. Anderson is an avid outdoorsman and skilled bow hunter.

Javier Beltrán is the Latin American and Caribbean research officer for the World Conservation Monitoring Center in Cambridge, United Kingdom. He specializes in issues related to the creation and management of protected areas. He holds a master's degree from the Universidad Nacional, Heredia, Costa Rica.

Christopher Bruce is a professor of economics at the University of Calgary where he has taught since 1973. He obtained his Ph.D. from Cambridge University. Although his research has primarily concerned the economic analysis of legal principles, Calgary's proximity to Banff National Park has recently spurred his interest in conservation and park management issues. Bruce currently holds a grant from the Donner Foundation to investigate alternative methods for resolving disputes over the use of public lands.

191

Peter W. Fearnhead was the first in-house resource economist employed by South African National Parks (SANP); he now acts as adviser to the chief executive officer of SANP. Fearnhead has also been instrumental in formulating the new commercialization plan for the organization, which is currently in the process of being implemented.

Holly Lippke Fretwell is a PERC research associate whose current research emphasis is on public land management. She holds a bachelor's degree in political science and a master's degree in resource economics from Montana State University. Fretwell has worked with Northwest Economics Associates in Vancouver, Washington, where she examined timber export regulation in the Pacific Northwest, and she has consulted for organizations including Plum Creek Timber and the Center for International Trade in Forest Products (CINTRAFOR). Fretwell has presented papers promoting the use of markets in public land management and has provided expert testimony on the management of U.S. national parks. She is the author of PERC's Public Lands Reports and numerous articles on natural resource topics.

Michael Green is chief conservation officer at the Broads Authority, the agency responsible for managing the Broads, an English wetland of national and international importance. Previously, he worked for many years on protected area issues at the World Conservation Monitoring Center in Cambridge, United Kingdom, an international nongovernmental organization that manages and networks information on the world's biological diversity.

Karl Hess Jr. is an environmental writer and policy analyst. He holds B.A., M.A., and Ph.D. degrees in economics, history, and ecology, respectively. He has spoken extensively on western land and national environmental issues and written on those topics in publications that include *High Country News*, *Reason*, *Human Ecology*, *Environmental History*, the *New York Times*, the *Washington Post*, and the *Wall Street Journal*. His published books include *Vision upon the Land: Man and Nature on the Western Range*, *Rocky Times in Rocky Mountain National Park: An Unnatural History*, and *Writers on the Range*. Hess is a senior associate of the Thoreau Institute of Portland, Oregon; a board member of the High Country Foundation; and a founding member of the *High Country News*' western writers group, Writers on the Range. In addition, he is working on community-based conservation projects in the Sangre de Cristo Mountains of Colorado and on the western slope of Mount Kilimanjaro, Tanzania.

George R. Hughes is chief executive of the Natal Parks Board, South Africa. He was born in Scotland and emigrated to South Africa after World War II. After extensive traveling and spending four years as a game ranger, he studied zoology and geography at the University of Natal in South Africa. There he completed a study of the sea turtles of South East Africa and earned his Ph.D. His research interest in sea turtles continues today, and he is an active foundation member of the International Union for the Conservation of Nature's Sea Turtle Specialist Group. He has authored numerous scientific papers, reports, and popular articles on conservation and sea turtle biology. He is the recipient of several local awards and very proud of the fact that the Natal Parks Board was awarded the World Wide Fund for Nature's Gold Conservation Medal in 1995. He is an enthusiastic trout angler.

Alexander James is a doctoral research student in the Department of Land Economy at the University of Cambridge. He holds an M.B.A. from Cornell University and a B.A. in economics from the University of California, Berkeley. He is a former PERC graduate fellow and has consulted for the World Conservation Monitoring Center in Cambridge, United Kingdom, and the Secretariat of the Convention on Biological Diversity, in Montreal, Canada.

Stephanie Presber James holds a Ph.D. in land economy from the University of Cambridge. Her dissertation applied her institutional approach to protected area management to the country case studies of Botswana and Namibia. She holds a master's degree from the London School of Economics and a bachelor's from the University of California, Berkeley. Her work experience is in the private sector, primarily mergers and acquisitions.

Sam Kanyamibwa is Africa regional program officer for the World Conservation Monitor Center (WCMC), Cambridge, United Kingdom. He received his Ph.D. in evolutionary ecology and conservation at the University of Montpelier in France. Before joining WCMC in 1995, he lectured at the University of Rwanda and conducted research in the montane forests of the Albertine Rift. He is founder and coordinator of the Albertine Rift Conservation Society and member of the World Commission on Protected Areas Task Force on Protected Area Management Effectiveness. Kanyamibwa's work involves technical assistance to countries in the areas of information management, biodiversity conservation, and protected area management.

Donald R. Leal, a PERC senior associate, has been carrying out research in natural resource and environmental issues since 1985. He received his B.S. in mathematics and M.S. in statistics from California State University at Hayward. Leal is coauthor with Terry Anderson of *Free Market Environmentalism*, which received the 1992 Choice Outstanding Academic Book Award and the 1992 Sir Antony Fisher International Memorial Award. *Enviro-Capitalists: Doing Good While Doing Well*, also coauthored with Anderson, received the 1997 Choice Outstanding Academic Book Award. He has published numerous articles in the popular press as well as specialized journals on such topics as fisheries, water, recreation, oil and gas, timber, and public land use policy. Leal's studies comparing federal and state management of forests and parks have fostered a new perspective on public land management. He is currently assessing the impact of individual transferable quota programs in fishery management throughout the world. Leal is coediting a book documenting cases where government programs have harmed the environment, and he is coauthoring a revision of *Free Market Environmentalism*.

Mariano L. Merino is completing doctoral research on the ecology and conservation of the endangered Pampas Deer at the University of La Plata, Argentina. He works for the Scientific Research Committee and consults for the Protected Areas Department of the Natural Resources Directorate of Buenos Aires Province, Argentina.

Michael J. 't Sas-Rolfes is a conservation economist based in Cape Town, South Africa. As an independent consultant, he has worked on various wildlife issues, ranging from park management to wildlife trade. His work includes the monograph *Rhinos: Conservation, Economics and Trade-offs*, published by the Institute of Economic Affairs, London.

PARTICIPANTS

Patricia Bean, Tango
Graham Child, WISDOM Institute
Robert Davis, University of Colorado, Boulder
Derek de la Harpe, Price Waterhouse
Joanna Elliott, African Wildlife Foundation
Curtis H. Freese, World Wide Fund for Nature
R. Judd Hanna, Lassen Loomis Museum Association
Peter J. Hill, PERC and Wheaton College
Steve Hodapp, consultant
Charles Kay, Institute of Political Economy
Wilford W. Middleton, WISDOM Institute
Michael Penfold, Montana Parks Association
Randy T. Simmons, PERC and Utah State University
Jeanne-Marie Souvigney, Greater Yellowstone Coalition
Jeffrey Tiberi, Montana Fish, Wildlife, and Parks